Connop Thirlwall, J. J. Stewart Perowne, Louis Stokes

Letters literary and theological of Connop Thirlwall

Connop Thirlwall, J. J. Stewart Perowne, Louis Stokes

Letters literary and theological of Connop Thirlwall

ISBN/EAN: 9783743373075

Manufactured in Europe, USA, Canada, Australia, Japa

Cover: Foto ©Lupo / pixelio.de

Manufactured and distributed by brebook publishing software (www.brebook.com)

Connop Thirlwall, J. J. Stewart Perowne, Louis Stokes

Letters literary and theological of Connop Thirlwall

LETTERS

LITERARY AND THEOLOGICAL

OF

CONNOP THIRLWALL

LATE LORD BISHOP OF ST. DAVID'S

EDITED BY

THE VERY REV. J. J. STEWART PEROWNE, D.D.

DEAN OF PETERBOROUGH

AND

THE REV. LOUIS STOKES, B.A.

CORPUS CHRISTI COLLEGE, CAMBRIDGE

WITH

ANNOTATIONS AND PRELIMINARY MEMOIRS BY THE
REV. LOUIS STOKES

LONDON
RICHARD BENTLEY & SON
PUBLISHERS IN ORDINARY TO HER MAJESTY THE QUEEN
1881

LONDON:
PRINTED BY J. S. VIRTUE AND CO., LIMITED,
CITY ROAD.

PREFACE.

BISHOP THIRLWALL'S Letters contained in this volume
were collected for the most part by his nephew and
executor, Mr. John Thirlwall, before he went to America,
and were by him intrusted to me for publication. I had
selected and arranged those I thought most likely to be of
general interest, and had intended to connect them by
such biographical notices as I might be able to glean from
the recollections of friends or from other sources, but was
prevented by a variety of circumstances, into which I need
not enter, from completing my task. Meanwhile a second
volume, consisting entirely of the Bishop's correspondence
with one friend during the latter years of his life, had been
edited by Dean Stanley, and was already printed and ready
for publication. It was desirable that the two volumes
should appear together; and to avoid further delay I consented, at the Dean's suggestion, to place my portion of the
work in the hands of the Rev. Louis Stokes, who undertook
to complete it. The whole of the Memoir is written by
him; and he desires through me to express his thanks
to the numerous correspondents who have replied to his
inquiries for information in his work. Unfortunately the
materials for a biography are of necessity scanty and
imperfect.* The Bishop had but few intimate friends; and

* " With regard to the Memoir," Mr. Stokes writes, " I have been led to
compile it from the remarks of Professor Plumptre (to whom I am much
indebted) in his able and exhaustive article in the *Edinburgh Review* for April,

of those who were his contemporaries at Cambridge, most had passed away before him. To the world at large he was known as the scholar, the historian, the theologian, foremost in the first rank of these; but of the man they knew little or nothing. Even the letters which have been collected do not cover the whole of his life. His correspondence with Lord Houghton, one of his oldest friends, perished with other treasures in the disastrous fire at Fryston some years ago. A few letters have been sent me in answer to inquiries which the Editor of the *Athenæum* kindly allowed me to make in that journal; but there are still lamentable gaps in the series.

It must be added that the Bishop's life was not an eventful life. It was essentially the life of the student and the man of letters; it presented few of those incidents which make the ordinary biography. With the exception of the remarkable episode at Cambridge, there was little in it that attracted notice. Men far less distinguished made more noise in the world. He rarely spoke in the House of Lords; he never threw himself into the strife of parties. No man governed a diocese better, and the difficulties of his diocese were peculiar; but he did not belong to the modern type of bishop, whose efficiency is measured in common estimation by his power of speech and motion. It was chiefly as a writer that he commanded attention; yet, even as a writer, he was not prolific. His literary labours ceased with the publication of the second edition of his *History of Greece*. With the exception of

1876. He there says that 'it would be a real loss to the intellectual life of England if the memory of such a man were to fade away without a record—more or less adequate—of what he was and how he spoke and wrote.' I am quite conscious of the extreme inadequacy of the accompanying record, but it seems improbable now that any other will be forthcoming, and I have therefore tried to put together such an account of 'the outward events of his life' as the paucity of material permitted me. I owe much in this part of my work to the constant kindness of the Rev. W. H. Thompson, D.D., Master of Trinity College, Cambridge."

those masterly Charges in which, every third year of his Episcopate, he reviewed, as no other hand could do it, the history of the Church, he published nothing after he became a Bishop but a few Sermons and Essays. He mentions in one of his letters written from Abergwili his extreme aversion to the use of his pen. I am not aware that he has left any record of his feelings with regard to public speaking; but it is surprising that a speaker of such acknowledged excellence should have taken so little part in the debates in the House of Lords. When he did speak he commanded the ear of the House. I have been told by those who heard his celebrated speech on the Disestablishment of the Irish Church, that no single speech had so much influence on the fate of the measure in the Upper House as his. Even while at Cambridge he had established his reputation for eloquence. John Stuart Mill has left on record in his *Autobiography* the extraordinary impression produced upon him by the first speech he heard Thirlwall make in a debating society of which they were both members, and on an occasion when they took opposite sides of the question. "Although," he says, " I dissented from nearly every word he said . . . . before he had uttered ten sentences I set him down as the best speaker I had ever heard, and I have never since heard any one whom I placed above him." This is the testimony of no mean judge. His eloquence, it is true, was not of that kind which appeals to the passions, or stirs the enthusiasm of the multitude ; it was of that far higher order, which disdaining the artifices of rhetoric and never condescending to inflame popular prejudices, yet glows with the fire of an earnest conviction, lays bare the sophistry of the special pleader, and crushes with splendid irony the pretender to knowledge or the hasty, hot-headed partisan, who can see only one side of a question.

But though, owing to causes such as I have enumerated,

there are comparatively few materials for a biography, the letters speak for themselves. They begin at a very early period, and range over a vast variety of topics. The earliest which has been found was written when Thirlwall was a boy of thirteen to a boyish friend of whom nothing more is known than his name. The correspondence between them was continued for several years, and must have been voluminous if his friend's letters were as numerous and as lengthy as Thirlwall's. These are essays rather than letters; and, considering the early age at which they were written, are remarkable for the variety, extent, and acuteness of their criticisms. The bulk of these are necessarily omitted; a few specimens only are given, as indicating the early ripeness of his powers. They must have been written whilst he was still at Charterhouse, but it is singular that they contain scarcely an allusion to the school or to his schoolfellows; they are wholly taken up with the books he is reading, the politics of the day, or his own future plans in life. It is said that at school he did not care to enter into the games and amusements of the other boys, but was to be seen at play-hour withdrawing himself into some corner with a pile of books under his arm. This passion for reading went with him through life. In one of his later letters from Abergwili he says, "I can read literally from morning till night without any interruption but ∙that of professional business. Eating, walking, or driving, I have always a book in my hand." The boy was father to the man. Fortunately the precocity of his genius did not prevent its attaining to its full maturity. He was not one of those who "have an overearly ripeness in their years which fadeth betimes." Archbishop Whately's remark, that "there is nothing less promising than in early youth a certain full-formed, settled, and, as it may be called, adult character," may be true as a rule, but certainly Connop Thirlwall was a striking exception to it. He was no exception, however, to another rule, that the tree which bears the finest fruit is not that which bears the most.

What will be gathered from these volumes is a record all too brief of one of the giant minds of our age. "Bishop Thirlwall," it has been truly remarked, "was not only foremost in the intellectual ranks of the clergy; he was, by almost universal consent, foremost in the intelligence of Great Britain." But that which was not known, or known only to a few intimate friends, was the inner greatness of the man. If he abstained from taking that part in public life which his uncommon powers justly entitled him to take, this was a sign of a character that concealed its strength. But it concealed also its gentler and tenderer side. There was a solitary majesty about him, owing to this reserve, which prevented the world at large from understanding him. Men thought him stern and severe because they did not penetrate beneath the mask of reserve. He was in truth the warmest and the most sympathising of friends. I am indebted to one who knew him intimately for the accompanying reminiscences of the Bishop's life at Abergwili, which set his character in its true light, and supply much that is wanting in the letters.

"Although the intellectual side of the Bishop's character was generally admitted, and, in the main, justice has been done to the memory of his great acquirements and the singular strength and fairness of his judicial mind, there was another side, as precious, which few recognised, that which represented the qualities of his heart, his affection, his sympathy, his tenderness. This failure of recognition, it must be allowed, was partly due to his own belief that he was, owing to what he thought defects of manner, unattractive, and without power to interest others in himself; thus he had often an appearance of reserve, through

which acquaintance who knew him slightly found it difficult
to break, and he therefore passed through life for the most
part misunderstood, and was credited with a coldness and
indifference entirely opposed to his true nature.   In reality
no one valued affection more deeply than he, or returned it
when given with greater truth and intensity of feeling.
All that concerned a friend was to him as personal as
if it related to himself individually, so completely did he
identify himself with the lives and thoughts of those dear
to him.

"The memory of the simple, studious, earnest life at
Abergwili is in itself a sermon full of impressive and noble
teaching, of strong and gentle influences.   The day began
with the early service in the quiet chapel.   The voice,
now silent, which made it solemn, and the 'grave earnestness with which he read the Gospel of the day, were absolutely an exposition of its meaning,' * while the calm
thoughtful face and dignified bearing made part of the
holy peace which seemed always to rest upon that time
and place.

"When alone he spent his day chiefly in 'Chaos,' as he
playfully called the library in which he used to sit ; and
except when he entertained guests, or had business beyond
Abergwili, he rarely went without its precincts.

"If he had friends with him he made a point of driving
to places of interest in the neighbourhood, and when there
was time to spare in the morning he would take them
along the walks near the house, and show them his golden
pheasants, peacocks, canaries, and other pets.

"In a small pond in the grounds, which had neither inlet
nor outlet, three pike were kept.   One morning when the
Bishop went to see them he found but two; not long after,
on his next visit, one alone remained.   He observed to a
friend, it was impossible to take any interest in a creature

* A remark referring to the reading of F. W. Robertson.

who could devour his own family, and added, 'I never looked at him again.'

" After breakfast the Bishop usually fed his geese, having abstracted whatever available pieces of bread lay within his reach for their benefit. In the depth of winter, when ice covered the ponds, and frost and snow were heavy on the ground, he never omitted his visits to them, for it was then, he said, they needed him most; and if remonstrated with for running these risks of catching cold, he would protest that it was to his geese he partly owed his health, because there were many days on which but for them he would not have ventured out of doors, and would have thus lost the air and exercise which contributed to it. They treated him, he used to say, very familiarly, flocking round him, and even seizing hold of his coat in their beaks to show their welcome!

" He would, on returning to the house, come to the drawing-room laden with books of all kinds and nations, which he had gathered from the recesses of 'Chaos' for the amusement of his guests, pleased to make known to them what had been of interest to himself.

" The afternoons were generally occupied by picturesque drives, and the evenings made pleasant by conversation, music, and sometimes chess or draughts. His cat, a great tabby, usually joined the company. She was a privileged creature, and would assert her privileges, jumping upon the Bishop's shoulder when he was reading, and even playing tricks audaciously with the paper knife with which he cut open the book that was lying upon his knee.

" He was very fond of music, especially of the songs of Wales and Italy, and he also had much feeling for art. He was sensitive to all forms of beauty. A lovely scene, early dawn, sunset, effects of light, and pictures in the clouds were all observed by him with rare appreciation. He had never made botany his study, yet flowers were to him as living friends, and he could not bear to see them gathered. He would hurry out of London, when that was possible, in order not to miss the glory of the thorns at Abergwili ; and while in town he perpetually lamented his loss of the sights and sounds of the country.

"For all conditions of life, from the tiniest insect upwards, he had sympathy, and the suffering of all creatures touched his heart : consequently his interests were never those of the sportsman. One evening a friend related to him the experiences of Count Z——, who had bought land in Algeria, and, on first going there, amused himself by stalking lions. For forty nights he had watched for them in vain ; on the forty-first night, having small hope of better success, he took but one charge in his gun, and stationed himself under a great fragment of rock. Soon, to his surprise, he heard the roar of a lion, which presently came out of the jungle and went close by him; he fired, and wounded, but did not kill it, and it retreated with cries of pain. The lioness, who was at hand, hearing them, rushed out after the lion, leapt the rock beside which Count Z—— lay concealed, and in leaping touched his shoulder with one of her paws. At this point of the story the Bishop was heard to say with emphasis, and under his breath, 'The dear lamb,' but happily the Count, who received no sympathy, did not need it, for he escaped unhurt.

" In winter time he delighted in the floods which swept over his own valley, in the pattering of the rain, and in the howling of the wind ; but they lost their charm for him when he thought of storms at sea, and the sharp struggle for life in which they might result. Keenly susceptible to variation of climate, he felt the cold of frost and snow all the more because they reminded him of the poor who had not his comforts, and whose sufferings, therefore, must be greater than his own. He considered

his 'icy' winter 'plunging bath' to be his best safe-
guard against the bitterness of the weather.

"He took an exceeding interest in Wales, his country on
his mother's side, her people, her language, her traditions.
His knowledge of Welsh was profound, and his Welsh
writing remarkable for its strength and purity; it was, in
short, scholarly and classical. Tegid, a well-known Welsh
poet and scholar, dedicated a MS. to him (which, unfortunately, has not been published) on account of his 'deep'
Welsh learning, as Tegid expressed it.

"Of his own acquirements he had but a poor opinion.
His *History of Greece* he rated much below that of
Grote, and thought he had 'little reason to be proud
of it.'

"His deafness—which varied—often interfered with his
enjoyment of conversation, and there is a story related of
his too evident candour, when, on hearing a remark about
the weather, which had to be several times repeated by a
friend before he could catch its meaning, he said musingly,
thinking aloud, 'Strange, how little one loses by being
deaf.'

"His concentration was remarkable, and was applied
with the same steadfast purpose to small things as to great
—to a simple game as to a subject of grave import.
One night at the house of a friend he proposed joining
in a game of whist, and played for many hours (contrary
to his usual custom, because he had early habits) with
unabated energy and eager interest in every turn of the
game. To him nothing was small, trifles were no trifle to
him but parts of a great whole, and the light of that
bright intellect and that understanding heart illumined
all he touched.

"Business and letter-writing, and the perpetual interruption incident to his occupied life, were irksome to
him, but he never set them aside on that account. He

often complained of his memory, but no one else would have found in it ground for complaint, except, perhaps, in the direction of names, which did not recur so readily to his recollection as events or subjects.

"In summer time he was glad to quit 'Chaos,' and to sit and read under the trees, and to listen to the soft rustle of the wind passing through their leaves and branches.

"Who that has seen it will not remember 'Chaos'? Its quiet light, its dim recesses, the cat purring on the hearth, the chairs all unavailable until cleared of the books and pamphlets with which, like the tables, they were crowded; the drawers full of unarranged letters, papers, MSS., into which the Bishop, opening them, looked with pitiful and perplexed eyes, yet when offered help would invariably answer, 'I can seldom find anything in them now, but if they were set to rights for me I should certainly find nothing then.' And, over all, the presence that made peace and pleasantness, the life in its outward seeming eventless, within how eventful!

"His large heart, his wide spirit of tolerance, and his faculty for seeing all sides of questions, together with the allowance he made for variance of opinion and for errors inseparable from humanity, naturally inclined him to optimism; and he observes in one of his published letters, 'I should myself hesitate to say, "whatever is, is best;" but I have strong faith that it is *for* the best, and that the general stream of tendency is toward good.'

"He prized the gift of life. 'Life,' he writes, 'is a good thing, be it long or short.' One summer afternoon, during a drive, allusion was made to the remark Colonel S.'s wife addressed to him when first she saw the Taj Mahal—words to this effect: 'I would die to-morrow if you could raise such a monument as that to my memory.' The Bishop turned to the friend sitting by him and said, 'Would you?' adding, very earnestly,

' I would not give up one day of life for all the monuments in the world.'

"The gift of life he so valued has been taken from him to be replaced by a better in the ' White World ' *
beyond his narrow grave. Those who visit that quiet spot in Westminster Abbey may see in the calm face and thoughtful eyes, carved in white marble, some faint memory of the days, serene and beautiful, at Abergwili ; and, thus remembering, may humbly believe that he is working still with others, dearly loved, at the noble work begun in darkness here, continued there in light among the ' spirits of just men made perfect.' "

J. J. STEWART PEROWNE.

DEANERY, PETERBOROUGH,
October 3rd, 1881.

* The three words in Welsh, "GWYN · EI · FYD," on the Bishop's tomb engraved on a riband scroll of brass are, literally, " White is his world," meaning " Blessed is his state."

CONTENTS.

CHAPTER IV.—CAMBRIDGE. 1827—1833.

CHAPTER V.—CAMBRIDGE. 1834.

CHAPTER VI.—KIRBY UNDERDALE. 1835—1840.

CHAPTER VII.—ST. DAVID'S. 1840—1860.

CHAPTER VIII.—ST. DAVID'S. 1860—1869.

CHAPTER I.

Boyhood. 1797—1813.

CONNOP THIRLWALL, the third son of the Rev. T. Thirlwall, came, as his name implies, from an old border family. The branch to which he belonged was an offshoot of the old Barons de Thirlwall, who held Thirlwall Castle, in Northumberland. His "name speaks of a time when some of his forefathers were thirling their way with might and main through the old wall" (of Severus) "which was the scene of so many hard-fought battles."[*] His Christian name was derived from his mother's family, with which he shared "whatever Welsh blood flows in Radnorshire,"[*] a fact interesting from the close connection of his name with that part of the kingdom in after times. His father was the Reverend Thomas Thirlwall, who was successively minister of Tavistock Chapel, Long Acre, lecturer of St. Dunstan's, Stepney, and rector of Bowers Gifford, Essex. He was the author of various pamphlets and sermons, and was for some time chaplain to Thomas Percy, Bishop of Dromore,

* Bishop Thirlwall's " Letters to a Friend," p. 26. Ed. Dean Stanley.

the editor of the well-known " Reliques of Ancient English Poetry."

Connop was born on the 11th of February, 1797, in
Stepney. He soon gave signs of the precocity of his
genius ; " at a very *early* period he read English so well
that he was taught Latin at three years of age, and at four
read Greek with an ease and fluency which astonished all
who heard him. From that time he continued to improve
himself in the knowledge of the Greek, Latin, French, and
English languages. His talent for composition appeared
at the age of seven," and in 1809 a volume of his productions was published under the title of " Primitiæ; or,
Essays and Poems on various subjects, Religious, Moral,
and Entertaining, by Connop Thirlwall, eleven years of
age." It contained an Introduction by his father, from
which the above remarks have been quoted, and has for
frontispiece a portrait of " Connop Thirlwall, ætat 11
ann." "in which," says a friend, " there is a striking like-
ness to Bishop Thirlwall as I remember him ætat 70 ann."
The publication of this book was a measure of doubtful
wisdom ; it was a source of intense annoyance to the
Bishop in after years, and he took every opportunity of
buying up and destroying as many copies as he could
find.* A few months after his appearance as an author
he was sent as a day scholar to Charterhouse, then under
the presiding care of Dr. Raine, and he " there fell in with
one of those golden times, which at successive intervals
crown the harvest to schools and colleges as well as to the
natural world." Contemporary with him were Grote,
Julius Hare, the two Waddingtons, Henry Havelock,
Cresswell Cresswell, Turner (Lord Justice), and others who
have since made their mark. During this period of his
life he was in the habit of writing elaborate letters to
favourite schoolfellows on all sorts of subjects in Latin,

* Bishop Thirlwall's " Letters to a Friend," p. 155.

French, and English. These early letters show the extraordinary extent of his reading, the manner in which he already began to weigh everything in the balance of his singularly judicial mind, the gradual ripening or modification of his ideas, and also afford interesting glimpses of his own career and of contemporary events. The first of these letters which has been preserved was written when he was a boy of thirteen. It was addressed, as were all at this period, to a friend named John Candler, of whom nothing further is known than can be gathered from the letters.

To Mr. JOHN CANDLER, Ipswich.

January 4th, 1810.

"DEAR FRIEND,

".... If you have visited Oxford, you have seen, in spite of what I said of my father's prepossessions, by far the finest of the two Universities. You should, as I have done, have seen Cambridge first. Its inferiority would not then have appeared so striking. I shall belong to the former. Your conjecture respecting Kirke White is, I think, a very probable one. He would have been a second Cowper, although he might not have enjoyed so long the use of his transcendent powers. From such studies and such honours may I be always free. I prefer a long life a thousand times to such immortality. Your compliment, however elegant and polite, will, I am afraid, be undeserved. Whatever honours I may reflect on Alma Mater will not, I believe, be acquired during my continuance under her maternal wing. In fact—the old lady must excuse me if I differ with her on some points—I do not really think the classics, *alias* the dead languages, objects of such infinite importance that the most valuable portion of man's life, the time which he passes at school and at college, should be devoted to them. And, furthermore, I am absolutely of opinion that there are other studies and pursuits which may render a man a more useful member of society than these. And even that a man who is not acquainted with a syllable of Latin and Greek may be more useful to the world than the profoundest scholar.

"I shall be content if my knowledge of the classics extends but a very little farther than my knowledge of French; so far, in short, as to be capable of enjoying the beauties of their poets, historians, and philosophers. For when I enter upon the great stage of the world I may meet with several opportunities of rendering these attainments useful and agreeable to myself, but very few, if any, of making them serviceable to the interests of society at large. I must therefore be excused if I do not devote the whole of the time which I shall spend under the walls of the University to these pursuits, which are held in such high estimation, and if I employ myself in collecting information which may be of use to me in the profession I shall hereafter embrace. You will say that by this I shall forfeit all pretensions to academic honours. Be it so. I really think that these honours, if they are to be purchased (and it is the only price) by nights and days of anxious toil, afford a very inadequate compensation. When I commence my classical studies I do not imagine that any great advantage will result from them to the world. And if I do not think that my own happiness will be increased by them, surely I am justified in rejecting them. I am aware that was I addressing a professed scholar I should draw down upon myself an indignant reply. But I am inclined to think that you will be of the same opinion as myself. Nothing, I think, can be more favourable than such a seclusion from the bustle of the world as a college presents. During your residence there you are enabled to collect materials for the benefit both of yourself and the world.   And this I consider to be its principal if not sole advantage.   I therefore look forward with hope and pleasing anticipation to the time when I shall there immure myself.   But those honours which are bestowed upon the proficient in the dead languages do not form the object of my ambition."

" I remain,

"Your sincere friend,

" CONNOP THIRLWALL."

To Mr. JOHN CANDLER.

April 14*th*, 1810.

". . . . I will confess to you that French poetry in general has hitherto appeared to me tedious and insipid ; on your recommendation, however, I shall certainly look into the 'Henriade.'   There is at the London Institution a most beautiful and complete edition of Voltaire's works.   Having read the greatest part of the 'Æneid' in the original, I have not felt any strong curiosity to peruse Dryden's translation. Pitt's I have never seen.   You are by no means singular in giving the preference to the latter.   If I may be permitted to guess at that of which I can have no certain knowledge, Pitt has attended more to the beauties of versification than Dryden, who, hurried along by the force of his genius, neglected the gratification of the ear.   It will be remembered, however, that the former had laid before him all the beauties and errors of the other to imitate and avoid.   Between the two poets no sort of comparison can be instituted—a twinkling star to the full moon.   The last visit I paid to the London Institution I was much pleased to find there Crabbe's new poem, and was gratified with the perusal of the first letter.   His description of the ocean strikes me more as natural than poetical.   It is indeed a beautiful picture. I shall take the first opportunity of reading the remainder, which promise at least still better amusement. I hear from good authority that the 'Lady of the Lake' will make its appearance in three weeks or a month. I shall be sorry to find either that the author's powers are diminished, or that the possession of public favour has made him negligent of its preservation. That politics are a baneful region is exactly my opinion; the necessity of entering it I do not comprehend. Respecting Sir Francis Burdett, I know not whether the late events which have taken place in consequence of his refusal to surrender himself have made any alteration in your opinion of him, which, I believe, was a favourable one, but I can assure you they have made none in mine. No unpatriotic speech or action can excite the least surprise from the mouth of one who has chosen Horne Tooke for his tutor and O'Connor for his friend, and who has associated with men whose principles and views have admitted not the least hesitation. But that he should suppose that his resistance could answer any reasonable end seems rather discreditable to the good sense which has been generally ascribed to him. He, however, trusted in a mob. And what have they done for him? After having broken the ministerial windows, accompanied him to the Tower, and pelted the soldiers with brickbats on their way back, they have gone quietly home and left him to his meditations on Tower Hill. . . . . I have had another opportunity of looking into Crabbe. There are two sorts of passages in which he is particularly happy; in those little stories which he inserts here and there, in the manner of Pope's Sir Balaam, such as those of Swallow, the attorney, and James Thomson, with many others, and in the idle gossip, instances of which are to be found in abundance in his letter on Clubs. As the antechamber does not please you, I shall not venture to introduce you into the gallery itself. If you have read through

'Gil Blas' you must undoubtedly remember his entering into the service of a literary Marchioness, and the company she held. I cannot resist the temptation of transcribing a few lines: 'On n'y disait guère que de lectures sérieuses : les pièces comiques y étaient méprisées. On ne regardait la meilleure comédie, ou le roman le plus ingénieux, ou le plus égayé, que comme une faible production qui ne méritait aucun louange : au lieu que le moindre ouvrage sérieux, un ode, une eclogue, un sonnet, y passait pour le plus grand effort de l'esprit humain.' With a critic of this cast, who requires less light and more shade, my pictures can have little chance of success."

To Mr. John Candler.

May, 1810.

" . . . . I said, I think, in my last, that the region of politics is a baneful one, but I did not see the necessity of entering it. Permit me to explain myself more at large upon this subject. Between friends, I still think that political discussion, especially in an epistolary intercourse, ought as a notorious breeder of discussion to be avoided, and the more so since, when once indulged in, it gains so much ground as to leave room for no other topic. I nevertheless think it highly proper if not necessary that every man should obtain such a knowledge of the subject as to enable him in every case to judge for himself. For my own part, I am at present neither capable nor desirous of gaining sufficient information to form a decisive opinion. I am at present, therefore, neutralist. The representations of either party I am always inclined to believe in some degree exaggerated, and therefore abstain from, or rather take alternately, both sides of the question. I shall never be a bigot in politics. For whither my reason does not guide me, I will suffer myself to be led by the nose by no man; and in every contest reason will point out some weak and some sound arguments of both contending parties.

"I have just been reading the debates on Parliamentary Reform. And I cannot let slip the opportunity of making a few remarks on the subject. This word reform had so often assailed my ears in all its variations of radical and temperate that I had begun to think it a vague sound, of which its most zealous advocates scarcely understood the import. Nor do I remember that the question was ever before reduced to a *tangible shape*. What I have read of Mr. Brand's speech I highly approve of. Party prejudice must own it rather contradictory to reason and common-sense that a population of one hundred persons should have two representatives, while four hundred thousand are without one. These are abuses which require speedy correction. It will, however, I fear, be long ere a reform so necessary takes place. I by no means confide in the immaculate purity of the motives of men in power. It is extremely convenient for a minister when attacked by a strong opposition, to be able to purchase votes at any easy rate, and for a profligate debauchee who has exhausted the whole of his patrimony to bid defiance for some years at least to the fangs of the bailiffs, and to defraud honest industry of its dues. Venality, however, may also have its advantages on the opposite side. And, I believe, had it not been for its magic influence that illustrious patriot, that firm, disinterested, and virtuous asserter of the people's rights, that mortal enemy to corruption, whatever form it may assume and however high it may hold its head—you will immediately guess the name of Wardle follows—would never have graced the Senate and blessed the people by his presence either at St. Stephen's or the London Tavern. No! the energies of his noble soul would have been damped and cramped in the walls of a spot very dissimilar to either of these places. But to be serious, that there are many more flagrant errors in the State is undeniable; that they should be immediately put a stop to is just. The only (and well-grounded) fear is this, lest in lopping off from the tree of the constitution those branches which impede its growth we infix a deadly wound in its trunk. . . . .

"Johnson has, it must be confessed, laid his paws rather too heavily upon 'Lycidas,' although I assent to several passages of his criticism. There is nothing in it pathetic, and pathos ought, I conceive, to be the principal charm in such a production. To your question I reply that I have wandered long from home, and have not yet returned. My house, therefore, is not yet prepared for your reception. Thoughts crowd upon thoughts, and when paper and ink are at hand the temptation of fixing their volatility is too strong to be resisted. I strike the iron while it is hot, but the misfortune is it grows cool before I have finished. An assertion so very contradictory to all my sentiments on the subject as that poetry may be arrived at mechanically I cannot pass over in silence. It is possible, I will allow, to obtain by dint of study the highest perfection in the art of versification, but that the midnight lamp can inspire those ideas and present those images which form the body of the line I shall always continue to think out of reason and nature. Never until genius may be purchased by industry will poetry become mechanical. It was in the power of Prometheus to mould the dull and unimpassioned clay into the human shape, but to impart animation to its features and motion to its limbs, he was compelled to steal a spark of celestial fire. . . . .

"You have undoubtedly read the 'Odyssey,' if not the original at least a translation. If, therefore, you must view these things with a classical eye, while you are rearing your curious plants, you cannot fail to remember the description in the twenty-fourth book, and Laertes may probably do for your grandfather as well as the 'fortunate senex.' By-the-bye, Dr. Raine tells us this book is a spurious performance. This I have no doubt is the case, but the writer will nevertheless rank high in the list of poets. If you approve of Ponsonby's speech, I think you must retract some sentiments in your last letter. Your approbation of the conduct and sentiments of Sir Francis must be very qualified indeed. . . . ."

To Mr. John Candler.

September, 1810.

" . . . . Epistolary correspondence is little more than a species of more methodical conversation. And this agreed on, I will tell you why the letters of James Howel have afforded me little entertainment, although confessedly excellent in their way. I may be easily supposed to be interested in a conversation in which I am myself a party, but when listening to the dialogues of others there must be something extraordinary in the speaker or what he speaks to arrest my attention. In like manner, when I am reading the letters of a man whose letters are all I know of him, if the matter be original, the manner being easy and familiar, and of course not at all times perfectly elegant and correct, deprives it of the effect it would have if arranged in a form adapted to the eye of criticism. When, on the other hand, I peruse the epistles of men celebrated for their piety, genius, or learning, I seek with curiosity and read with avidity all those passages where the author is lost in the man. Of James Howel I never read even the name but as connected with his volume of letters, and the familiarities which in the great men I have mentioned are the principal charm of the correspondence, are in him uninteresting and impertinent. A collection of the letters of Young, Addison, Swift, Johnson, and other great geniuses, whose works have afforded me so much satisfaction, would be one of the richest banquets the whole range of literature can furnish.

"As to Adam and Eve's question, there is a solitude of the mind as well as of the body, and both perfectly distinguished one from another. A hermit distant a hundred miles from any human beings may be mentally transported to the bosom of society, and a philosopher treading the streets of our crowded metropolis may be fixed in the country, in the sea, or the stars. I have frequently considered the subject of Cowper's beautiful lines, 'The Pleasure of Retreat,' and the result of my contemplations is this. The pleasure the poet mentions depends entirely upon the mind and dispositions of the reader. Upon no subject have men been more frequently and grossly disappointed and deceived than on this, nor is there a more pitiable object in Nature than a man who has expected happiness in retiring from the busy scenes which once occupied his sole attention, and who, in view of the repose he had anticipated, finds himself the slave of the hideous monster, for which, because perhaps it is a stranger to us, we have invented no title, but have been compelled to borrow the foreign one—*ennui*. . . . .

"Oxford has, indeed, received a most violent attack in the person of their champion. As an impartial spectator, I think the Reviewers have besmeared the disputant with their own mire, and have been themselves sprinkled by the shower they intended altogether for him.* . . . .

"A peasant, whose literary knowledge extended, perhaps, no farther than the mark he made use of for his

---

* Referring to a controversy in the *Edinburgh Review* (April, 1810) respecting the studies pursued at Oxford.

name, was observed to listen with great attention and apparent interest to a classical debate carried on in a classical language. 'Do you know,' asked a spectator, 'what these men are talking of?' 'Not I,' said the clown, 'but I can tell which has the best of it as well as you.' 'How?' 'Why when one falls into a passion it's easy to see that the other's a match for him.' And the clown was no fool. Of the grounds of this dispute I know, perhaps, as little as the peasant of the one he was witness to. This I can see, that the Reviewers have lost their temper. But his sovereignty refused its homage, what critic was ever known to preserve it? In good truth they are a set of porcupines, a *genus irritabile.* And the epithet, to a certainty, is infinitely more applicable to them than to the objects of their critical anatomy. Nothing would give me greater pleasure than to see some Don Quixote start up among them, whose motto might be *Debellare superbos.* With what ample employment would their pride, insolence, and injustice furnish him!

"Walter Scott has lost none of his fire. His 'Lady of the Lake' is as animated as any of her predecessors, but not quite so interesting. I cannot, however, give a decided opinion, for I have not finished the perusal. Yet, on reflection, that is the strongest proof I could give. What I have read has not afforded me so much gratification as 'Marmion,' which I still think his finest work." . . . .

To Mr. JOHN CANDLER.

WOOD STREET, *October 24th,* 1810.

" . . . . On the receipt of your letter I reperused the admirable essay you mention. And this perusal, with another circumstance or two, gave rise to some ideas which may perhaps afford you amusement, and of which this letter will be a very proper vehicle. I read lately in a preface to a book containing the meditations of Mr. Pascal, a truly pious, learned, and ingenious character, that after having made a great progress in the sciences, he, at the age of thirty, laid aside every pursuit in which he before excelled, and devoted the remainder of his life to the study and elucidation of the Holy Scriptures. How greatly would the imitation of so excellent an example redound to the honour and advantage of every scholar ! . . . .

" For my own part, I intend, if I should live long enough to carry my designs into execution, to follow the example of the great man I have mentioned, and at an early period to abandon every literary and scientific pursuit for more noble and profitable studies. And if, in spite of the multitude of accidents which may intervene to put an end to our intercourse, we should continue this correspondence until that time shall arrive, you will serve me by bringing back my present resolution to my re-membrance. . . . .

" I read lately in Cowper's ' Tirocinium ' a passage which at the time very much startled me, and which I cannot reconcile to any ideas of mine upon the subject. He is endeavouring to strike a deadly blow at the root of public education by demonstrating the pernicious effects of a spirit of emulation. I say he endeavours, because I do not think that he has succeeded. . He considers Emula-tion as but another name for Envy ; between which I esteem the difference as great as between Piety and Fana-ticism, Liberality and Ostentation, or Perseverance and Obstinacy. I have always supposed Envy to be both active and indolent, Emulation only active. I have be-lieved Envy to desire not so much its own exaltation as the envied object's downfall ; while Emulation seeks to promote its own superiority without detracting from the possessions of others. What law of justice, honour, or religion discountenances such a principle I have yet to learn. With regard to the great question of public or private education, I decidedly prefer public to particular instruction. But the intercourse of a number of boys, apart from their literary studies, I think fraught of necessity with all the evils the poet mentions. I should, therefore, wish for a school which should be only the place of assemblage for the students, who on their departure thence should immediately separate. Such a plan would embrace all the advantages attendant upon a spirit of emulation, while it avoided the pernicious effects of the boarding-houses, the common appendages of a public school. From a variety of causes such an arrangement will, I fear, never take place. I at present enjoy as a day scholar all these advantages.

"Milton's 'Paradise Lost' may with great propriety be called a divine poem. Not merely on account of the subject, although that alone would entitle it to the appellation, but in it *Materiem superabat opus*. It bears marks of a genius so far elevated above every other, that it seems almost an indignity to call it human. Nothing in this admirable work fills me with so much admiration as the perfect propriety and correctness with which he treats the most lofty subjects, and adapts them to every (Christian) sect and denomination. Nevertheless, in such a poem it would be strange if some parts of the performance did not meet the disapprobation of some readers. I myself, little as I like cavillers and Zoiluses, did not think some few passages entirely consistent and correct. Milton in several places describes gems and gold, that 'precious bane' out of which the fallen angels erected their Pandemonium, as the pavement of heaven. The passages brought to my recollection two similar ones—one in a romance of the infamous Voltaire, where the as infamous hero travels by supernatural means into a hitherto unheard of region, where the road dust is gold and the stones precious, and where he saw a multitude of children playing, whose garments were formed of the glittering metal. He imagined these to be princes of the blood royal, but he was informed that they were only the poor children of the villagers. Such a spot was the Valley of Riches mentioned in the 'Tales of the Genii,' where precious gems of exquisite beauty dropped like buds or blossoms from the trees. Such scenes were more consistent than those which the poet depicts. For it is to me at least somewhat difficult to conceive palaces of gold, such as we see it, the habitations of spiritual beings. But he most likely conceived this to be the image most capable of conveying an idea of beauty and excellence to the generality of readers. . . . . .

"These opinions may, perhaps, be contested and refuted. But should they be admitted in all their force, they would not diminish the unrivalled excellencies of 'Paradise Lost.' Whether we consider its design or its execution, it stands pre-eminent above every work which human genius has hitherto accomplished. But for a full explanation and elucidation of its beauties the inquisitive need only apply to the admirable critique in the *Spectator*, where its superiority over the two great works with which it has been compared is demonstrated, fully at least to my satisfaction. I must yet hazard another observation on a passage which on my perusal of it bore the appearance of an inconsistency. The bard, in his admirable description of the battle of the angels, makes 'the girding sword with discontinuous wound' pierce the fallen Archangel, and a sanguine stream issue from the gash. In a few lines farther he says that spirits cannot receive 'mortal wound in their liquid texture.' If this be the case, I cannot imagine how the uptorn hills which were hurled on them and their engines could bruise and pain although they might confine them.   Let us, however, dismiss these perhaps hypercritical and presumptuous remarks.   How far different is the style of Cowper and the pleasure we receive from it!   His 'Task' is, as far as I can judge, a poem without previous parallel.   Nor do I know under what class of poetry to place it.   It seems to have been begun without design like a morning's ramble, and to have been continued and completed without labour. Nevertheless, in this walk how many beautiful and even sublime objects rise upon the view.   Cowper appears to bear in his style a very great resemblance to the Roman Ovid.   There is in both the same elegance of diction and unstudied easiness of expression.   But the Christian poet must be allowed to bear the palm from the Pagan in sentiment if he is equalled by him (which I do not think) in other respects.   The pious fervour which goes through the page of Cowper will preserve it from oblivion, while the blasphemous scoffings of a witty infidel, should they pass down to another generation, will be viewed only with mingled indignation and contempt.   I have read lately in the *Edinburgh Review* a critique upon Walter Scott's new poem, and it very justly complains of a want of novelty. In truth, as soon as a new work of this poet is announced we instantly know the characters and the scene of action, and should he make a fourth attempt he will, I think, discover that the public are satiated with courteous lords, and gallant knights, and ladies fair, with the Scottish borders and the ages of chivalry. . . . ."

To Mr. JOHN CANDLER.

January, 1811.

". . . . On the subject of the education of the poor I most cordially coincide with them (the Edinburgh Reviewers).   Their satirical observations upon Mandeville and other men of better intentions, who would limit the information of the poor, are not more cutting than just; and your remark that 'where there is nothing but bigotry on the one hand and an enlightened scheme of liberality on the other, truth must force its way,' which, I thought, as I applied it to the question of religion, wore the appearance of illiberality, I can adopt on this head. The distinction which wealth and poverty, power and subjection, make between man and man is sufficient, without adding that of learning and illiteracy. The knowledge of reading, writing, and arithmetic must benefit and cannot injure the most obscure peasant. Could (what from obvious reasons cannot take place) an acquaintance with the whole range of literature be added to these, the advancement of the general good would, in my opinion, be the result. For, as the Reviewers very justly observe, until learning shall fill the purse or the stomach its universal diffusion will not deprive our plains of husbandmen and our shops of mechanics.. And I would ask the advocates for confining learning to the breasts of the wealthy and the noble, in whose breasts are the seeds of sedition and discontent most easily sown? In that of the unenlightened or well-informed peasant? In that of a man incapable of judging either of the disadvantages of his station or the means of ameliorating it? Or of one who possesses opportunities of knowing the necessity of subordination and distinction? In Scotland I believe the peasantry are far better educated than in this country. And the effects are visible. In genius and intelligence Scotchmen of the lowest rank in their own country are scattered over every part of Europe, and receive wherever they go the respect which constantly accompanies merit; while in England a genius whose lustre might have enlightened nations, unable to penetrate the mists of ignorance which surround it, may make its entrance and departure without once emerging from the

shades of obscurity. These were long since my sentiments. Nor, indeed, have the major part of the arguments of the Reviewers made any alteration in my ideas.
The only doubt I ever entertained of the excellence of
Lancaster's plan was founded on religious considerations.
I questioned the propriety of a system on so broad a basis.
These doubts the *Edinburgh Review* has removed. It
appears that Lancaster, although he makes his pupils read
the Scriptures, leaves it to the parents to apply what they
have read according to the religion which they design
them to embrace. . . . .

"Southey's genius is, I think, obscured by affectation.
He is a sort of literary fop who will either lead the fashion
or own none. Irregularity seems to be a rule with him;
and, if I may be allowed the expression, perpetual devia-
tion is his constant line. To such an extent does he
carry his eccentricity that he would not call his 'Madoc'
an epic poem because, forsooth, the title has been frequently abused and degraded. With equal reason might
a man refuse to go by the name of John and Thomas
because they have been borne by a tyrant and an infidel,
or to read Homer because he has been travestied. He never
indulges his readers with rhyme, which, indeed, I could
very well dispense with, if he gave me always harmony
instead. Nay, I could even console myself under the
want of this if he supplied the deficiency with sublime
thoughts and poetical expressions. But it frequently
happens that his least harmonious lines are his tamest.
He, perhaps, calls it simplicity."

To Mr. John Candler.

April, 1811.
". . . . I read lately in the *Edinburgh* and *Quarterly*
Reviews two critiques upon Southey's new poem, 'The Curse

of Kehama.' The two reviewers are considerably at variance. The latter speaks of it in terms of nearly unqualified approbation. The former, as he always does, mingles his praise with censure. For my own part I approve of the view which the latter takes of it. I detest that malignant spirit of criticism which constantly directs itself to the faults of a performance while it overlooks its beauties. The 'Curse of Kehama' is in my opinion a poem which will last—I mean will be read—as long as the mythology on which it is founded : I believe I may say longer. For the work contains an explanation of itself, and the reader, who never before heard of the religion of the Hindoos, may rise from the perusal of this work with a tolerable insight into it. This was precisely my case. Before it fell in my way I was perhaps as little acquainted with the mythology of the Hindoos as with their language. Southey has thrown into my mind a sudden ray of light. In every other respect I have rarely met with a poem which has more elevated, surprised, interested, and amused me. The story, resting as it does upon the most wild and extravagant fictions that ever entered the head of man, can never be reproached for wandering beyond the bounds of probability. It is of necessity full of impossibilities, and those of the most gloomy nature. Yet with so much wit has the poet contrived his tale that the whole appears but a pleasing fiction. The incidents are ever new and varying, and in general happily contrived. The characters being for the most part superhuman do not admit of much variety. But the passions, when by accidental circumstances they are not excluded, are admirably depicted. The descriptions are perhaps in some places too minute, but they are for the most part inimitably beautiful. Never did the poet furnish better materials for the painter than are to be met with in the lines which precede the utterance of the dreadful 'Curse.' The collected scorn, hatred, and thirst of vengeance, which we may suppose to mask the features of the Almighty man, and the silent despair of the defenceless object of his resentment, would have afforded an admirable subject for the best painters of the Italian school.   Nothing can be more exquisite than this description, as also the passage in which Kailyal after the loss of her charms expresses her confidence in the unabated affection of the Glendoveer.   As for the metre, if the poem can be said to have any, it is perfectly adapted to the story. The one is as irregular and unconfined as the other is wild and extravagant. . . . .

"Our affairs have of late assumed a more favourable aspect.   I congratulate you, as a friend to 'liberty and an enemy to oppression, upon the forced retreat of the French Invaders.   As a philanthropist I condole with you upon the miseries attendant upon war, and I commiserate the. ill-fated inhabitants of its theatre, the Spanish Peninsula. At the same time I despise while I deplore the folly and weakness of the wretched slaves of a tyrant whom ambition has steeled against every sentiment of humanity, and who, 'in no hesitative mood of justice or of mercy,' can calculate with as much composure upon the destruction of thousands as a manufacturer upon the consumption of his tools. . . . ."

To Mr. John Candler.

St. John's Street, London, *October* 8*th*, 1812.

". . . . It is my design before I enter into the ministry to acquire a competent familiarity with the Hebrew, and to be enabled to compare the original dictates of inspiration with the translation which forms the groundwork of our faith.   Such a comparison cannot but be attended with equal pleasure and improvement.   If this venerable and ancient language should answer the expectations I form of it, I shall perhaps be tempted to make farther efforts, and to extend my progress in the literature of the East. But my motto must be, *Labor omnia vincit improbus.* . . . ."

To Mr. JOHN CANDLER.

December, 1813.

". . . . I am at present preparing myself in the most compendious method for the University, although without those expectations which you seem to have formed for me, and without imagining that my future happiness depends upon their being realised. There are many pursuits which are held in great request at the University, to some of which I attach little importance, and to others of which I do not find my taste, or, perhaps, to speak the truth, my abilities adapted. In those pursuits to which my inclination leads me, my disappointments (which I apprehend will be very few) will not be owing to my negligence or indolence. There is one particular in which I hope to differ from many of those envied persons who have attained to the most distinguished academical honours. Several of these seem to have considered the years which they have spent at the University, not as the time of preparation for studies of a more severe and extended nature, but as the term of their labours, the completion of which is the signal for a life of indolence dishonourable to themselves and unprofitable to mankind. Literature and science are thus degraded from their proper rank, as the most dignified occupations of a rational being, and are converted into instruments for procuring the gratification of our sensual appetites. This will not I trust be the conduct of your friend. Sorry indeed should I be to accept the highest honours of the University were I from that time destined to sink into an obscure and useless inactivity."

CHAPTER II.

Goes to Trinity College, Cambridge — Scholarships — Degree — Classical
Medallist—Elected to a Fellowship—Tour Abroad—Acquaintance with
Bunsen—Letters from Cambridge and Abroad—Correspondence in
Foreign Languages—Study of Ancient History—Biographies—Twed-
dell's Remains—Byron—Desire for Foreign Travel—Improvement of
Morals and Manners at Cambridge—Dislike of Mathematics—Acquire-
ment of Italian—Cicero, &c.—Choice of a Profession—Resolution to de-
vote himself to the Bar—Aversion to Legal Pursuits—Desire for Literary
Retirement—Acquirement of German—Comparison between Protestant
and Roman Catholic Worship—Bunsen—Religious Tendency of his
Studies—Remarks on his Brother's Ordination.

THIRLWALL left Charterhouse in December, 1813. In
February, 1814, he was admitted at Trinity College, Cambridge, and went into residence in the following October.
At Trinity he happened on another "golden time;" in the
same generation of undergraduates with him were Whewell, Sedgwick, Hugh James Rose, Kenelm Digby, Hamilton, E. B. Elliott, and his old schoolfellows, Julius Hare,
and George and Horace Waddington. In February, 1815,
he was elected Craven University Scholar, he and Professor Kennedy, being, with Porson, the only instances of
this honour having been gained by Freshmen. The Bell
Scholarship was gained the same year. He took his degree
in 1818 as 22nd Senior Optime, the Seniors of the tripos
being Shaw-Lefevre and Hind. This comparatively low
place was more than atoned for by his position as First
Chancellor's Classical Medallist, the Classical Tripos not
being instituted till 1824. In October, 1818, he was

elected a Minor (*i.e.* B.A.) Fellow of his college.* Among those elected with him were the late Dean Hamilton and his inseparable friend, Julius Hare. By gaining his Fellowship he was enabled to fulfil the "most enchanting of his day dreams," and to carry out the long-cherished idea of a tour abroad. He left England at the close of 1818 and journeyed on the continent for more than a year, visiting France, Switzerland, and Italy. During his residence in Rome he formed that close friendship with Bunsen which lasted for half a century. In the "Life of Baron Bunsen" allusion is made to Bunsen's influence on Thirlwall's choice of a career; and in the "Memoirs of Baroness Bunsen" (pp. 138—141) an interesting letter is quoted showing how prepossessed the Bunsens were in Thirlwall's favour; how assiduous he was in cultivating their acquaintance; and the widened sphere of culture and information that it opened to him.

To Mr. John Candler.

July, 1815.

" . . . . My motive, as I have before said, for making a foreign language the vehicle of a familiar correspondence was to acquire a facility in the use of it, which I foresaw would be of the highest importance and utility in my academical career, and might be a source of benefit and amusement in the course of my future life. That end is now in some degree answered. A letter in the one language costs me no greater effort than one in the other, and I flatter myself with the hope, that in proportion to the number of the Latin letters you receive from me (for I do not intend wholly to drop the exercise) you will find the stiffness

* The Major Fellowship followed in due course in 1821. This distinction was done away in 1860. A difference of stipend still remains, which will be abolished when the new statutes are confirmed.

of my first attempts relax, and their roughness insensibly wear away. . . . .

"I have for some time back been much more conversant with Greek than Roman history. The former we have the peculiar satisfaction of receiving from the pens of writers of the most acknowledged information, talents, and industry, and who for the most part took a share in the events they commemorate. I shall watch both these historical streams to their confluence, and then direct my undivided attention to the mighty flood of Roman grandeur which, growing in its progress at once broader and more dull, loses itself at length in what, to pursue the metaphor, I may call the stagnant pool of the dark ages. I shall not, you may be sure, stop there, but with renewed pleasure accompany it when it emerges from that deep and motionless expanse, divided into a number of rivulets vying in strength and rapidity, though not in extent and magnificence, with the parent stream. I therefore perfectly coincide with you in considering history and biography as the basis of polite literature. They are the inexhaustible sources from which poetry derives her characters, eloquence her examples, and to which writers of almost every class have been indebted for ornament and illustration in their several subjects. To the greater portion of mankind, however, the uses of biography are more obvious and unquestionable than those of history. To the vast majority whom fortune has fixed in a station too humble to interfere with the general interests, whose virtues or vices, wisdom or folly, can influence the happiness only of a narrow circle, narratives of battles and sieges, of conspiracies and revolutions, of the rise and fall of nations, contain little to edify and instruct, little which they can apply to the regulation of their conduct and the direction of their affairs. But as there is no man who lives isolated from the world, whose activity or indolence does not produce some effect upon a part of society, there are none whom the example of persevering virtue may not stimulate to exertion, and whom the contemplation of its rewards may not encourage in their career. It was in consequence of this reflection that the ingenious though fanciful Rousseau, whose speculations, among several extravagancies, contain many just and useful observations, was induced to regret that the gravity of history so seldom descended to record traits of private character in illustrious men, and that he gives the preference in point of utility to Plutarch's lives over the more dignified and elaborate compositions of Thucydides, Xenophon, and Polybius. Yet there are cases in which the perusal of history affords a pleasure not to be derived from any other class of writings. The source of this pleasure is to be found in one of those circumstances which distinguish the great kingdoms of modern Europe from the little republics of ancient Greece, and from Rome before the period of its degeneracy and decline. The circumstance to which I allude is the vastly great number which at present exists of speculative geniuses, of men whose talents are either entirely buried in obscurity or known to the world only through the medium of the press. I shall not, I believe, be too bold if I affirm that the greater part of the most eminent writers of antiquity were men who spent their lives in active employment, and who were as well known by their actions in their own day as they are by their writings in ours. We have, it is true, remaining the feeble though laborious productions of some rhetoricians who turned their periods in the closet for others to deliver in the forum, but the number of such writers is far overbalanced by that of the historians and orators who led armies, who presided in councils, and who served the State by their exertions either in the field of battle or in the rostrum. Such characters were, among the Greeks, Herodotus, Pericles (whose orations, though no longer extant, attracted the admiration of Cicero), Thucydides, Xenophon, Demosthenes, Polybius.   Among the Romans the instances are more rare because literature began to flourish but a short time before the overthrow of liberty.   But Cicero and Cæsar afford striking examples of men who made literary pursuits the amusement, not the business of their lives.   Nor do historians and orators afford the only instances.   We know that Socrates was not content with instructing the youth of Athens under the shelter of the groves of Academus, but that his arm resisted the enemies of his country in the field, and that his voice opposed the insolent injustice of an overbearing faction at home.   Of the three great dramatic poets, Æschylus is recorded to have borne an active part in those combats which one of his dramas has commemorated, Sophocles was the colleague of Pericles in one of the high offices of the State, and Euripides was admitted to a familiar intercourse with Archeläus. . . .

"The quarto you speak of has not yet met my eye, but I am not unacquainted with the subject of it.*   He was one of the brightest ornaments in the college to which I belong, and I have seen some monuments of the elegance of his genius and the variety of his attainments, and have felt a sympathy in a fate in its period so premature, and in its circumstances so romantic.   I should express my joy at the conversion of Lord Byron if I could bring myself to believe that his doubts had been ever sincere. The French Revolution may have produced wretches so

* The quarto alluded to in the above letter was a volume of the " Remains' of John Tweddell, published in 1815.   He was a distinguished young scholar of Trinity, had been Chancellor's Classical Medallist in 1790, and had carried off a multitude of University and College prizes.   The exercises for these had been published in 1793 under the title of "Prolusiones Juveniles," and were afterwards incorporated in the "Remains," and much studied by classical men.   Tweddell travelled a great deal.   He died from fever caught during a stay in Athens in 1799, and was buried in the Temple of Theseus.

hardened by crime as to render it necessary to persuade themselves into the idea of a disbelief of a future state of existence; but that since that mania has passed, and in this country, where the contagion never spread to any considerable extent, such scepticism should have become the settled conviction of a highly cultivated mind, is a phenomenon which it would be more difficult to account for than the supposition that the vanity of a youthful poet might have induced him to throw over his works the melancholy tinge of so gloomy an idea. . . . .

" I am well aware that no extensive and lasting reputation was ever acquired by compositions in a dead language, and I should perhaps be tempted to wake again the strings of my long-sleeping lyre, but that the horrible and appalling denunciation of our master Horace rings in my ears: *Mediocribus esse poetis.* You know the rest. Seriously, I believe my powers, if I have any, to be more adapted to prose composition. I have no doubt of my ability to construct verses which should fill the ear with their cadence, but whether I could produce a poem which should elevate the fancy and satisfy the judgment, is a question of a very different and much more doubtful nature. For whatever efforts I may hereafter make for reputation, I am now, and shall for some years be, employed in paving the way. One of the great advantages, as Rousseau observes, which the geniuses of old times had over those of the present day is, that whereas the ancients spent the whole of their time in thinking, the moderns spend half of theirs in collecting material for thought.

To HIS UNCLE, JOHN THIRLWALL, Esq., Alnwick.

December, 1815.

" . . . . I set off for Cambridge without writing a single line to the oldest and most valued of my correspondents. I write not in the ease and leisure of a long vacation, in which I have nothing to do but to pursue the fancies of my own brain, but under the distraction of two powers, of which one impels me in one direction and the other draws me back in another, under the disquieting apprehension of two not very distant examinations, one of which will require a little share of mathematics, and the other scarcely anything else.

" Moreover, if I abandoned for you a difficult problem or a complicated demonstration, you would not be under any great obligation to me for my preference ; but I now quit, to take up my pen, something infinitely more adapted to my comprehension and agreeable to my taste, a volume of ancient history. . . . .

" As I am not destined, I believe, nor perhaps qualified, for any active occupation, and yet feel in myself a certain restlessness of disposition which will not suffer me to remain idle, the substitute for such employment the most congenial to my inclinations would be travelling, a means of enjoyment and improvement which will perhaps be never in my power, but of which, nevertheless, if I were cut off from the hope altogether, I should lose a considerable share of the pleasures of my existence. When I say travelling, I mean of course travel beyond the limits of our own island ; which although it contains much that is curious and interesting, is not to be compared in point of attraction to those parts of the continent to which I should wish to direct my course. You suggested, I think, some time back a mode of accomplishing this much-desired object, but your scheme, as I observed at the time, although I might accept it if I despaired of bringing any other to bear, would be very inadequate to the complete fulfilment of my wishes. My notions on this head are perhaps somewhat peculiar. I should be by no means content with an opportunity of crossing the

Channel or the German Ocean, and traversing the first country on whose shores I might chance to land. . . . .

" There are, in fact, but three legitimate ends of travelling. One, the contemplation of the great and the beautiful in the scenes of nature'; another, the inspection of works of art, the surviving test of departed genius, or of places which derive an interest from some memorable transactions of which they were the theatres, and are now the monuments ; and a third, the most useful and important, though not calculated to excite such strong and vivid sensations of delight, observation upon the manners, government, and general condition of arts, sciences, religion, and morals among the subjects of foreign States. . . . .

" This reverie of mine, however, upon travelling, leads me to make an observation or two, one founded upon the account you give of your travels through this town, in which I am now writing, and another which has been long in my thoughts. First, the little specimen you met with of Cambridge manners may have induced you to suppose that you are better acquainted with the habits of our academic youth than you really are, and it may happen that you have split upon the rock of which so very few travellers have had the dexterity to steer clear, that I mean of mistaking a particular incident which has befallen themselves for the general custom of the country they are visiting. And again, you may have fallen into the error of which a traveller would be guilty, who, having in his youth visited foreign parts and noted the customs and manners of the inhabitants, should in his old age publish an account of them to the world as a faithful representation of the state of things among the generation living at the time of the publication. As a general maxim I need not remind you that to the end of the world there will be in every large society a great diversity of habits and inclinations, and that it will be as impossible for some to form a relish for refined and intellectual pleasures, as for others to accommodate their palate to those which are gross and brutal. There will even be some who enjoy the one, and yet sometimes descend to the other. But at the same time it is equally certain that in proportion to the progress of refinement and decorum in the great mass of the community, will be the advancement in those respects in the places of polite education. I can further inform you that such improvement I have heard remarked in conversation, and I have seen noticed in a very admirable modern publication, as having taken place in Cambridge within the space of a comparatively small number of years, and that this very circumstance has from its notoriety been insisted on as a proof of the gradual progress in decorum, if not in morality, through the country at large. Here I might say many fine things according to my old and highly commendable custom, for you cannot but remember that it used to be my practice to make my letters to you the vehicles of sundry moral apophthegms highly valuable (if not for their originality) for their truth, and to enliven them by the best similes and metaphors I could bring to bear on the subject, and without some of these I never used to think a letter complete. That I could have tacked some of these to the subject I have just quitted you ought not to doubt from the fertility of invention displayed by me on former occasions. But somehow or other my turn for this species of communication has considerably diminished of late, and whether it is that I read and think more, or that I grow more lazy and indolent, certain it is that I write much less than I used.

"The period of my return to Cambridge has revolved, and with it the annual tribute of a letter, which I have been long accustomed to pay you. I am returning to Cambridge in a somewhat melancholy frame of mind in consequence of the anticipation of above a year of trouble and labour which I have to encounter. I must first shorten and finally abandon the worship of the Muses for that of the Sciences. . . . .

" I console myself partly by the prospect of the respite I shall enjoy as soon as the term of labour has expired, and partly by the occasional relaxation I obtain in the interval. I have added to my stock of acquirements the Italian language, in which I make as much progress as the extreme scantiness of time I have to devote to it will allow. I am almost in doubt whether it be not in general more valuable than the French, to which in poetry at least it possesses a decided superiority. My principal object in acquiring this as well as others I may hereafter learn, is to provide myself with greater variety of entertainment. But although I look to my library for the chief fruits to be derived from it, yet I have still another object in view, and I do not despair of being enabled to derive at some time or other an additional advantage from the acquisition. I certainly was not made to sit at home in contented ignorance of the wonders of art and nature, nor can I believe that the restlessness of curiosity I feel was implanted in my disposition to be a source of uneasiness rather than of enjoyment. Under this conviction I peruse the authors of France and Italy, with the idea that the language I am now reading I may one day be compelled to speak, and that what is now a source of elegant and refined entertainment may be one day the medium through which I shall disclose my wants and obtain a supply of the necessaries of daily life. This is the most enchanting of my day dreams ; it has been for some years past my inseparable companion. And apt as are my inclinations to fluctuate, I cannot recollect this to have ever undergone the slightest abatement. In fact, whatever plans of life I propose for myself, this always constitutes a part of the outline, and I do not know that any prospect of advantage would induce me to part with the hope of its gratification. As soon as I shall have gone through the trial which is to close the approaching period of labour and anxiety, my spirits will be lightened of a considerable load, and my inclinations will meet with little farther constraint. I shall be at greater liberty to embrace any opportunity of present enjoyment, and to look abroad for the most eligible scheme of future happiness. In fact the only object to the pursuit of which I shall be attached will be a fellowship which I shall content myself with endeavouring to earn, without suffering my tranquillity to be very much disturbed either by eagerness for the possession or regret for the loss of it.

" P.S. [by his father] The *Trinitarian* has left me room to inform you he has gained a prize Latin essay in his college as well as is enrolled in the second class, a much higher rank than he expected from his deficiency in mathematics. He is, however, pursuing that science with great ardour, and expects he will gain a respectable honour, even in that region which he least delights in. I am glad Connop has taken up his pen to you.—T. T."

To Mr. John Candler.   *January 17th*, 1817.

" Your last letter did not merely afford me the pleasure of a transient emotion, but supplied me with an occasional subject for thought, during the remainder of the term. I have determined to make provision against my own dilatoriness by beginning an answer thus early in the vacation, a precaution which receives an additional justification from the length of the sheet I have chosen, in which at least I think you will find it difficult to surpass me. I shall as usual save myself the trouble of inventing a subject by following your observations in their own order. The favourable opinion I entertained of the moral character of the great Roman orator was formed in consequence of the perusal of his epistolary correspondence, the only source I apprehend from which any conclusion on the subject could without temerity be drawn. That opinion is not shaken by any argument contained in your letter. You lay particular stress on the encomium upon Cæsar delivered in the oration of thanks for the restoration of Marcellus. If I felt my opinion hard pressed by this panegyric I might be eager to acquaint you that a German critic, probably the most profound and acute scholar of the present day, has pronounced an opinion that this oration is not the production of Cicero. I might add that my last perusal of it inclined me very much to concur in that judgment, partly from an air of sophistical and elaborate declamation which pervades the speech, and partly from the recollection of a passage in one of Cicero's letters (I cannot now remember which) in which he acquaints us that he had not intended to speak on the occasion, and was only induced to rise from what took place after he had entered the Senate. Now as on the one hand I cannot imagine Cicero to have misrepresented the fact on so trifling an occasion, so I cannot easily conceive it possible that an oration of the cast of that now extant should have been unpremeditated and delivered under the influence of transporting and irresistible emotions. I do not insist upon the elegance of the style, which either constant exercise might have placed at his command or a subsequent revisal have polished; but the consummate art and caution visible throughout the whole performance, the skill and judgment with which his praise of Marcellus, Cæsar's enemy, and his panegyric on Cæsar, so lately his own, the review of the past, and the prospect of the future, are balanced and adjusted, tend in my judgment very much to support the conjecture (of the grounds of which I have never been informed) that the whole is the fabrication of some learned and elegant sophist. But as far as the character of Cicero is concerned I might have spared this little piece of criticism, nor have I the least occasion to resort to any such conjecture for an argument in his defence. In fact, supposing the oration to have been delivered, I could discover upon a very late perusal nothing which could be reasonably construed into a desertion of his previous political sentiments. That part which you probably consider as the most objectionable appears to me nothing more than an exemplification of one of the most common, obvious, and innocent of rhetorical artifices, and that too used for the best of purposes : that, namely, of conveying a tacit and forcible admonition to a man whose intentions were not avowed, under the veil of a strong presumption in favour of their integrity and honour. When, therefore, the orator, in praising and thanking the victorious general for an act of clemency, takes occasion to inform him that his work was not yet accomplished, his conquest not yet complete, that the Republic was fixing her eyes in anxious expectation upon his conduct; that, exhausted by a long and cruel series of contests, she expected from him refreshment and repose, the re-establishment of those judicial proceedings which had been suspended by the violence of party, the assurance of respect to the laws, whose voice had been drowned by the din of arms, that she expected, in short, the restoration of all which she had lost; that, consequently, brilliant as had been his past achievements, she hoped their glory would be lost in the lustre of those which were to come, and that without this happy consummation the character of those prior exploits would remain to all posterity as it was in his own day ambiguous and contested; when, I say, the orator addresses the victorious general in this strain, I do not perceive that he is guilty of any inconsistency with his past conduct, or that he in the slightest degree binds himself for the future. His panegyric is obviously, and, indeed, expressly, conditional; nor do I think if, instead of Brutus, he had himself held up the dagger reeking with the blood of Cæsar, there is a passage in this oration (that is, any sentence sufficiently illustrated by the context) which he might not have heard repeated without a blush. Here my defence of Cicero may close; for your argument, if I mistake not, was entirely founded upon this single speech.

"But, unable as I am to agree with you in your attack on the character of Cicero, I can still less admit the excuse which you are willing to allow him, when you impute his inconsistency to ignorance of the Ethics of the Christian Philosophy, 'which would have taught him never to surrender his integrity for the attainment of any object, however desirable.' The observation which follows, 'that the Machiavellian policy, which sanctions unlawful means for the attainment of a lawful end' (by the way, where does the Florentine politician sanction this?), 'was not then scorned and dreaded by statesmen as it is, or ought to be, now,' this observation raised a smile from more causes than one. I was amused by your original contrast of the principles of ancient and modern statesmen, and still more by the interlinear clause, by which you destroy all the meaning of the observation. The fact is, that the proportion of the corrupt to the honest statesmen appears to have been nearly the same formerly that it is now, after all due allowance has been made for the difference of ancient and modern forms of government, and for the progress of a certain sense of decency, which is of recent diffusion, and which must be distinguished both in time and character from the effects of the propagation of Christianity. We have our Chatham, and Athens had her Aristides and her Phocion (of course, I am instancing and not enumerating). But what I wished particularly to animadvert upon was the notion you seem to entertain of the ignorance prevailing among the heathen (I mean their men of education and reflection) respecting the nature and sanctity of moral obligations. I can scarcely express how widely I differ from you on these points. I am firmly of opinion that the detestable maxim of the end sanctifying the means was never adopted in theory or practice by any class of any people in any age or climate (as in the case of the Fathers of the Church, who have, I believe, the honour of being its authors, and of the Church of Rome, and particularly its champions the Jesuits), except, I say, where, as in the instances I have mentioned, superstition blinded the judgment, or interest deadened the heart. I believe it impossible that men could ever have given their assent, secret or avowed, to such a maxim before they had either recognised a guide superior to reason, even when in opposition to it, or had become rebels to its authority even while they acknow-ledged its legitimacy. As to the heathen philosophers, so totally erroneous is your opinion of their ignorance (for when you speak of Cicero it ought to be remembered that you are speaking of a man who was perfectly acquainted with the dogmas and the arguments of every sect which had existed to his day), that there was but one sect of philosophers which professed the principle of parting or dispensing with any moral obligation on the ground of expediency, and that even the most celebrated doctors of this sect contended that to make this dispensation was never expedient, and that finally after this proviso the sect was branded with peculiar opprobrium by the rest on this very account. But as to Cicero himself, in whom the whole question originated, there are a multitude of passages in his own book, 'De Officiis' (in the third book, I think, in particular), which set in a very clear point of view his sentiments on the Jesuitical (for so I would rather call it than Machiavellian) policy I have been speaking of, and show that if he had actually been guilty of an adherence to it in practice, his philosophy might more reasonably and more forcibly have been quoted against him than his eloquence.

" You may possibly recollect that in my last letter I expressed an opinion diametrically the reverse of that which your judgment on Cicero called from you, namely, that the Christian religion had introduced with it no innovations at all in ethics, that it had laid down no principle of morality which had not been acknowledged and inculcated by either all or the best of the heathen writers long before. I still retain this opinion, which was originally founded upon the unbiassed view I had taken of the ancient philosophy as I met with an exposition of it in the works of Cicero. I am persuaded that this opinion is perfectly compatible with a belief in the divine origin of our religion ; and, to go a step farther, although I am very willing to admit that Christianity did effect (whether directly or indirectly is of no consequence) a material and sensible improvement in the practice of morality, yet I should be not only surprised and perplexed, but to a considerable degree shocked and pained, to discover by any convincing proof that any of its essential doctrines were unknown before that revelation. The improvement I mean consisted in bringing forward to more general notice, and more warmly recommending to practice, some of the less brilliant and conspicuous but more useful and amiable virtues. But I repeat, that I still remain to be informed of any one moral precept of Christianity which is not to be found either positively delivered by some heathen moralist or deducible from some part of his system by easy and natural inference. In what the peculiarity, excellence, and necessity of the Christian revelation really consisted is a question of some doubt and difficulty, on which, as it has no intimate connection with our present subject, I shall avoid entering into any disquisition. But as you follow up your particular attack on Cicero by some language of general contempt towards the heathen philosophy, I shall simply remark that your observations on it appear to be founded on a very indistinct, and consequently erroneous, conception of its merits. I am aware that it was formerly the fashion to depreciate it among superstitious Christians, and that it has been lately the fashion among men who call themselves philosophers. But I entertain as low an opinion of the Christianity of the former as of the philosophy of the latter. The fact is, much of this abuse originates in the indolence of our earthly nature, which finds it an easy and gratifying substitute to underrate that to which it cannot attain without exertion. If I may venture to speak from my own experience, I may truly declare that I recollect no book which ever produced a more deep impression on my mind and furnished me with more abundant food for interesting speculation than that volume of Cicero which comprises his philosophical treatises ; nor was the preference I gave to the Epistles founded on their superior intrinsic value, but on their superior peculiarity and originality. And so widely do I differ with you in my estimation of this branch of ancient literature, that if access to it had been the only fruit resulting from all the labour I have spent on the study of the languages I should have esteemed it amply repaid, and if my views of future life had not been changed this would have been the pursuit I should probably have cultivated with the greatest interest and assiduity. I am not quite sure whether I understand the bent of what you say as to danger to be apprehended from 'the elegance, the ingenuity, and the seeming wisdom of some part of the heathen mythology.' I have never heard but of one instance in confirmation of your suggestion. There is, I am told, a man now living who is an exceeding admirer of Plato, and who sacrifices to Jupiter. But if this be true he is certainly unique. Gibbon was a notorious sensualist, and consequently incapable of understanding feelingly any religion whatever. I feel little respect for his taste or his philosophy. As to the three other celebrated men you mention, Salmasius was a pedant who was likely to derive as much edification from Achilles Tatius as from David's Psalms and Paul's Epistles. The consciences of Grotius and Erasmus could best decide whether the fascinations of profane literature had seduced them from any particular of their duty to God or man. But I may remark that theirs was a religious age, and I conceive no great compliment is paid to religion by those who insinuate that there exists a natural connection between learning, philosophy, and infidelity. But I am sensible of the inutility of these general remarks. The subject which I am now quitting naturally leads to questions of greater interest and importance, but for which I have not enough either of leisure or, perhaps, information and ability.

" My aversion and contempt for the artifice of concealing ignorance of a subject under vague and general observations upon it will prevent me from saying much upon Locke. I have not yet read his essay, not so much because I could not find leisure for it, as because I was unwilling to enter at all upon metaphysical reading without being able to pursue it beyond one or two popular works. I cannot, therefore, presume to decide upon the grounds of Locke's reputation. I hope, however, before I quit the university to have it in my power to form a tolerably fair estimate of his merits, although I may perhaps never enjoy sufficient leisure to extend my researches into the study itself so far as I could wish and its importance deserves. Still, having thus candidly made you acquainted with my ignorance of the subject, I cannot refrain from observing, that the merits of Locke as a philosopher have been of late called into question by men for whose talents and acquirements I entertain very high esteem and respect. The originality of his system has been denied by one and its truth by another. It has been charged with a tendency most pernicious to the interests of morality and religion, of which the author was himself not aware. On the justice of this charge I must repeat I am yet incompetent to decide ; but it will certainly prevent me from taking up the work with that superstitious veneration with which the generality of readers apply themselves to it ; and I may add, that the only specimen of its philosophy which ever happened to fall under my notice has by no means tended to counteract the impression produced by the preceding attacks upon it. Locke's reasoning on the subject of free will, in which he is followed by Jonathan Edwards, and I believe some other writers, appears to me unphilosophical, the doctrine in general to debase our nature, and to shake the very foundation of our hope and our faith in suggesting to us the fallacy of our most powerful convictions. I am hence led to suspect that your warm admiration of Locke may have arisen in a great measure from his work having been the first on the subject on which your thoughts have been exercised.

"I do not dislike your definition of metaphysics which,

if my memory does not deceive me, does not differ very widely from one given by Coleridge in a note in the 'Friend.' It is certainly a curious fact that the term itself by which the extensive branch of literature or rather philosophy is known should have no other actual import than the place which a treatise on the subject held in the collection of Aristotle's works. But when you proceed to distinguish between investigations of the properties and of the nature of thinking beings, I apprehend you to have fallen into two mistakes. In the first place I cannot agree with you in your opinion that the consideration 'of the manner in which we acquire, compound, and associate our ideas is the noblest of merely human studies that can occupy the attention of man,' although I confess that our difference may possibly arise from my want of knowing the bounds by which you conceive studies 'merely human' to be circumscribed. But, at all events, I consider these as topics belonging to an inferior branch of metaphysics. And here I may observe that on these topics I believe the merit of Locke to be acknowledged even by his opponents; but this will not entitle him to the rank of a great philosopher. The subject, for instance, of free will, which I mentioned a little before, appears to me to belong to a very different class and to be of incomparably greater interest and importance. In the second place, when you speak of the nature or essence of the soul of man, of angelic spirits, and the Divine Being, you appear to me to summon up a defunct absurdity, or rather, perhaps, one which never existed, for the purpose of expressing your contempt and neglect of it. For although the heathen philosophers had many disputes on the nature of the soul of man for instance, yet I apprehend these not to come exactly within your meaning. For the main point in these discussions was whether the soul was or was not immaterial, which I apprehend to be no improper subject of investigation. But that any man ever was guilty of such an excess of ignorant presumption as to enter into a consideration even in thought of the essence or substratum of the soul, admitting it to be a spiritual or immaterial substance, I cannot bring myself to believe, and I am really at a loss to conjecture what can be the mark against which you levelled these observations. No modern writer surely can have been guilty of the folly you point at. The mention of Locke calls forth the most puzzling queries, and the more so as I cannot perceive their relation in whatever manner answered to the two axioms whose universality you seem to question.

"The tradition of Ossian's poem has I suppose continued uninterrupted to the present day, but Macpherson's forgery may have given it a freshness which it has not possessed for many centuries since its origin. Your second query as to the conversion of Constantine is, if possible, still more perplexing. I have not read the life of Constantine in which the account of the miracle is contained, but I do not believe that any information on the subject is to be found in the original, which might enable me to form a more correct opinion upon it than may be deduced from Gibbon. The evidence of Eusebius, a man whose general character does not certainly exempt him from all suspicion of sacrificing truth to adulation, carries with it little weight. But were the external evidence for the miracle tenfold stronger than it is, I should upon mature reflection decidedly reject it. There are two things necessary for my belief of a miracle, that the fact should be well attested and that an adequate reason should be assigned for the interruption of the laws of nature. In the present case there is every reason to believe—1st, that the miracle did not produce the immediate and particular effect which was to render it a cause of general benefit; 2ndly, that general benefit did not actually result from it; and 3rdly, that, admitting the consequences to have been really beneficial, the same would have taken place in the common order of events. To explain my meaning, I think, first, that history sufficiently proves that Constantine never was converted to Christianity— that from first to last he professed it without ever feeling in his heart or exemplifying in his practice its genuine excellence. The arms of his soldiers adorned with the figure of the Cross were no bad illustrations of the character of their Emperor. The instruments of rapine and violence bore the visible sign of a religion of peace and love; exactly as the hard, cruel, and ambitious heart of Constantine was disguised under the profession of the same mild and benignant creed. Is it to be imagined that the great Searcher of hearts should have stretched forth the arm of His omnipotence to form a nominal proselyte to His worship, or that in providing for the salvation of multitudes He should have neglected to rescue from perdition the man himself who was His elected organ, His chosen vessel? But without searching for an argument into the unfathomable depths of the eternal wisdom, it is more than doubtful whether the Church of Christ did not receive from the event itself of the profession of Constantine more injury than benefit. The injury is obvious, the advantage a matter of uncertain speculation. The patronage of Constantine, as far as it extended to the Church then existing, was unquestionably detrimental. The trappings of wealth and power accorded ill with the simplicity of a religion whose professors were taught to expect that they should be here militant and hereafter only triumphant. It is from the conversion of Constantine that I should date the visible and rapid decline of Christianity, as, if your friends shall ever begin to erect schools or colleges for the instruction of their youth in liberal studies, I should fix upon this period as the point at which the society will begin to fall to utter and absolute decay. On the other hand, I would not positively deny that if the power or influence of Constantine, even by means the most repugnant to the spirit and precepts of the Gospel, accomplished the introduction of some barbarous nations into the pale of Christianity, although his contemporaries had no reason to congratulate themselves on his conversion, it may still have been the means of promoting the greatest interests of generations then unborn. The early inhabitants of our own island were threatened or allured into a Christianity scarcely less contemptible and unprofitable than the superstition they abandoned for it. Yet perhaps as much of genuine and vital religion now prevails here as in any other country of Europe. The question, therefore, whether Constantine did the greater service or injury to the general interests of the Gospel will depend in a great measure upon another, whether in a civilised nation the introduction of a new or the reformation of an old religion be a work of greater difficulty. But in whatever way this question be decided, it is tolerably obvious that in the time of the supposed miracle Christianity was becoming the predominant religion, that it would consequently in the common course of things soon have found its way into the palace, and that the Divine wisdom would scarcely have anticipated by a miracle a conversion which ere long would have been accomplished by the ordinary workings of the human passions.

"I almost regret that I have spent so much of my paper upon such a subject; and as I am unwilling both for your sake and my own to begin a fresh sheet, I shall omit entering upon a topic on which I had proposed to make a few remarks relating to the study of languages, that I may have room to answer the concluding part of your letter, in which you give me your advice on the choice of a profession. It is a subject which has long occupied my thoughts and distracted my will, and on which I scarcely know whether I have yet decided, for I have learnt from experience to distrust my own resolutions and intentions. The present state of my mind, however, strongly inclines me to follow your advice and devote myself to the bar. My disinclination to the Church has grown from a motive into a reason. But be assured that if I do give myself up to the law it will not be with the elation of hope and ambition. Not even the brilliant objects with which your friendly partiality gilds the prospect in the distance, if I were as fully persuaded of their reality as I am convinced of their emptiness, would console me for the sacrifice I must make in the pursuit of them. I must surrender all tastes, views, and wishes which have possessed me during the greater part of my past life since I became capable of reflection and imagination. I had hoped to be able to pass my life quietly though not indolently, and obscurely though not uselessly ; to have gratified eye and ear and mind and soul with the sights and sounds of nature, and the finest productions of the human intellect. I hoped to have been able to add to my acquirements all the most valuable of the modern languages, and by that means to have gained access to the stores of modern as well as ancient literature. I had intended to have made myself master of all that was important in the universal history of mankind, and to have followed the researches of ancient and modern philosophy, and from all these sources to have collected certain principles and maxims both of taste and philosophy which might supply the place of books, if ever their perusal should become more toilsome than agreeable. Nor had I purposed to confine my pleasures to those of either sense, or reason, or understanding, whose barrenness I well knew when unaccompanied by the exercise of the social and benevolent affections. In the indulgence of these I had anticipated that the desire of communicating happiness might in many instances make amends for the deficiencies of fortune. But it is useless to dwell on a vision which has past. The painful reality is that some profession is necessary, and the law seems that which circumstances have marked out for my adoption. I must exchange the retirement with the prospect of which I have hitherto amused my fancy for the noise and bustle I have always detested, and mix in the crowd of men pursuing like myself one sordid object. I must feel my most valuable acquisitions dropping away for want of leisure to bestow on their cultivation, and a metamorphosis gradually taking place in my whole frame without the possibility and scarcely with the wish of resisting it. You may easily suppose then that I shall not enter upon the study of the law with large views and swelling hopes and glittering projects. No! I shall rush into the pursuit with a desperate activity, propelled by the single forlorn chance of amassing a competent fortune in time sufficient to free myself from the trammels of business, before my views and tastes and sentiments have undergone a total change. If this can be accomplished, I may perhaps console myself for having wasted the elasticity of youth and the glow of fancy on the routine of a barren and unanimating occupation (barren, I mean, in all that can rouse the imagination and interest the heart), and in finding 'the glory and the freshness' of my early dream succeeded by a gloomy and monotonous reality. But ere thirty or forty years have elapsed who can tell what I may have become? The seeds of avarice and ambition now dormant in my breast will perhaps very soon be awakened into life. I shall mistake the fever of restless and unnatural desires for the ordinary and healthy warmth of my moral constitution; and I doubt not if this letter should again reach my eye, that I should read it with a false and hollow mirth, mingled, however, with glimpses and shadowy recollections of the past, ten thousand times more bitter than the melancholy with which I am now writing. Horrible anticipation! I do not dislike your Indian scheme: certainly the prospect of the great ocean which would be to divide me from my country and my friends for a moderate term of years would be infinitely less desolating than the view of the great city, contemplated with the possibility of being a sojourner in it for life. You may imagine that I do not quit such a subject for want of words."

To Mr. John Candler.

June 11th, 1818.

" . . . . At the time when I received your last letter containing an account of your Scottish excursion my whole attention was engrossed by the approach of an examination on which my future prospects in a considerable degree depended. I determined, therefore, to defer my answers till I should be in a humour better suited to the purpose of repaying you for your very entertaining narrative. That time, it is true, has not yet arrived; I am as I was then absorbed in the future, with no present enjoyment to satisfy my wishes. . . . . I once hoped that I should this summer have realised the wishes I have so long indulged of visiting those parts of the continent whose scenery has in all ages ravished the eye and warmed the heart of every spectator capable of enjoying the beauty and sublimity of nature. In this hope I have been disappointed, and shall perhaps for a year or two more be confined to the same routine of study in which I have been for many years past engaged. . . . . I am sick I confess of the confinement of

the closet.   The uniformity of this way of life wearies and
oppresses me. . . . . I have begun to learn German, but
as my home views forbid me to relax my attention to
the classics and mathematics, and my project of a continental tour induces me to wish for a familiar acquaint-
ence with French and Italian, I have not much time to
devote to this new pursuit, which certainly does not require
the least share of it.   Of this, however, I am certain, that
no modern language will so amply repay me for my time
and labour."

To HIS FATHER.

ROME, *March 2nd*, 1819.

" . . . . In as far as regards its exterior the Catholic
worship presents at the present day an appearance which
is probably precisely the same which it has borne for five
or six centuries back. The same ceremonies are performed
with the same circumstances on the same occasions. If
you wish to know my opinion of these ceremonies in
general, I must own that I am not disposed to condemn
them with that severity which most Protestants appear to
think necessary to support their character, either as members of a Reformed Church or followers of an enlightened
philosophy.   Some of these rites depend, it is true, upon
articles of faith peculiar to Catholicism ; others seem to be
nothing more than customs derived from notions once
popular and now no longer prevalent even among the
Catholics themselves.   But, putting these out of the
question, I am not at all convinced that the use of forms
and ceremonies necessarily destroys the spirituality of devotion, and am rather inclined to conclude that wherever
a stated return of public worship is instituted, some appeal
to the eye and ear ought to be made to excite religious

feeling in those who do not happen to bring it with them. The form of prayer used by the Church of England, as it is the only public manifestation of a religious sentiment, is, wherever the sentiment is not felt, an empty ceremony, but a ceremony which, from its extreme simplicity, is perfectly adapted to the expression of devotion where it exists, but which can scarcely excite it in the mind where it lies dormant. The Catholic worship combines the advantages of forms which affect Protestant spectators in a variety of ways, but which are certainly found imposing by the Catholics themselves, with the most perfect liberty of private devotion. For those who do not feel disposed to join in the public service of the Church no place and no time is prohibited for the expression of the particular feelings or desires. . . . .

"I have been fortunate in the acquaintance of a Prussian who has married a cousin of Monk, and resides here to transact the affairs of the Prussian Catholics with Rome. He is a man of very various acquirements and considerable abilities, and his wife a most amiable and accomplished woman. He has introduced me to several learned Germans, whom I meet occasionally at his house, and lends me from time to time some good German books, which are still more scarce at Rome than Greek books.

To Mr. JOHN CANDLER.

FLORENCE, *August* 12*th*, 1819.

" . . . . I read with a smile the extract you give me from one of my early letters. I recalled with pleasure the ardour of resolution, the sensibility of the great and beautiful in morality which was one of the best features of my boyhood, and which I hope, in spite of my more extensive intercourse with the world, I have not wholly lost. I was at the same time much amused by the recollection of the sort of vow of which you remind me, and which, as I well remember, I made after reading not the Works of Pascal, but only a notice of his Life prefixed to an English translation of, I believe, his ' Thoughts.'   I was the more amused, as it happened that a short time before, during my stay in Rome, I had read the entire Works of Pascal, and not only with deep attention, but when I was in a frame of mind perfectly fitted to receive the same impression which his memoirs made upon me before his religious opinions, or in fact religion in general, had ever been presented to me as a subject for examination.

" . . . .   In the meanwhile I think I may say that I have already begun to fulfil my boyish vow, not in the letter but in spirit, not by devoting my time and attention to one particular book or class of books, the sure way to cramp the intellect and prevent the attainment of truth ; but by fixing my thoughts frequently and earnestly on the great principles of religion and morality, and referring to them in ways more or less direct everything I read and observe.   I hope to do so on my return to England in a still greater degree, and although, if I am forced to enter into the commerce of the world, a great portion of my time must be devoted to a different pursuit, I feel convinced that these meditations must be henceforth the great employment of my leisure, my refreshment from the wearisome routine of affairs, and, I hope, will be a guide and assistance in the conduct of them. . . . ."

To his Brother Thomas.

Genoa, *August* 30*th,* 1819.

" . . . . The news of your ordination came upon me unexpectedly enough, but it occasioned more of pleasure than surprise. Your reflection, that to decline associating with the present clergy because their ancestors probably differed from them on points on which you agree was to exercise a delicacy carried to excess, appears to me very natural and just. I only wonder that it did not strike you sooner. The prospect of filling a station in society which affords means of great utility ought not certainly to be sacrificed to a punctilio. Paley is certainly right in giving the founders of the English Church credit for perceiving that on articles which are subject to opinion there never can be an universal uniformity. The only misfortune is that any article which is subject to opinion should have been admitted into any creed. The English Reformers, in selecting from different confessions the tenets they considered necessary, opened a door into the Church towards opposite quarters of the theological horizon. In so doing they exposed it to as many attacks from without as any of the others, and gave occasion to more internal dissensions than the rest appear to suffer."

CHAPTER III

Lincoln's Inn.   1820—1827.

THIRLWALL returned from the Continent to settle down to
work.   What this work should be had been with him a
subject of long and anxious consideration.   The idea of
embracing a clerical career, apparently the fixed intention
of his boyhood, had gradually grown distasteful, and was
now put aside from ' distrust of his own resolutions and
convictions.'   He seems to have been guided in a great
measure by the solicitations of his friends (pp. 45-60), and
" the long-balanced deliberation on the choice of a profession
came to a conclusion " by his being entered as a law student
at Lincoln's Inn in February, 1820.   But his aversion
to the law was never concealed, nor his total absence of
ambition in that profession ; and he evidently looked
eagerly forward to the time when he might throw off his
wig and gown and devote himself entirely to his favourite
literary pursuits.   An anecdote is preserved telling of a
humorous picture that Thirlwall once gave a college friend
of a successful lawyer's life and death.   " After setting
forth the drudgery and thankless efforts of a rising Junior,

and the utter want of leisure of his successful seniors, he said, 'I think it was Sir Matthew Hale who observed that a successful lawyer commonly died in his bed surrounded by his family; which, I suppose, is intended as some compensation for the little happiness he has enjoyed in this life, and his very doubtful chance of happiness in that which is to come.'"

The drudgery of his work was lightened by the lengthened tours he took every autumn; by the leisure hours he devoted to German literature; and by the brilliant and intellectual society into which he was thrown. In Mill's Autobiography there is an interesting passage which gives a glimpse of this period of Thirlwall's life. In the society founded by the Owenites called the Co-operative Society (the occasion was a debate on Population), " the speaker with whom I was most struck," says John Stuart Mill, " though I dissented from nearly every word he said, was Thirlwall the historian, since Bishop of St. David's, then a Chancery barrister, unknown except by a high reputation for eloquence acquired at the Cambridge Union before the era of Austin and Macaulay. His speech was in answer to one of mine. Before he had uttered ten sentences I set him down as the best speaker I had ever heard, and I have never since heard any one whom I placed above him." The interest aroused by this debate led to the formation of a debating society, which included, besides Mill and Thirlwall, Macaulay, Charles Austin, the present Earl Grey, the late Lord Clarendon, Romilly, the two Bulwers, Samuel Wilberforce, Albany Fonblanque, and, later on, Frederick Maurice and John Sterling. In April, 1823, Thirlwall became the pupil of Mr. Basevi, the brother of the well-known and unfortunate architect, and uncle of the Earl of Beaconsfield, and studied conveyancing under him. In the summer of 1825 he was called to the Bar, his surety on call being his old school and college

friend, George Waddington.   He afterwards joined the
Home Circuit.   The year 1825 was 'also marked by the
publication of the translation of Schleiermacher's 'Essay on
St. Luke,' with a remarkable introduction by the translator,
showing that his mind still retained its theological bent.
The publication of this book was an epoch in the history
of English Theology, and in Thirlwall's own life, owing to
the part it played in his future prospects (p. 159).   Julius
Hare and Thirlwall at this time " were probably the only
Englishmen thoroughly well-versed in the literature of
Germany," and the letters to Hare show the wide range of
German reading which the preparation of the work entailed,
and the earnestness with which he devoted himself to it.
The dryness of his investigations (p. 73) was relieved by
the translation and publication in the same year of two
of Tieck's Tales—The Pictures (" die Gemälde "), and The
Betrothing (" die Verlobung"), accompanied by an elaborate
preface.   The *Quarterly Review* (No. LXXVII.) referred to
the translator as " a man of great talents," and to the
Introduction and Preface as " sufficient_to place him in an
eminent rank."

In 1827 came the great change in his life, and he
abandoned the legal for the clerical profession.   His
Cambridge friends have attributed this change to his deep
interest in religion, but there is not the slightest evidence
to show that it was anything more than the exchange of a
legal for a literary career.   Strange as this may seem in
these days, it was quite in accordance with the spirit and
practice of the times.   In the letter to his uncle, at the
beginning of the next chapter, Thirlwall explains and
defends his motives.   Bearing in mind his aversion to
the practice of the law, and his utter repudiation of all
desire for forensic honours, it is difficult to say what might
have been his future position.   It is certain, however,
" that Equity lost in him an incomparable judge.   It is

not difficult to imagine the serene ratiocination with which
he would have rivalled even the greatest masters of the
modern Equity Bench.   But he carried the temper, and
perhaps the habit of Equity, into all his subsequent work."

To JOHN THIRLWALL, Esq.

February 16*th*, 1820.

"I feel much obliged to you for your early congratulations on my arrival in England, and for the interest you
continue to take in my proceedings and prospects. . . . .
As to my future plans, the most precise intelligence I have
to give you is, that last week I was entered a member of
the Honourable Society of Lincoln's Inn, and kept my first
term.   So that you will next congratulate me on the long-
balanced deliberation on the choice of a profession having
come to a conclusion.   I would not, however, have you
infer too much from the outward act, nor suppose that all
or any of my objections to the profession have been
removed or lost their weight.   The theory of the law is a
useful branch of knowledge, as necessary to that profound
and minute acquaintance which every man who has leisure
for it ought perhaps to acquire of the history of his own
country.   But to the practice I shall look forward with
the same aversion as ever.   The studies belonging to it
tend I think to cramp the intellect and kill the imagination,
and thereby to stop the sources of the purest and noblest
pleasures of life ; and the qualities most instrumental to
insure success are precisely such as I would wish to assume
with the wig and gown, and with them to lay aside, when
I was about to enter into any good company, to transact
any fair business, and to prosecute any liberal study.
Nevertheless, two considerations prevent me from regretting
the step I have taken, though not the necessity which

caused it.   One is my firm determination not to suffer the study of the law to engross my time so as to prevent me from pursuing the other branches of knowledge of which I have been so long acquiring the rudiments, and which, though in the common sense of the word less lucrative, are much more essential to my well-being.   If by economy of time or intensity of application I can render the two objects compatible, I shall consent to suffer my progress to be slower than I could wish.   If not, I know which to prefer. And by the same means I shall probably escape the misfortune into which several members of the profession, who, perhaps, entered into it with feelings similar to mine, have fallen, that, namely, of being unable to retire from it, long after all rational inducements of interest had ceased to exist, because they could not fill up the void which would ensue in their occupations by any pursuit of interest sufficient to counterbalance the love of gain.   The second consideration is, that I have entered into no engagement which binds me any longer than suits my pleasure or convenience; that I do not make myself answerable for the maxims or doctrines of any set of men whatever, but continue to enjoy a full independence in thought, word, and action, which is not only formal, but, real as it is, not even violated by an additional interested motive. . . . ."

[In reference to a tour abroad with his brother.]

To John Thirlwall, Esq.

October, 1820.

". . . . We made a most interesting and delightful excursion to the Grande Chartreuse, situated in the mountains at a short distance from the frontier of Savoy. This was the birthplace of the Carthusian order which distinguished itself among the monastic orders by the severity of its rule and the princely magnificence of its establishments; to one of which, you know, I owe the rudiments of my education. About nine hundred years ago S. Bruno led a little colony into this wilderness, as it was then justly called, to the greater glory of God and edification of mankind. The retirement of these pious settlers was frequently broken in upon by admiring and consulting visitors, who were eager to testify their veneration or gratitude by donations, which, after the first resistance had been overcome, were showered profusely on the growing settlement. Roads were opened through the pathless wood into the hallowed retreat; the simple oratory rose into a church; the rude huts of S. Bruno and his companions into a spacious convent, which has, of course, received in the lapse of ages numerous alterations; the adjoining forest was in part cleared, cultivated, and peopled for the benefit of the fathers, who became proprietors of all the adjacencies of their retreat. Nevertheless, although much has been done to facilitate the approach to it, and the surrounding region has assumed a different aspect, it is difficult to imagine a spot better adapted to monastic seclusion. It is a valley of irregular shape, whose sides present a woody wilderness only broken by the convent itself and a little pasture ground immediately surrounding it; they are crowned by a wall of steep bare rocks, which contrast surprisingly with the mass of foliage below, and at the bottom a little stream feels its way over fallen trees between huge fragments of rock. At each extremity of the valley the sides close suddenly in, and two lofty overhanging precipices only allow a passage to the stream and the only road which gives entrance into this majestic solitude. Some of the monks who had been driven from their cells at the beginning of the revolution have returned and partially repaired the plundered and disfigured buildings, and continue to exhibit the rule of the Order in all its austerity.　No female is allowed to enter their walls; all flesh, even for the use of strangers, is excluded from their kitchens; they invert the natural order of rest, and labour for the mortification of the flesh and the weal of. the soul, and at the hour when the generality of men retire to sleep rise to spend the greater part of the night in the repetition of long offices or silent meditation; they are allowed one another's society only at rare and measured intervals, and even the majestic spectacle which surrounds them is opened no oftener to their view.　To soften the rigour of these painful restrictions and injunctions they are permitted to follow the bent of their genius in the disposal of the small number of their solitary hours which are not assigned to stated acts of devotion, and to refresh the mind—after exercises which, whether they are the overflowings of pious fervour or merely prescribed and mechanical repetitions, must equally exhaust it—with a gentle, regular, and voluntary exertion.　It was principally this spot—which has acquired additional celebrity since Gray wrote in 'The Traveller's Album' a few Latin stanzas,* which have been as often quoted as any of his works—that attracted us into Dauphiny. . . . ."

[In reference to a tour in Scotland.]

To JOHN THIRLWALL, Esq.

EDINBURGH, *August* 15*th*, 1821.

" . . . . I spent last Sunday at Glasgow, and I believe saw everything very remarkable. . . . . Unluckily Dr. Chalmers was out of town, a circumstance which I did not learn till the afternoon, and attended his church both services in hopes of hearing him.　In the morning I heard a very heavy piece of Presbyterian divinity, which I had

* Commencing " Oh tu, severi religio loci."

hardly time to digest in the interval. I was, however, highly gratified in the afternoon by Dr. Chalmers's coadjutor (a Mr. Irving, I think),* who is one of the very small number of powerful and original thinkers I have heard from the pulpit, and whom I should be willing constantly to attend. . . . ."

To Monsieur Bunsen, Rome.

November 16th, 1821.

". . . . Seit meiner Rückkehr von Italien habe ich mich, den Wünschen der Meinigen zu folge, auf das Studium unsrer Gesetzen gelegt. Das ist mir freylich für sich genommen nicht zuwider, aber ich hätte gewünscht mich anderen Studien ganz zu widmen ; die mit den Juristischen mir wenig in Berührung kommen. Leider ist jetzt in England mehr vielleicht als anderswo die Ansucht herrschend die Dinge von der Seite der Brauchbarkeit oder vielmehr des Gewinnes betrachtet. Diesem Handelsgeiste gelten sogar Kunst und Wissenschaft mehr als Waaren die man erst zu Markte bringen soll, um sie recht zu benutzen ; nicht das Mittheilen soll Zweck seyn der erworbnen Kenntnissen und Fertigkeiten, sondern das Vertauschen. Ja! den Meisten kömmt eine verschiedene Denkungsart unbegreiflich oder gar verwerflich vor.

"Diesen Ansichten kann ich mir unmöglich beystimmen : ob es aber mir gelingen wird den Schein der Weltklugheit zu erhalten ohne auf alles was mir wirklich werth ist versicht zu thun, oder ich werde endlich die Maske abziehen müssen und mich von dem Schauplatze entfernen—darüber wird die Zeit entschieden. . . . .

"Seitdem habe ich mich auch mit immer steigenden

* Edward Irving's public career began with his acceptance, in 1819, of Dr. Chalmers's invitation to become his assistant at St. John's Church Glasgow.

Lust und grösserem Nützen auf die Deutsche Literatur gelegt. Besonders haben mich Tieck's Schriften eingenommen, und ich muss gestehen dass seine Genovefa scheint mir das vollkommenste Gedicht das in den neueren Zeiten irgendein Deutscher Schriftsteller hervorgebracht hat.

"Ich habe Waddington seit seiner Rückkehr noch nicht gesehn; durch seinen Bruder aber habe ich die unangenehme Nachricht erhalten dass Ihre Gesundheit in einen misslichen Zustande gewesen ist. Es würde mich sehr freuen, wenn Sie Gelegenheit bekämen mir einen Brief zu senden, aus Ihren eigenem Munde von Ihrer volligen Genesung zu vernehmen.

"Ich bitte Sie Frau Bunsen in meinen Namen zu grüssen."

[TRANSLATION.]

". . . . Since my return from Italy I have, in accordance with the wishes of my family, applied myself to the study of our laws. I certainly have not an intrinsic aversion to this, but I had wished to devote myself to other studies which have very little to do with the law. Unfortunately, the predominant inclination just now, in England more than elsewhere, is to regard. things from the side of utility, or rather of gain. This commercial spirit values even art and knowledge simply as wares which shall only be brought to market in order to make the best use of them ; not imparting but exchanging shall be the aim of the acquired knowledge and skill. Ay ! to the most part a different way of thinking appears inconceivable and altogether to be rejected.

"It is impossible for me to assent to these views : whether I shall succeed in keeping up the appearance of worldly wisdom without betraying all that I really value, or whether I shall at last be obliged to tear off the mask and withdraw from the stage, time alone will decide. . . .

"Since then [his return from a tour abroad] I have been engaged in German literature with ever-increasing pleasure and greater profit. I have specially taken up Tieck's works, and I must confess that his 'Genovefa' seems to me the most perfect poem that any German author has ever produced in modern times.

"I have not seen Waddington yet since his return, but I have received from his elder brother the unwelcome intelligence that your health has been in a critical state. I should greatly rejoice, if an opportunity should arise for you to send me a letter, to ascertain from your own lips your complete recovery.

"Pray greet Madame Bunsen in my name."

To J. C. HARE, Esq., Trinity College, Cambridge.

LONDON, *November* 8th, 1822.

"I have at last determined to continue my experiment upon the law for some time longer, and am for that purpose just come to town, when Stair put into my hands a composite letter from you and Robert Grant. All things considered, I find it would not be worth my while to go into your rooms for the remainder of your half-year, and I should not wish—if it were practicable—to take them for any considerable time longer upon my own hands. I have, therefore, taken a set of lodgings at 19, Southampton Row, where I shall probably remain during the winter.

"I feel hardly interest enough for Robert Grant to bring me to Cambridge, and yet I should rather like to give a vote against Lawyer Scarlett, and should certainly most bitterly regret my absence if it were to prevent his defeat or the triumph of the good cause.* But, in fact,

---

* At the election of M.P. for Cambridge University, in November, 1822, Mr. Scarlett (afterwards Lord Abinger) was defeated by Mr. Banks and Lord Hervey.

if I were to go down now, the election would be little more than a pretext; for the strongest attraction would be the prospect of spending a day or two with you, and satisfying my senses of your new state of existence. I was, however, not much surprised, and, upon the whole, very glad to hear of your translation.*

"I could, perhaps, have wished you a somewhat wider channel for your activity, but it is certainly good, and as the course of the world runs fortunate to have one at all, especially one which it is possible to enlarge, and anything is better than the torment of being distracted by two opposite objects, or rather by the complete contradiction of the reality and the ideal.

"From what I have been able to observe I rather doubt the success of the Trappist in his vigorous attempt to take the kingdom of heaven by storm.

"That he possesses the zeal of St. Bernard I am ready to believe, but it is a different generation that he has to deal with, one from which he is more likely to receive the crown of martyrdom than the honours of a saint. We must talk more about him when we meet, which will, I hope, be either here or at Cambridge before long."

To Monsieur Bunsen.

19, Southampton Row, London, *January 20th*, 1823.

"I found your very acceptable letter on my return from a tour which I made last summer in Portugal and Spain. I came to town too late to take advantage of H. Waddington's journey to Italy, and I have been since waiting in vain for an opportunity of committing these lines to the care of a friend. I can no longer defer my thanks for

* Julius Hare quitted the study of the law to become assistant tutor at Trinity.

the interest you express in all that concerns me, and for the instructive hints which some of the subjects of my letter have occasioned. These hints would in their turn afford me abundant matter for observation, but in proportion to the extent of the inquiries to which they lead I feel the imperfection and insufficiency of this mode of communication. At the distance which separates us I should be loth to enter into a long discussion which might possibly turn on a misconception of your meaning. In an hour's conversation we should understand one another much better than after two dissertations upon paper, however long and elaborate. In the hope of renewing before long that closer intercourse to which I look back with so much pleasure, I shall here only describe my present opinions and feelings on some of the points in question.

" It would be impossible for me to feel the full force of your remarks on the dignity and importance of the study of the law, without a more distinct notion of the sense in which you wish them to be understood, or of the historical views on which they are founded. I suppose, indeed, that the study to which they refer is of the most general, comprehensive, and philosophical kind, consistent with the peculiarity of national circumstances. But it appears to me that statesmen possessing minds gifted for and cultivated by this study, who have certainly been rare in all countries, have not been more common in England than elsewhere. Now, too, among our legislators we have some able lawyers, but as at other times they who distinguish themselves most in the one quality perform the least in the other. A really great lawyer, who should combine a deep and accurate knowledge with a large and statesmanlike view of his subject, is, in the present state of our law, a phenomenon not to be hoped for, scarcely to be imagined, any more than an accomplished mathematician who should be at the same time a great philosopher.

Indeed, much less, for of all studies I can conceive none which has a more direct tendency to cramp the intellect and unfit it for all high and generous speculation than that of our law in its details. It is difficult enough even for the strongest heads to emerge, even at intervals, from the artificial sphere within which they are circumscribed by precedent and analogy into a higher and clearer region, more nearly approaching the pure ether of absolute reason ; but constantly to keep in mind, while threading the mazes of this immense labyrinth, the plan, design, and relations of the whole, seems to me almost to surpass the ability of man. And hence it is, to revert to my own particular case, that I can perceive here no link of connection with my other pursuits and inquiries, far less any central point to which to refer them all. Thus is the unity of my intellectual life utterly broken, and I find myself in the painful and unnatural necessity of devoting the greater part of my time and attention to that which appears to me petty and uninteresting, and making the great business of my thoughts an accidental and precarious appendage to it. Some kind of employment at the University to which I belong would, as you rightly suppose, be infinitely more congenial to my inclinations, but, in order to fill any station there which would be more than temporary, it would be necessary to enter into the Church, a condition which would deprive such a situation of that which constitutes its chief attraction for me. But who is there that has not often experienced similar obstacles to the attainment of objects which appear to him most conducive not only to his happiness but his usefulness? My chief consolation in this state of divided activity is, that I am perhaps more likely to make the best use of these less frequent opportunities, and in less danger of being misled by prejudices or diverted by minor objects from the investigation of greater and better things than if I were able to devote all my time

to the pursuits I love.   Perhaps, too, what I lose in dura-
tion I gain in intensity of enjoyment.   I consider these
short intervals which break the return of my ordinary life
as a kind of sanctuary reserved for higher and more solemn
thoughts, and into which I therefore admit only some
select companions.   Upon the whole, too, I find myself
better so than if what I have followed hitherto for its own
sake were to become connected with any prospects of outward advantage and success in the world.   I have always
felt a peculiar horror of simony—and surely the name is
as properly applied to the sale of the ordinary as of the
extraordinary gifts of the Spirit.   And as we love men
more for what we do for them than what we receive from
them, so my studies are more endeared to me by every
hour I give to them subtracted from more gainful occupations.   And then, compared with the field of human
intellect, how trifling is the difference between the longest
and the shortest life, the most extensive and contracted
opportunities !   The things most essential are a steady will
and a well-directed tendency of pursuit.   The want of a
right direction of intellectual energies is perhaps the greatest
that England now suffers.   For the age appears to me to
be scarcely less fruitful in men of extraordinary powers than
any in our history.   But the very productions which bear
the strongest stamp of their genius prove most decidedly
the want of a steady aim and distinct perception of the
extent, the limits, and objects of art.   We do not, indeed, now
groan under the tyranny of absurd and borrowed rules, but
we are exposed to all the perversities and extravagancies
of powerful minds which have broken loose from the old
arbitrary restraint, and are governed by no self-acknow-
ledged well-grounded principles.   And such must continue
to be the case till the spirit of true and vital philosophy
shall descend upon this chaos, pregnant hitherto with
scarcely anything but abortions and foul and ominous

shapes, and shall order and organize the whole and every part.   Some of the better spirits of the age have expected this regeneration from Germany, and have in consequence attempted to naturalise among us some of the speculations of your philosophers.   But although these attempts, as they were excellently meant, have been far from useless, I am inclined to doubt, first, that it would be possible through any medium to familiarise even our best cultivated intellects with your philosophical theories ; and, secondly, still more, that by so doing the object would be accomplished.   Such systems would, I think be always something foreign and uncongenial to our peculiar intellectual character, and would therefore have either no general influence, or a wrong and mischievous one on literature, art, and science. It is as you say, from England, from some original and independent English thinker, that we must expect this restoration of philosophy, which appears unhappily to be still very distant. . . . ."

To JOHN THIRLWALL, Esq.

May 2nd, 1823.

". . . . I took my post some days ago in the office of a conveyancer, who is introducing me into not the least intricate or lengthy windings of the interminable labyrinth, the law.   The effect of this engagement will be to detain me a close prisoner in London till the beginning of autumn. Whether it is that in the fine season people are more given to marry or make their wills, or to buy estates, than at other times, the fact is that the spring and summer are the conveyancer's harvest-time.   So I shall spend the next four months very differently from the same period in the last three or four years.   Instead of ranging at discretion over hill and dale, through field and city, forest and flood,

I shall be obliged to confine my discoveries to a dark room of a few feet square, in which, as in a camera obscura, I shall be amused with an unsubstantial and floating image of what is passing in the world without, shall thread the mazes of voluminous family settlements, and trace to their source the sinuosities of ancient titles, which sometimes after many a wearying turn suddenly lose themselves underground and elude the research of the disappointed inquirer. There are some men to whom the prospect of a summer, and in fact a life, so spent has nothing gloomy or forbidding in it ; who, indemnifying themselves by the evening's amusements for the severe application of the morning, are content to divide their whole existence between the two opposite hemispheres of business and pleasure. To me, if I even took a greater share in the amusements of London, my time would appear nearly equally wasted.in both. There are but two worlds which have any interest for me—the world of nature and the world of books. I once hoped that what constitutes the highest enjoyment of my life might also be the great business of it. At present it scarcely answers any nobler purpose than that of refreshing and invigorating the mind after an occupation which exhausts the attention without awakening a single feeling of interest—subjects on which the highest faculties of the greatest men of all ages have been unremittingly employed must for the present fill up my scanty and precious leisure. I suspect you will shake your head at this confession, which would certainly excite a stare of astonishment or a smile of contempt on most of the plump and ruddy as well as the long and care-furrowed faces which meet me in my morning's walk across Lincoln's Inn. You will draw from it no very promising augury of my professional elevation. To say the truth, the ermine and the mace do *not* terminate the vista of my waking dreams. When I escape into the regions of fancy, my airy castles are not framed of any materials borrowed from the realities which surround me. Perhaps, however, the object of my hopes and wishes, though less obvious, is more attainable than that of the crowd in which I am now not so much pressing as pressed forward, an involuntary and unambitious competitor. Certainly in *my* road to happiness, whenever I am able to diverge into it from the beaten track, I shall not be in much danger of being jostled. . . . .

"By the by, I suppose your quidnuncs at Alnwick are almost as busy in conjecture on the event of the Spanish war as they were some eleven or twelve years ago on the French invasion of Russia. It seems as if the causes of war in Europe were never to end. For certainly if any circumstances ever appeared to ensure a long period of tranquillity, it was those which succeeded the battle of Waterloo. It seemed as if the exhaustion alone attending so long and violent a struggle would have kept the nations for one generation in repose. And the peace of the world is broken by our friends the Bourbons; scarcely settled on his throne, Louis XVIII., whom some of his friends have supposed to regret his retreat at Hartwell, begins to form schemes of conquest, and to revive the plans of Louis XIV.! I confess that I feel more than usual interest in the event of this war, not only for the sake of the principles and interests it involves, but on account of the recollections which its different stages will recall to my mind. Of one circumstance I am firmly convinced, that whatever success may attend the French arms, they will never be able to restore the dominion of Ferdinand in any part of the Peninsula which they do not hold in military occupation; and that his throne, should they raise it once more on the ruins of the national liberty, will rest on the crater of a volcano which sooner or later will bring it and its supporters into irrevocable ruin. I am obliged to close the sheet in haste, and indeed I have not much more room or matter, if indeed what I have already written deserves the name."

To JULIUS HARE, Esq.

19, SOUTHAMPTON Row, *May* 29th, 1823.

" I have just written to Peacock, who sent me, *ex officio*, the information contained in your letter.   It is useless to regret the combination of circumstances which has transferred me from a congenial element into one which can never be anything but loathsome to me. But I took the leap, though not *motu proprio*, yet *ex plenâ scientiâ*.

" My aversion to the law has not increased, as it scarcely could, from the first day of my initiation in its mysteries. Moreover, it has me faster in its toils than ever.   It is not a month since I began to drive a quill at a conveyancer's.

" To compare the life I am now leading to that which I should have chosen for myself would be only tormenting. The loss of the Greek Professorship, however, if I am to reckon that among the things I have sacrificed by withdrawing from Cambridge, will not greatly embitter my regret.   I hope Monk will have a worthier successor.*

" I should like to know how long you mean to stay at Cambridge, and whether you shall be there at the triennial when our great Apostle will honour us with his presence. I have been expecting the appearance of Landor's Dialogues.†   I suppose they are buried by this time under three or four more recent strata.

" Let me know when or where I may have a chance of seeing you."

* Mr. Dobree succeeded Professor Monk in the Regius Professorship of Greek at Cambridge in 1823.

† Julius Hare edited and brought out W. S. Landor's "Imaginary Conversations," the author being resident in Italy. Some of them came out in the *Philological Museum.*

To JULIUS HARE, Esq.

BRIGHTON, *October* 28*th*, 1823.

" I met Barnes here the other day, and learnt from him that applications have been making to the Master for a long time back for the next Lay fellowship. I have not heard of Chambers's fellowship having been actually vacated, though I have been expecting to hear of it every day.

" As I do not want to lose my chance for want of a timely application, I should be obliged to you to send me word how the case stands, for otherwise the fellowship may be disposed of before I hear of its being vacant. Unless it is certain that everybody who wishes for the fellowship has applied upon the mere prospect of a vacancy, I should think it better to wait till it has taken place. I only want to do what is necessary and usual on these occasions, as the applying sooner or later will, I should suppose, have very little effect on the Master's intentions. I shall be in town in the course of a fortnight, but whatever information you possess at present on the subject, direct to me at 50, King's Road, Brighton.

" How are the ' Dialogues ' and Niebuhr going on ? I have been reading two books lately which have given me a great deal of pleasure, and which I think I would recommend for a place in your next order from Germany. One is ' Theodor, Eine Bildungs—Geschichte Eines Evangelischen Geistlichen.' It is by Schleiermacher's colleague, De Wette, but without his name in the title-page (two little volumes from which I have learnt more than from anything else I have read for a long time past). The other is ' Büsching's Vorlesungen über die Ritter Zeit.' Bohte had just received two copies one day as I looked in, one of which he designed for Sir Walter Scott.

" My cargo arrived, I believe, some three weeks ago, and I am rather impatient to open it."

To JULIUS HARE, Esq.

52, LINCOLN'S-INN-FIELDS, *May 5th*, 1824.

" Your valuable packet has reached me. As my design is to draw up in my leisure hour a sketch of an introduction which I may afterwards fill up as I meet with the books which I shall have occasion to refer to, it will not be of much consequence in what order they come into my hands. I have inquired for Veysey's book without success.

" The dispute about Marcion seems to me to be of considerable consequence certainly to Eichhorn's theory, though Hahn's objections to it, if well founded, would be equally applicable though Marcion and his gospel had never existed. But I do not at present see how the decision of this question affects Gieseler's hypothesis, which, it appears to me, will stand equally as well in either case. Indeed, as his hypothesis is in every respect the very reverse of Eichhorn's, it would be strange if it derived confirmation from the same fact which Eichhorn labours to establish in favour of his. The presumption, however, is, I think, strongly in favour of Hahn's opinion. My great doubt and difficulty at present is as to the possibility and the manner of reconciling Gieseler with Schleiermacher.＊

" There is so much appearance of truth in both their arguments that I should be unwilling to think them incompatible. And yet I do not clearly see a medium.

" I foresee that I shall have my hands well employed for the greater part of the summer, especially as I am just

---

＊ Eichhorn's theory was, that there existed an " original Gospel" from which the three synoptic Evangelists drew all that they have in common, and that Marcion's Gospel was derived directly from this. Hahn showed almost conclusively that Marcion's Gospel was that of St. Luke, altered to suit his own particular views. Gieseler's hypothesis is, that whatever is common to the three Gospels is due, not to the existence of an original Gospel, nor to mutual copying, but to the fact that by the time the Gospels were written " the apostolic preaching had already clothed itself in a settled or usual form of words."

entering into office and with a yoke-fellow of most indefatigable perseverance. My great consolation is that it is
a work of supererogation, and that I am not confined to
time.

"The reading of Gieseler's book has redoubled my
interest in the question.

"I will see in the course of a few days what materials
I can extract from Plato."

To Julius Hare, Esq.
52, Lincoln's-Inn-Fields, *July 28th*, 1824.

"I believe there will be nothing to prevent me from
breaking out of town next Monday, August 2nd, in which
case I shall go down to you by the 'Times.' I leave it to
you to find me a suitable set of rooms to sojourn in.
If you bethink yourself of anything I can do for you before
I leave town send me word.

"I am afraid you will think I have not made so much use
of your books as I ought, for I have as yet done nothing
more than trace in my mind the general plan of my
introduction, and have committed nothing to paper. I
hope, however, that my stay at Cambridge will produce
some visible fruit. It will, at all events, pretty nearly
determine the amount of the service I shall be able to
render to Schleiermacher's book."

To Julius Hare, Esq.
Bowers, near Rayleigh, Essex, *October* 10th, 1824.

"It is time, I am sorry to say, to inquire about your
motions, as mine will a good deal depend upon them.

"I am particularly anxious to see you when you pass

through town, and if you will be there any day after the 18th I will make a point to meet you. But as I should not otherwise leave the country quite so soon, I shall be glad if you can send me a line to let me know as nearly as you can the *latest* day that you expect to be in town.

"'Schleiermacher' will by that time be ready for the press, unless I should find it necessary to copy a few sheets. You will not probably be much surprised to hear that my Introduction or Preface, or whatever it is to be called, is not quite finished. I still want some of the materials. 'Veysey,' I had the mortification to learn, had been sold about two months when I inquired for it. But I still hope I may find a copy on my return to town. As I confine my notice to the works which have appeared since Marsh, which, in fact, comprehend the whole controversy, I should not like to omit mentioning any book of importance, and have therefore sent for one or two which I daresay will arrive as soon as I want them. I hope, however, that I shall have dispatched the books I have borrowed from you, so as to enable you to take them back with you to Cambridge.

"I should like you to see what I have done, which will give you a tolerable notion of the whole, and indeed comprehends some of the most important points. In the meanwhile, partly to relieve the dryness of some of these investigations, and partly to counteract the effect of too strong a dose of theology, I have filled up some of my leisure hours with translating those two exquisite pieces of Tieck's 'die Gemälde,' and 'die Verlobung.' I have bestowed pains upon them, and though I do not flatter myself with having done full justice to the original, or overcome all its difficulties, I think, with a few more touches, they will form, even in English, a pretty book. Direct to me as above by return of post, as I am to send notice to town of my coming. Pray remember me to Lady

Jones and Augustus, if he is with you.   I long to see the result of your united labours in the good cause."

To JULIUS HARE, Esq.

BOWERS, near RAYLEIGH, ESSEX, *October* 16*th*, 1824.

".... Perhaps you will return to town in the Christmas vacation in time to see my additions to 'Schleiermacher' before they go to the press, which is the thing I most desire, and you would then see them in their finished shape, though probably a great deal the worse for not having met your eye before. See them you must, at all events.   I shall take an early opportunity of reconveying your books after my return to town, and as a great deal of what I have to say will depend upon what I find and do there, I shall put it all off till then.   I only write now in hopes of saving you a part of the day which you have been kind enough to reserve for me, and which I am unlucky enough to lose.

"Could you ascertain before you leave town whether Taylor would like to publish Tieck's 'Novellen'?   I believe I cannot very well avoid offering the other bargain to Whittaker, as there is a sort of family acquaintance between us, and he has often expressed a wish to publish something of mine. If you have an opportunity of seeing Taylor on the subject, you can send a line to Lincoln's-Inn-Fields."

To JULIUS HARE, Esq.

52, LINCOLN'S-INN-FIELDS, *October* 31*st*, 1824.

". . . Of the 'Schleiermacher' nobody certainly has so good a right to dispose as yourself, to whom I am indebted both for the knowledge of the book itself and for almost all the materials of my Introduction. I found Taylor at home, and as he was going into the country in a day or two I sent him my manuscript of the 'Novellen,' though a part of it was not in the state in which I should otherwise have wished to produce it. He was obliged, however, to leave town for a few days last Monday, and when I called upon him after his return on Thursday I found that he had only read about a quarter of the first novel (I suppose I must not call them novelles ?). I was not much surprised to observe that the impression he received was not the most favourable.

"The dialogue predominated more than he seemed to expect, and he remarked that discussions on the arts did not excite so much interest here as they seemed to do in Germany; and as in this precise part my translation bore a great many more traces of the original than I meant it to retain, he very naturally began to augur ill of the whole. I am not sure, indeed, that his objection will be quite removed even when he has finished them both, though he will perhaps then begin to suspect at least, if he does not clearly see, that there is not in either a single speech or sentence which is superfluous even to the narrative, and which is not indispensable either to the development of character or to the progress of the tale. Still, as the subject of the first is not certainly one of universal interest, and many of the touches which constitute the greatest beauty of both are so fine that they may frequently escape observation, even should they be happily rendered, I am not very sanguine of success. And indeed *I* should be quite content with a limited circle of readers. . . . .

" I have got Paulus's 'Commentar,' with an additional volume containing the first part of his St. John. I should have been much better pleased to have seen Lücke. His ' Essays in the Conservatorium ' I have found very useful, and as I shall still have occasion to consult it I have kept it till my copy arrives. If, however, you have any need of it I will take a note or two, and send it down to you immediately. Of all the rest I have, I think, extracted the essence. It may, perhaps, appear rather too condensed, but as I have still a good many points to discuss, and what I have written will, I think, fill upwards of fifty pages, I shall not be able to give it a greater expansion without swelling the Introduction to an unreasonable size. Its present contents are an examination of the question of inspiration—a critique of Marsh, of Eichhorn (in which I have discussed at some length the question of Marcion's Gospel), of Grätz, and of Gieseler. The latter. I have studied very attentively, and have at last satisfied myself upon the most material points. As to the question of inspiration, I have thought it better to take it up at the point where it was left by Marsh and his critics. I do not know whether there are still people capable of reading the book who have not yet reached that point. If there are, I do not wish to disturb their prejudices. You see by this that I have still a good deal to do. Taylor said that the printing of 'Schleiermacher' would take between two and three months, and as I wish to state nothing upon the authority of others without examining for myself, that time will, with the little leisure I have, not be at all more than I shall probably require. I am much obliged to you for leaving me Weber's pamphlet ; it contains useful materials ; the argument is well stated, and one or two points I had not seen elsewhere. I am regretting that in my last order I did not send for Schmidt's 'Einleitung.' I believe you have not it. Schleiermacher speaks of Schmidt in his letter to Gass on the first Epistle to Timothy in the highest terms of praise. By the way, whenever you are disposed to enjoy a very rich critical treat and to see a spurious work completely detected, read that letter. . . . ."

To Julius Hare, Esq.

52, Lincoln's-Inn-Fields, *November 1st*, 1824.

"I had just come in for the purpose of writing to you when I received your parcel. The enclosed one shall be forwarded to-night to the coach-office. I had intended (as you will, I suppose, have observed) the letter enclosed with your books which I sent off this morning for the post, having forgotten that the Post Office in London is never guilty of a breach of the Sabbath. I have been spending almost all the morning with Taylor. He had not yet finished the second Novelle, but what he had read had produced the natural impression of delight and admiration which I·thought it could not fail to make. He also liked the 'Schleiermacher' very much, and will send it immediately to the press. He gives me a hundred guineas for it, which I think a sufficiently liberal offer on his part, and as I shall have spent nearly half the money in collecting materials, not an extravagant compensation for me. The plan of the *Athenæum* is very tempting, though I am afraid I shall not be able to make much use of it. Still I think I can hardly decline so flattering an offer.

"When I was at Cambridge, and looking into Eichhorn's 'Bibliothek,' I neglected to compare his article on the Urevangelium, in the fifth volume, with his Einleitung. I should like to know whether the former contains any account of the early Gospels, or, in fact, anything besides the analysis and the statement of his first hypothesis. I want to know nothing more than the general heads. I shall be excessively glad of Veysey, though I am not advising anybody to commit felony for my sake. My books seem to be dropping in by driblets. I have just received an ascetical treatise of Tauler, which at some future time will probably prove very edifying."

To JULIUS HARE, Esq.
52, LINCOLN'S-INN-FIELDS, *November 12th*, 1824.

" I must tell you an amusing fact, though I have nothing else to communicate. When I wrote to you last I had left Taylor apparently very much delighted with the half of the 'Verlobung' which he had read—an impression which I thought would not be weakened at least by the remainder. He told me he had some friends coming to him the next day, and among them a religious lady, to whose case he thought some things in the novel were very applicable. If I had no objection he would entertain the company by reading it to them. I was, of course, perfectly willing. About a week after I received from him a parcel containing the MS. and a note, in which he expressed his regret at being obliged to inform me 'that for particular reasons, which would have no weight with me, he would rather *not* publish the German stories. He nevertheless considered them as very ingenious compositions, and of a class which would succeed admirably if attempted by an English writer.' As he made this communication with a reluctance which showed that he was apprehensive he might be hurting my feelings by it, I called on him the next day to relieve him from all uneasiness on my account, and at the same time to ascertain one point which his language still left ambiguous. After assuring him that I was not even surprised by the intelligence conveyed in his note (which, although I certainly did not expect it, was really the case), I begged to know whether his motive for declining the publication was that he thought the work unsaleable, or whether he had any other. He assured me that it was solely a conscientious one. He had received and imparted a great deal of pleasure at the public reading of the novel, but the result of his own reflections and the suggestions of his friends was that he should be doing an injury to the cause of godliness by publishing it. I was too much delighted with this practical illustration of Tieck to make the slightest attempt to shake Taylor's determination. We had a good deal of conversation about that and other subjects, apparently agreeing most cordially upon them all, and parted the best friends in the world, as indeed he is a very amiable man, whom nobody can fail to like and esteem. This incident certainly has not induced me to abandon all thoughts of publishing my translation, though I shall let it lie by for the present..

"'Schleiermacher' is to be printed on the same scale with 'Landor.' It will make, I suppose, about 500 pages. I have not yet been able to meet with Conybeare. If I find it necessary to take notice of him he will come in quite at the end. I have been attempting to read Theile, but it is the longest book I have yet opened on the subject, and I despair of getting to the end of it.

"You hinted some time ago at coming to town some day this month. If you do, let me know if you can beforehand, that I may keep myself at liberty."

To JULIUS HARE, Esq.

November 26th, 1824.

"I have been waiting some days in the expectation of being able to let you know whether my translation of Tieck is destined to see the light. I think it most probably will, though I am not yet absolutely certain. . . . . .

"I have been correcting the first sheet of Schleiermacher, which will now, I hope, proceed without interruption. I believe we shall put thirty lines in the page, though in the sheet they sent me, owing to some mistake, there are only twenty-eight. I mention this that you may not be surprised if it is sent to you, for I told Taylor I should be glad if he could let you see it.   If you do, let me have the benefit of your opinion, and also of any alterations that may occur to you.   In the page you saw three of the places you marked were, as you probably supposed, typographical blunders.   In the other two I have not thought it advisable to make any alteration, for the following reasons.   I had originally translated ' der Zusammenhang im Ganzen ' as you suggest, but it afterwards appeared to me, as it does now, that the original words themselves would be ambiguous and vague if they were not defined and explained by the context, and to *that* the expression ' in general ' seems to me to refer more distinctly by its contrast to that which follows ' in the details ' than the mere epithet ' general.'   I was much annoyed at not being able to render ' Zusammenhang ' here by a single equivalent word.   Your other remark about softening the doubt expressed by Schleiermacher as to the authenticity of Matthew's Gospel is of more consequence. But I think you will find that in his comparisons of Luke and the other two he betrays very evidently his doubt as to that fact, and indeed that some of his conclusions are hardly admissible if it be considered as unquestionable, and therefore this seems necessary to prepare the reader for an impartial examination.   Besides, the suppression of it is a liberty which I feel a scruple in taking.

" I now want your opinion on one point.   Some of the allusions to Paulus will be obscure, I am afraid, unless they are explained.   If this is necessary, where is it to be done ?   In the introduction there will be no fit place for such remarks.   If they are added in the shape of notes at the end, will it not seem strange to add to such a work only five or six short notes ?   Yet any further commentary is quite out of the question. . . . ."

[In reference to a pamphlet entitled "A Layman's Letter
to the Author of the 'Trial of the Witnesses.'" It consisted
of four letters, written by Augustus and Julius Hare in
defence of the Gospel narrative of the Resurrection. *See*
Professor Plumptre's Introductory Memoir in "Guesses at
Truth," p. xviii.]

To JULIUS HARE, Esq.
52, LINCOLN'S-INN-FIELDS, *November 29th*, 1824.

" I have to thank you for two or three hours spent very
much to my satisfaction over the 'Layman's.' I received,
perhaps by mistake, four copies instead of two. One I
have delivered to Starr, and the remainder, if you have no
directions to give about them, I will endeavour to dispose of to the best advantage.

" Well, the united force of the two Universities has
produced a very interesting, instructive, and convincing
pamphlet as far as argument on these subjects can convince and somewhat further. The Oxford Layman's letters
seem to me written in the vein of Tertullian. At least
they have reminded me more than anything else of the
leading features of the controversial style of that powerful
polemic, but with considerable advantages on the side of
the modern. His arguments are as fine, and they are of
firmer temper; his sarcasm is as strong, and it is softened
by a great deal more of the spirit of charity than commonly breathes through the disputations of the old Hære-
simach. Never, certainly, was unhappy abortion more
completely despatched, demolished, strangled, or smothered.
Augustus may well exclaim, as Epiphanius is wont to do
at the conclusion of a heresy, ' Now, by the grace of God I
have crushed this amphisbæna, let us now with the divine
assistance proceed to attack another scolopendra, &c.'

" I think at the same time that some of the orthodox
persons who will most highly approve of the design of the

work will stare a good deal at some passages, and shake their wigs and be rather at a loss what to make of their unknown ally. Nobody, certainly, will wish the fourth letter shorter or in a different place. It has the effect of allaying whatever excitement of a passionate kind might be produced by the foregoing three, while it gives them a firm foundation, and at the same time forms an appropriate transition and preparation for that delightful conclusion. There is a point or two in it on which I have some doubts ; I am not satisfied as to the force of the argument, which seems to imply that there were apocryphal Gospels in existence anterior to our four.

"Now, all the inquiry I have been able to make on the subject has impressed me with the conviction that we know of no Gospel earlier than our own, and that all of which the names have been preserved to us are later than the end of the first century. The only objection I am aware of to this opinion is the Πολλοὶ of Luke, which has always perplexed me very much.

"I know of only two ways of explaining it : either by supposing that some complete Gospels existed when Luke wrote of which the very names have been since entirely lost, or that Luke referred to the compilations which Schleiermacher supposes. But I must not get on these topics now. What reason have you for supposing the ancient manuscripts to have been commonly so gigantic as you represent them ? Were they not sometimes in the form of a modern book only rolled round their axis ?

"Schleiermacher's doubt about Matthew is now irrevocable, and if it is likely to do mischief I hardly know how to remedy it. I had not intended in the Introduction to notice any of the details of the book except as far as they may enter into my discussions. But even if I should find an opportune place for touching upon this subject, or, not finding, should make one, I am afraid I should be in danger of making matters worse. The doubt is evident, and cannot be explained away. I am not disposed to undertake the vindication of Matthew's Gospel, nor would that be the way to save Schleiermacher's credit. On the other hand, much as I respect him, I do not think myself bound to make any attempt to justify his suspicion, though I share it with him at the expense of our delightful Gospel.

" Thank you for suggesting a word for Verlobung, though I am afraid I must not venture to utter a new one when the dictionaries have supplied me with one already. And yet God knows with what reluctance I have put at the head of that lovely tale such an awkward, heavy, drawling combination of sounds as ' Betrothment.' If anything better and not too bold occurs to you before it is too late let me have it, for a title is of some importance."

To Julius Hare, Esq.

52, Lincoln's-Inn-Fields, *November* 30*th*, 1824.

" . . . . Whittaker says German tales are now the rage, and he wishes to take the benefit of the mania while it lasts. And so I have sent off my MS. to the printers this morning. I feel there ought to be a Preface, and probably shall prefix something, though you know that fully to explain the two novels would require a book larger than themselves. On looking over Schleiermacher I have the satisfaction to find that he fully justifies his doubt as to Matthew, and that no one who reads him through will charge him with having thrown out a random paradox. This, perhaps, I may have an opportunity of noticing in the Introduction. . . . ."

To W. J. BAYNE, Esq., Edinburgh.

52, LINCOLN'S-INN-FIELDS, *Easter Sunday,* 1825.

"I am conscious that my long silence must seem to you inexcusable. . . . . And I must therefore let you into a little secret, which, otherwise, I should not have communicated quite so soon.   I have been engaged in addition to my ordinary occupations (which as I shall now be called to the Bar in about two months I could not wholly suspend) in sending two little works to the press.   They are both translations, but one of them will receive some additions of my own which have cost me more time than I had imagined when I undertook the task they could possibly do, and hence I have been obliged to defraud the law of a part of the time I used to allot to it, for which I must make up by redoubled application when I am once more at liberty.   Neither of the two publications has yet appeared, and therefore I will not say anything more about them now, and as they will be anonymous you need not mention what I have been saying to any one.   My labours are not yet at an end, but Easter has brought with it an involuntary pause.   Notwithstanding this extraordinary occupation, I still take some shame for not having answered you sooner; but really time flies so fast when the attention is distracted by a great variety of calls upon it, that till I looked again at the date of your letter I did not think my delay had been so long as it has. . . . .

"Unless you find the bad qualities of the atmosphere counterbalance all the advantages of Edinburgh, I confess I envy you your residence there.   To a single man, who is not quite satisfied with animal enjoyments, nothing can compensate for the total absence of beautiful forms, either natural or artificial, in the neighbourhood where he lives. Books cannot continually divert a man's mind from the realities around him, and if he happens to be endowed with a tolerable perception of beauty in nature or art, to be confined to a place where this sense can scarcely ever be gratified is really a melancholy thing. With respect to domestic happiness certainly all places are alike ; for those who seek only gain or what is called pleasure, or even perhaps literary intercourse, there cannot be a better than London, but for one constituted and situated as I am, it certainly is the dullest capital in the civilised world. You were very right and wise in resolving to cling to your profession as long as you can, and I do not see why anything should force you from it. Health, of course, is the object of first importance to which every other must be postponed ; but this is only a motive for regulating your medical studies by your internal feelings, and sacrificing to the latter the seeming advantage of close application, but not for abandoning the profession altogether. This, I should think, as long as your health permits you to pursue any studies at all, can never be absolutely necessary, and certainly a very obvious necessity ought to appear before you deprive yourself of what will infallibly become a means of extensive and constantly increasing usefulness and happiness, for so very precarious a source of enjoyment as college leisure earned by no previous exertion and filled by no one great and useful pursuit. I certainly say this without prejudice, being at this moment heartily sick of London, and having fresh in my recollection a most delightful fortnight which I spent last long vacation at Cambridge, and looking forward with eager longing to next summer, when I hope to spend a month in the same way. But to expect to enjoy leisure without toil (that is without a fixed and forced occupation) is as great a delusion as to think of enjoying a feast without hunger. . . . . ."

To W. J. BAYNE, Esq.

BOWERS, near RAYLEIGH, *October 2nd,* 1825.

"I am extremely obliged to you for conveying to me the information which I probably should not have received by any other channel for a long time to come. At the same time I think it highly improbable that the event you mention can at all affect my future prospects. .... The only motive that could justify me to myself in changing my present pursuit for another would be the hope of finding in the new sphere opportunities of more useful exertion. Otherwise I should not feel easy amidst all the enjoyments of a college life. My great objection to the law in this respect is that all the labour and all the ability I bring to it are utterly wasted and useless to society. I learn only what others know, and I do only what if I were not in being there would be hundreds to do just as well. The number of candidates for employment in the profession is so great that their competition has ceased to produce any advantage to society. As to any improvement, theoretical or practical, that law as a science or an art is capable of receiving, I know too well the turn of my own mind and the measure of my powers to believe that I am destined to produce any. This conviction would render me very open to temptation from any opportunity of exerting myself in some way more peculiarly suited to myself, and therefore more useful to others. But as to the precise station which poor Dobree has left vacant, I should feel very great doubt in occupying it whether I were not doing more harm than good. At least I should be quite sure that it might have been much better filled by another man.[*] .... I am now getting up some law for the Chelmsford Quarter Session, which opens the 18th of this month, till when I shall be very sufficiently employed....."

[*] Mr. Scholefield succeeded Professor Dobree in the Regius Professorship at Cambridge in 1825.

To W. J. BAYNE, Esq

52, LINCOLN'S-INN-FIELDS, *April* 11*th*, 1826.

"Nothing but engagements to which I am now forced to make all others give way would have prevented me from answering your letter as soon as I received it. I had been anxious for one from you for a long time, and it gave me very great entertainment ; but it reached me just as I was on the point of starting on one of my professional excursions, and I have been campaigning either at Assizes or Sessions till within these few days, and this is the first evening I have since had to myself. I wish it was in my power to repay you in anything but thanks for the amusement you have afforded me. But you know that in London there is never anything new but what you see in the papers. The last thing that enlivened us was the "panic;" that is now grown stale, though the blackness which then gathered on all faces on 'Change is not yet removed. One of its bad effects has been to give political economy a greater preponderance than ever in our literature, for a person is ashamed, and indeed is hardly fit, to appear in society without a theory respecting the cause of our mercantile convulsions.

" You could hardly have applied to one less competent than myself to direct you in the selection of a French library. You know, I believe, that I have always attached little, possibly too little, value to the French literature, which is generally either overrated or depreciated in this country. All I can do is to give you a few very general hints on the subject. If I were forming the collection you propose to make, I should endeavour, in the first place, to acquire the works of the principal chroniclers, biographers, and poets who have given a picture of the nation during the ages of chivalry and the continuance of the feudal system—neither of which long survived the reign of

Louis XI. Of these I cannot pretend to give you a list. But the works of Joinville, Brantôme, and the biographers of Bayard and Duguesclin will immediately occur to you. The notes of Sainte-Palage to his *Memoires sur la Chevalerie* will supply the names of many others, and will probably suggest to you the great utility which may be derived for this purpose from the *Fabliaux* and old romances, both in prose and verse. The next interesting point is to observe the transition from the feudal system and chivalrous habits to the absolute despotism of Louis XIV. and the unbridled licentiousness of the Regency. For this end you must collect as many as you can of the historians and biographers who flourished in the interval between Louis XI. and XV., always directing your especial attention to the contemporary writers, Philippe de Comines, Sully, Retz, &c. These *Mémoires* grow more numerous every century—you must choose the best, not neglecting the great historians Du Thou, Mézeray, &c. Now occurs that singular phenomenon, the literature of the French Augustan age. Here nobody wants directions. I would only remind you particularly not to omit Bossuet whatever he may cost. The next epoch is the Revolution, comprising the events out of which it grew. For the outline of this it may be worth while to procure some general history (I do not believe there is any good one). The most valuable details you will find in the *Mémoires* of the principal actors, from which also you will get the best account of Napoleon's reign and fall. But there is still left a very important part of French literature which is absolutely necessary for every one who wishes to understand the present state and the future prospects of the nation. This is composed of the works of a class of writers who have been called up by the reaction which followed the Revolution, and who are accused of wishing to restore the old *régime*. There are among them several men of very great genius and reasoning powers. I should particularly recommend Fievée Bonald and Le Maistre. Chateaubriand and La Mennais I can only mention.

"These will bring you down to the age in which we live. The first part of this collection will cost you the most trouble and money, but it will, I think, well repay both. The later writers you will find at very moderate prices in the new editions of the French classics. By the by! Shade of Voltaire! I had nearly forgotten the revolutionary literature. This, of course, you will not neglect, and I need only observe that Diderot is as essential in this as Bossuet in that of Louis XIV.

" I suppose you know that the next Cambridge election is expected to produce a warm contest. Lord Palmerston is the only candidate favourable to the Catholics. Hare has just taken orders. . . . . . I only. mention these facts because you spoke of the dearth of news you experience at Paris. Let me hear from you soon. Adieu!"

CHAPTER IV.

CAMBRIDGE. 1827—1833.

In 1827 Thirlwall quitted for ever the "brawling courts and dusty purlieus of the law," and went into residence at Trinity. He was ordained Deacon in the same year, on his fellowship, by Bishop Sparke, of Ely ; and Priest in the next year by Bishop Gray, of Bristol. His return to Cambridge was also marked by the commencement, in conjunction with his friend Hare, of the translation of Niebuhr's "History of Rome." This translation played an important part in opening a new method of historical study to English scholars. The first volume appeared early in 1828, and a second edition of it was called for and published in 1830. It was bitterly attacked in the reviews, notably in the *Quarterly*—so much so that in 1829 an answer was published by J. C. Hare, in a pamphlet called "A Vindication of Niebuhr," &c. A postscript was annexed to it signed "C. T.," in which Thirlwall took his full share of the implied blame. He declared that there was "nothing inconsistent with their profession in giving publicity to a historical work containing two or three speculations not sanctioned by the most approved commentators on the first ten chapters of Genesis." It would have been pitiful ostentation to have placed on record their rigid orthodoxy by entering a protest against questionable passages. The reviewer had said, " Pity that such talents should be wasted on the drudgery of translation." Thirlwall took exception to the term. " Intellectual labour voluntarily undergone for the purpose of communicating to others what has excited feelings of the warmest delight and admiration in ourselves appears to me no fit subject either for shame or regret." The second volume was published in 1832.

In 1831 Hare and Thirlwall started the publication of the *Philological Museum* with the object of forwarding " the knowledge and the love of ancient literature." It " shared the usual transitory fate of such learned periodicals, but during the period of its existence it furnished more solid additions to English literature and scholarship than any other of the kind that has appeared." * Thirlwall contributed several essays to it, the one " On the Irony of Sophocles " being a " masterpiece of philosophical criticism." The journal ran through six numbers and lived till 1833.

All this literary labour was carried on amid a full share of college and clerical work. From 1827 till 1832 Thirlwall filled the various college offices of Junior Bursar, Head Lecturer, and Junior Dean. In 1828, 1829, 1832, and 1834 his name appears as one of the Examiners in the newly instituted Classical Tripos. In 1832, when Hare left Cambridge for Hurstmonceaux, Thirlwall succeeded him as Assistant Tutor. In this capacity he gave classical lectures to the undergraduates on Whewell's " side." Like Hare he took Aristotle, and delivered two courses on the Ethics and the Politics. They were of the most

* *See* Dean Stanley's Memoir of Julius Hare prefixed to the " Victory of Faith." Ed. Prof. Plumptre.

exhaustive and elaborate kind, and notes of them are still extant. His lecture room was always crowded, among his audience being Lushington, Thompson, and all the rising young classics of the time.

There is an entry in the Conclusion Book at Trinity dated April 19, 1829 : "That Mr. Thirlwall be recommended to the Bishop of Ely for the sequestration of Over." This place, which is a village about eight miles from Cambridge, was then without a vicarage house, and Thirlwall undertook the charge of it for some time and diligently performed its duties. Some of his friends used occasionally to ride out from Cambridge to hear him preach. He had resigned this charge before his appointment to the assistant tutorship.

In 1834 came the great controversy about the admission of the Dissenters to degrees, which is described at length a little farther on.

To John Thirlwall, Esq.

October 6th, 1827.

". . . . I remember that some time back, in noticing my retirement from what is called active life to a quieter scene, you expressed your regret that the change, if made at all, was not made sooner. In so thinking you no doubt share a very general opinion, and one which, so far as it is general, is also my own. For I am perfectly willing to admit that a long fluctuation in the choice of a profession always implies something wrong or unfortunate in the individual or the society, or both. Which is the case in the present instance it is not for me to determine. But I see no impropriety in making two or three remarks which may perhaps tend to diminish your regret, whether it relate to what has happened or to the time of its happening.

The first is that the change which has taken place in my pursuits is much more nominal than real. It is great, perhaps, in the eyes of the world; from my own point of view it is one, not of substance, but merely of circumstances and accidents. My own inclinations and convictions as to the kind of occupations for which I am formed, and in which alone I take interest, have never undergone any alteration. I cannot remember the time when I felt a different wish or ambition from that which now possesses me. But the mode in which I might best gratify my inclinations, and might lay out myself and my faculties to the greatest advantages, is a point on which I have certainly been long doubtful, and have more than once changed my mind. Nor is this, I think, all the circumstances considered, a thing very much to be wondered at, or to be violently censured. Society possesses two or three strong, stiff frames, in which all persons of liberal education who need or desire a fixed place and specific designation must consent to be set. Which of these frames is the best adapted to the nature of the individual, and allows him the largest and most commodious room for exerting his powers for his own and the public good, is a question not in every instance very easy to determine. Fortunate, indeed, are they to whom it presents no difficulty, when the promptitude of decision arises from clearness of conviction and not from the absence of thought. But, on the other hand, it is not always just to attribute even a long fluctuation to levity or caprice. I must further observe that the particular change which has led to these remarks is of no very uncommon occurrence, but one of which I could produce a great number of examples ancient and modern. I may mention the late Dr. Parr as one in which nothing but the peculiar character of the individual prevented it from being of considerable advantage to the public. This, however, is accidental. What is more to the purpose is, that I see no reason for wishing that the change had taken place sooner. I am not sure that I could have employed my past time more profitably (by which I do not mean either more pleasantly or more lucratively) than I have done. And I am very sure that there is much less harm and danger in deferring than in precipitating all irrevocable steps. I do not perceive that in consequence of the delay I am belated or disqualified for any useful purpose ; and I think I have gained by it a clearer insight into the nature of the ground I have to tread than I could have done by any other means.

" One of the things which inclines me to look with complacency at the particular epoch of this change of profession is, that if it had occurred at any other time, earlier or later, I should in all probability never have been engaged in what will perhaps be the most useful labour of my life, the work about which you express your curiosity in your last letter. In anticipating its usefulness I do not mean to express an expectation that it will ever be a popular work, that is, that the number of readers who will understand and enjoy it will at least for a long time be very great ; for in this respect, notwithstanding the attention that has been drawn to it, it may very possibly share the fate of my other literary attempts ; but I do trust that the effect it produces will, however confined in extent, be deep and salutary. As to its condition and progress, when I left Cambridge about one quarter of the volume had been printed. Unless some unforeseen obstacle intervene, I believe it will be published soon after Christmas. The concert with the author which you have seen announced in the advertisements will, I hope, afford us some peculiar advantages in the course of the work, but I do not expect that it will produce any effect on the first volume. This is owing to accidents which prevented us from opening any direct communication with the author in time to turn it to account. But this is not the point on which the superiority of our translation over that of the first edition will depend. It is the difference between the two originals, between a first outline and a finished work, that will principally distinguish the two translations. So far as the translators themselves are concerned there will be the difference between one pair of eyes and two, a difference greater than any one who has never been himself conversant with these tasks can imagine. Some utterly groundless rumours have been industriously propagated about the book, for the chance of the effect they may produce before its appearance, which will instantly expose their falsehood. . . . ."

To JOHN THIRLWALL, Esq.

ENFIELD HIGHWAY, *July* 23*rd*, 1829.

". . . . It would undoubtedly have been most natural and proper that on my return to Cambridge from the North I should have written to you immediately to inform you of my arrival ; and probably I should have done so but for the following circumstances. I found at Cambridge among several letters which required answers one by which I learnt that a very distinguished foreigner, Dr. Schleiermacher, of Berlin, a person whom of all others in the world I had always been most desirous of seeing and knowing, was then in London, and meant during his stay in England to visit Cambridge, and that he had expressed a wish to become acquainted with me. I lost no time in proceeding to town, where I found him, and accompanied him to Cambridge, which I left again for London in order to hear him preach there. All this took up some time, and for a good while drove everything else completely out of my head. . . . .

". . . . I believe this [a tour in Ireland] will be the last excursion I shall be able to make for two or three years; for at least so long I expect to be confined to Cambridge by some literary engagements which will allow me no interruption. I have also taken the charge of a church in the neighbourhood, so that I am almost afraid I shall have too much on my hands. . . . ."

[In reference to Mr. Keightley's " Mythology of Ancient Greece and Italy."]

To THOMAS KEIGHTLEY, Esq.

TRINITY COLLEGE, *May* 16*th*, 1831.

"I congratulate you on having opened to English students. an entirely new field of knowledge and thought, and I hope that you will be rewarded by seeing your work very soon supersede and banish from our shelves all the miserable compilations on the same subject by which our literature has been so long disgraced, and one of the most captivating and fruitful of studies has been rendered generally disgusting to young minds and contemptible to the more mature. Your book is one of those which encourage me to hope that the next generation will be much wiser than our own. As it will, it is to be hoped, pass through several editions, I cannot better show my gratitude for the honour you have done me than by directing your attention to some points where I think it may still be improved. I do not mean to enter into a discussion of questions on which I differ from you in your general views, because that could not be done without explaining my own, for which I have no room here and shall probably find opportunities elsewhere. I must, however, just observe that I cannot help feeling some compassion for the fallen fortunes of the Egyptians and Phœnicians. Once the greatest powers in the realm of

Greek mythology, and allowed to give away the principal places, they are now banished and outlawed; the Egyptians confined within their own valley, the Phœnicians closely watched and prevented from landing on the shores of Greece. An attempt has even been made lately in our cyclopœdias to deprive them of a large part of their foreign commerce. For these reverses in their affairs they have certainly to blame the injudicious zeal of old Creuzer more than any one person besides. They are now suffering from the violent reaction which was the natural consequence of the temporary success they obtained through his impostures. But while I admit that Voss and Lobeck were very justifiable in the severity with which they have treated that arch-mystifier whose book is one of the most provoking that ever was written, I cannot forget that they are polemical writers, and have done much more in the way of exploding errors than in the way of establishing truth. And I think when party heats have subsided, it will be generally admitted that the early intercourse between Greece and Asia produced more considerable effect on the mythology of the former than they and their school are willing to admit. . . . .

" The theory you have unfolded has been long so familiar to me that I was startled to hear it called a hypothesis, only I do not see any reason for supposing that man gradually became a polytheist by losing his original knowledge of one God. This, indeed, is a hypothesis, and one which seems to me irrelevant in a survey of a national mythology, unless there are any facts which cannot be explained without it. But this is so far from being the case here, that one rather misses a proof that the facts are reconcilable with such a hypothesis, and that the process which you so happily describe would still be the same in a society where a monotheistic creed was co-existing but gradually losing ground. In developing the history of mythology you collect instances which illustrate the composition of heroic genealogies, but some further steps are wanting to bring us to a myth.   As to Cœur de Lion, it must be remembered that Samson and David slew their lions and bears though they took no titles from them.   I do not understand how you conceive the origin of Hyacinthia to be immediately connected with the flower; if this were so we should expect to hear of more than this single festival called by similar names.   On the other hand, Hyacinthus appears to me to belong to a large class of mythical persons, and his connection with the flower to have been merely accidental.   At all events, a more appropriate example of the proposition would be desirable to learners. . . . .

" If the legend of Psyche became popular, this was owing to the poets and artists who took the hint from the philosophers.   But the true philosophical myths were scarcely known out of the school.   I see no great objection to speaking of personifications of the sea and the sun, &c.   I understand by it that act of the mind by which the attention is withdrawn from the real sensible object, and is fixed upon an invisible imaginary person to whom attributes and operations are ascribed, resembling those which belong properly to the object. . . . .

" The remark of Herodotus shows no partiality for the system of representing the gods as deified mortals.   Wolf's argument is stated fairly enough, but I cannot consider it so conclusive as you seem to do, and, indeed, several of the grounds you lay stress on are clearly untenable.   He admits, on the evidence of Herodotus, that the Ionians used skins for writing before they imported the papyrus, so that it could not have been the want of materials that prevented them from making volumes.   Their preference of the more convenient material when they became acquainted with it cannot prove that the less commodious had been but a short

time in use ; in fact, the contrary is implied in their
retaining the old name. It seems probable that as soon as
they had established a friendly intercourse with the inland
barbarians they found them in possession of such manuscripts, and I have sometimes been inclined to suspect that
it was in this way they acquired their alphabet. But, at
least, the time when parchment was manufactured cannot
affect the question ; it was, no doubt, a more elegant
instrument than the old skins—though the Persians were
content with these for centuries—but was not cheaper or
more abundant. As little can I assent to your argument
drawn from the difficulty of keeping the plan of the
poem (which, according to your view, is not one of any
wonderful art) in the mind's eye. At the utmost this
would only be an objection if the work were held to be a
mere creation of the poet's fancy, which I do not believe
anybody now supposes. As to the plurality of Homers,
the burden of proof clearly lies on the negative side, and if
eighteen books of the Iliad are allowed to belong to the
same age it will be very difficult to show cause why they
should not have been the work of one person. Even your
illustrations carry us no further than a possibility. . . . ."

To MONSIEUR BUNSEN.
TRINITY COLLEGE, CAMBRIDGE, *November* 21*st*, 1831.

" I seize an opportunity which very rarely offers itself
of sending you a few lines to keep alive the remembrance
of a time to which I shall always look back with pleasure
and gratitude—that in which I enjoyed your society at
Rome. In my mind the recollection of that interesting
period of my life was revived with redoubled freshness by
the perusal of your work on Rome, which recalled to me,
not merely as it might to many others, a vast variety of

memorable scenes and objects, but the person of the author. I felt at the same time a desire to communicate a part of the pleasure and instruction I had received; and this desire I was enabled in some degree to gratify by a new journal to which I had been requested to contribute. The article,* which you will find in the volume which Dr. Haulthal has been good enough to take charge of for you, is, I am very conscious, in a literary point of view, quite undeserving of your notice, and if you should take the trouble to read it, I hope you will remember that in writing it I had no other object than to make the work known in England by a general account and a slight specimen of its contents. If I have succeeded in raising the curiosity of that part of our public to which your literature is accessible, and so to contribute something towards the circulation of the book itself, my highest aim will have been fully reached. But as a token of personal regard I send it with greater confidence that it will not prove wholly unacceptable to you.

"I have enclosed in the same number the first numbers of a new *Philological Journal* which we are trying to set up here. The articles signed 'J. C. H.,' which you will probably think the best as well as the largest part of the volume, are from the pen of my friend Hare. I was called on for a contribution rather suddenly, and at a time when many things were pressing on me, and the result has been an effusion which I am afraid you will think would have been better reserved for more mature reflection. In reading this trifle (it is headed Ancæus†), if you should be struck by the appearance of an odd mixture of extravagant conjectures with commonplace learning, I must beg you to remember that many things are new in England that are familiar and even stale in Germany, and that I was there-

* In the *Journal of Education*, vol. ii. p. 260 (July, 1831).
† Reprinted in "Bishop Thirlwall's Remains," vol. iii. p. 106.

fore compelled to say something to justify the thought that I had bestowed on a seemingly trivial subject. The two chronology essays are by Fynes.Clinton.

"Our translation of the second volume of 'Roman History' will, I hope, appear soon after Christmas ; and I trust that the pains we have taken to do justice to the wonderful masterpiece of genius will not have been thrown away. I was agreeably surprised to hear that the first edition of the first volume of our translation was very soon disposed of, notwithstanding the ruggedness which I hope will be found very much softened in the second edition. The second volume will probably be more generally interesting to the English public than the first. I have not yet heard any account of the condition in which the third volume, or rather the materials for it, have been left, but I trust that they are in such a state as will permit them to be published, and that we shall be able to perform one duty more to the memory of the great departed.

"I do not know whether you remember that on the evening when I took my last leave of you, you predicted that I should live to be attacked in the *Quarterly Review*. I little imagined that your prophecy would be literally fulfilled,* and you can yourself scarcely have anticipated the occasion. In Germany I hear most persons were at a loss to conceive on what grounds Niebuhr could have been assailed in England as irreligious. But our irreligious atmosphere is a very peculiar one, as may be supposed when it is known that we are beginning to be very fluent in unknown tongues, which are now attracting crowds to one of our meeting-houses. The millenarian persuasion is become so universal that any man who doubts the certainty of the Messiah's appearance on earth being now near at hand is denounced by, I am afraid I may say, a majority of the persons who claim the epithet religious by way of

* See *Quarterly Review*, No. lxiii. (June, 1825), and No. lxxvii. (Jan. 1829).

eminence as a downright infidel. That persons of this description would be scandalized by Niebuhr's divergency from the book of Genesis I knew to be an unavoidable misfortune, and I only hoped that his speculations might not fall into their hands. But I had scarcely imagined that the *Quarterly* would have degraded itself by such a stupid and bestial attack as that with which it evaded the more difficult task of reviewing the book. The *Edinburgh*,* which has no great reputation for sanctimony, could not extricate itself in the same way, and has, perhaps, managed matters still worse; for it has committed the manufacture of an article on the subject to a young Scotch lawyer, supremely ignorant of all matters connected with it, and who has not even taken the trouble to read the translation (the original was beyond his reach) with common attention. You will find a little specimen of his qualifications at the end of the *Philological Museum.*

"May I beg to be remembered to Mrs. Bunsen. I hope you will be preserved from the arrows which are now flying about Europe, and are, I am sorry to say, beginning to strike us.

"A year ago I received a letter from Mr. Brandis, in which he held out some hope that we might see you this year in England. I am afraid that prospect is now at a greater distance than when he wrote."

To MONSIEUR BUNSEN.

TRINITY COLLEGE, *December* 16*th*, 1832.

" . . . . I felt sure that you would sympathize with us in the attempt we have been making to revive the taste of the English public for philology in the highest sense of the word—in that sense from which, as I re-

---

* *Edinburgh Review*, No. cii. (July, 1830) and No. cxii. (Jan. 1833).

member you remarked in a letter I received from you some years back, it has been degraded in this country to a spiritless, pedantic, mechanical craft. I fully enter into your views as to the important functions which philology might and would discharge in England if it had been cultivated among us as it has been in Germany. But, alas! the obstacles both to its cultivation and to the application of its resources are at present greater than a foreigner can easily conceive, and its friends have to fight a battle almost without hope. Still the experiment is well worth the trial, and God forbid I should despair of the final result. Let our journal only live, and I am sure that it would improve and would work good. But I have at present great difficulty in keeping it alive ; our most able and active contributors have been all taken away from us at once, and I find the burden devolved mainly upon my own very incompetent shoulders.

"With regard to the application of philology to the various branches of theology, I see still less prospect of the hopes of real well-wishers of our Church being speedily realised. It contains many disinterested and enlightened friends, who perceive its defects and would wish to remedy them. But the present anxiety about its temporal relations to the State so completely engrosses all other subjects connected with it that it would be absurd in any one to propose any scheme of internal reformation. The Church remains powerless for any new good, and at the utmost only able to preserve itself from ruin.

" Nevertheless, as this crisis must certainly pass, I am not without hope that when a period of tranquillity returns it will be accompanied with a spirit of reflection and of earnestness which will lead to some important changes in the discipline and forms of the Church. That a reform in both these respects is wanted I clearly see ; I believe it to be also inevitable. I only hope that it may be effected by our friends, and not be a consequence of the assaults of our adversaries.

" Among the things most indispensably requisite to the stability of the Church of England I hold to be a revision of her liturgy. I fully appreciate the beauty of many parts of this composition, and decidedly prefer an established form to an unlimited license in the management of public worship. But yet it is painful to have to choose between two extremes, to see an opportunity of calling forth the noblest feelings and faculties of our nature wasted by lifeless formality or unmeaning extravagance. The service of the Church ought, according to my view, to be regarded as the highest work of art. If it does not purify and elevate the soul, as inferior productions of art sometimes do, the question is whether this is to be ascribed to the incurable apathy of the persons who take part in it or to the indolence and unskilfulness of those who conduct it. I am one of those who enter fully into the feelings of the Dissenters, while at the same time I am sure that they are opposed chiefly, if not entirely, to what is really faulty in the construction of our liturgy. You are probably aware that there are many dissenting congregations who adopt the liturgy of the Church, a proof that it contains much that commends it to all unprejudiced feelings. But it is also true that many persons are driven out of the communion of the Church by their repugnance to its liturgical form, a repugnance springing from the purest and most enlightened conviction. A remedy for this mischief can only be found in a reformation of our Church government. This will undoubtedly take place. I only pray that it may be brought about without schism or convulsion. I have no fear about any danger that may appear to threaten our religious convictions from political differences. I shall be extremely anxious to see your work on this interesting subject. As you mention that you directed M. Perthes to send a copy to *Oxford*, I hope that there has been no mistake in the address that may prevent me from receiving it. Among the many things for which I have to thank you is the indulgence you have shown to my young friend Milnes, whose character I think you have justly appreciated. Before this letter reaches you, you will, I suppose, have become acquainted with my friend Hare, a person like whom we have very few to produce. Would that I could be present at your conversations! When I left Rome I thought it was impossible I should never see it again. Now I hardly venture to cherish the hope."

To Monsieur Bunsen.
Trinity College, *May 5th*, 1833.

". . . . I shall request Mr. Ramsay to convey with this letter the last number of our *Philological Museum*, which I have been keeping alive as well as I could in the absence of Hare and some others of our best contributors. In the course of another fortnight I hope to be able to bring out the sixth number, which will complete the second volume. I should have been glad to have sent it to you at the same time, as it will, I hope, prove rather more interesting than the one you now receive, in which I was induced by the publisher to insert several papers bearing on the subject of our Cambridge reading, but containing nothing worth your notice. In the sixth number I have more freely followed the bent of my own taste.

"Beside your two letters, I have to thank you for procuring me the pleasure of perusing that to Dr. Nott, to which I am indebted for many new conceptions, and for a clearer view of the whole subject than I had ever attained before. It has made me very eager to see your liturgy and the *Gesangbuch*, which I have not yet received.

"It is singular enough that your last letter should have brought me the first intelligence of the projected revision of the liturgy which you mention. I believe that the want of such a change has long been felt by some of the most enlightened members of our Church ; but, nevertheless, I did not anticipate that it was to take place soon, and I have still great doubts about it. There are two impediments in its way, one of which, indeed, is perhaps gradually losing part of its force, but the other is, I am afraid, rather strengthened by the actual circumstances of the Church. The one is an indiscriminate and passionate admiration and love for the liturgy as it is, a feeling which in some cases is merely the result of education and habit, in others is also intimately connected with political opinions or prejudices, and in both shrinks from every alteration of a work in which it can perceive no fault or defect, and which it reveres as sacred. This, however, is an honest and good feeling which needs not to be weakened but only to be enlightened. But there is another obstacle to all plans of alteration in the liturgy which I am afraid is much more powerful, and which is produced by motives much less respectable. Among many of those who are not only sensible of the imperfections of our liturgy, but perhaps scarcely do justice to its merits, there is a dread of admitting the existence of the former, though it be for the purpose of correcting them and heightening the latter, partly because such an admission might tend to weaken the attachment of those whose affection for the liturgy is grounded merely on prejudice and habit, and who are supposed to form the largest part of its admirers, and partly because all change is apprehended to be contagious and progressive, and therefore, however minute at the beginning, and however desirable in itself, to threaten the safety of Church and State. The present aspect of public affairs seems, as I have observed, to confirm the fear of these cautious politicians, and to justify them in resisting every innovation till it has been forced upon them. On the other hand, as projects without number are now afloat for amendments in other branches of our ecclesiastical constitution, so it is very natural that to many this should appear the most convenient season for reforming the order of public worship. When, however, I consider who the persons are from whom such a reformation among us must proceed, I do not think it likely that it will be rashly undertaken or intemperately conducted. The real danger I apprehend to be, that whatever is done may prove a half measure, producing all the evil of change with but little of the benefit of reformation, and shutting the door, as you justly observe, for a long time against any wiser and more salutary plan.

"That some considerable change will before long take place in the constitution of the English Church as a temporal establishment seems to be much more certain. That there is great room and need for it everybody feels. You have probably seen Dr. Arnold's and Dr. Pusey's pamphlets on the subject.* The latter contains a proposal with regard to diocesan seminaries which, I imagine, you would approve of. The former impresses every one who reads it with a great respect for the author, but seems to me more deficient in a practical point of view than I could have expected, and if I am not mistaken betrays great want of information as to the views and feelings of the Dissenters, whom it aims at conciliating. But on all these points the first and great question is not what is to be done, but who is to do it. Is the reform of the Church to be consigned entirely to politicians and economists, who only look at the goodly stones and gifts of the temple, some with an anxious, others with a greedy eye, and care nothing about

---

* Dr. Arnold's "Principles of Church Reform" (three editions); Dr. Pusey's "Remarks, &c., on Cathedral Institutions."

the service of the sanctuary nor the edification of the worshippers ? Or will any part of the work be put into the hands of sincere and zealous and enlightened lovers of the Church ? In the latter case we may securely hope for the best. In the other it is to be feared that if beneficial changes ever take place, they will have been purchased by great losses and a disastrous experience. . . . .

" I look forward with the greatest eagerness to the continuation of your work, the beginning of which afforded me a pleasure only second to that which I scarcely hope to enjoy, of revisiting Rome itself. It is still the capital of the world, for it is the only one which makes those who have seen it long after it as a home. Pray present my respects to Mrs. Bunsen."

To MONSIEUR BUNSEN.

TRINITY COLLEGE, *October* 10*th*, 1833.

" . . . . Since the last letter I sent to you, which was, I think, by Mr. Ramsay, I have had a great many marks of your kindness to acknowledge, first of all your beautiful hymn-book, and then the first volume of your 'Rome,' and the first part of the second. I wish, beside my thanks, it was in my power to send in return anything similar in kind, or approaching in value to either. You will not, I trust, suppose that I imagine myself to be so doing when I accompany this letter with the sixth number of the *Philological Museum.* I could have wished, for several reasons, that so large a part of the contents had not come from my hand. For though they may be accepted as proofs of my good will toward the undertaking, they at the same time betray the melancholy fact that I am unable to fill up the volume by any other means. Nothing but the pressure of scarcity would have induced me to insert the smaller articles towards the end, which I wrote after having been disappointed of contributions on which I had relied when I undertook to bring out a new number. I am sorry to say that it is not only the latest number, but that according to present appearances it is likely to be the last of the series. The publishers find the sale so slow that they fear a considerable loss on the two volumes now completed, and will not venture to go on at their own risk. The prospect of a continuation seems to depend on the disposition there may be in the directors of our University press to bear a part of the expenses. It still remains to be seen whether they can be prevailed on to do so ; but it is a thing rather to be wished than hoped for.

" This apparent want of a market for the only work of this kind at present existing in England is particularly mortifying to those who have set it on foot, because though during the last twelve months peculiar accidents occasioned an extraordinary scarcity of contributions, those causes have now ceased, and there is every reason to think that the work, if it was allowed to proceed, would become more valuable and be better conducted than it has been. From another point of view there will be still stronger motives for regretting its cessation. For it was an effort made, not without urgent need, to rouse the interest of educated persons for ancient literature and the various subjects connected with it. The excitement produced in the public mind by the events of the day may undoubtedly have had a share in deadening this interest, and so far there may be hope of seeing it revive. But I cannot help thinking that we are in great danger of sinking into that state of general confirmed indifference to this branch of knowledge which the revolution and the system of Napoleon have produced in France, where, I believe, a taste for it is generally considered as a kind of fancy not much more respectable than that of a bibliomaniac, and as an indication of a somewhat weak head.   It is true that we can never come to this point so long as the study of the ancient languages continues to form a part of what commonly passes for liberal education. But it is by no means certain that this will always be the case, and I am afraid that symptoms may be discerned of a growing tendency towards the opinion that such studies are frivolous, or at least of very slight importance. I do not know whether in Germany it would be possible to meet with an educated man capable of thinking and saying that the value attached to the classical languages was a mere fraud practised on the credulous by those who found it their interest to keep up the price of a worthless commodity which they happened to possess. We sometimes hear such opinions in England from persons far above the rank of Jack Cade. When we see an evil or a danger we naturally inquire after a remedy or a preservative. In the present case it seems clear that the source of the mischief must lie in the system of education hitherto pursued in England, and I think it must be admitted that this has hitherto been, and still is, very imperfect, both as to the matter and the form. With regard to the former, the main cause which has tended to bring ancient philology into disrepute has undoubtedly been that both in our schools and colleges an infinitely minute branch of the subject has been severed from the rest and treated as the whole. The good sense of the age has revolted against this absurdity, but generally without perceiving its real nature or proper correction. The exertions of a few individuals can produce little effect as long as they are opposed to a vicious system in schools or universities, or both, and the schools and universities depend intimately on each other. It is, however, in the latter that most remains to be done, and it is in them that the introduction of a better general system would seem most practicable. But here the great difficulty arises from the peculiar form which has been given to their institutions by the accidental circumstances which determined their origin and growth. To these purely casual and irrational claims we owe the remarkable feature of a system which partakes of the nature of the school and the university, the individual colleges being, in fact, no more than private schools, which, together with their particular means of instruction, offer an opportunity of enjoying those which the university presents to all its members. There can, I think, be no doubt that this subdivision not only stands in the way of the introduction of any better general system, but that it would probably tend to weaken the efficacy of any that might be introduced. There is one very obvious mode of meeting this difficulty—the radical one : sweep away the particular societies (with or without respect to existing individual interests), and then remodel the general one on a better plan. I should, however, lament such a change, even if it were made with the best dispositions towards · literature and science, because I am convinced that the peculiarity of our system might in able hands be directed to very useful purposes. But how to accomplish this, and particularly without disturbing the property of the several corporations concerned, is certainly a very arduous problem. Then there is another question arising, which to many appears of much greater importance. The Dissenters loudly demand admission to all the benefits of education afforded by the two Universities. The demand seems very reasonable ; but those who look not only to the thing in itself, but to its consequences, believe that such a measure would subvert the Universities as ecclesiastical establishments, and this is probably the reason why the claim of the Dissenters will be supported by many who would otherwise be indifferent to it. To impartial and disinterested men the only question can be, how far it is necessary or expedient that the Universities should continue to be in their present state ecclesiastical establishments, and this question again depends on the whole of our Church system, which I have here no room and no inclination to discuss.   I have not yet seen Hare in his parsonage, but I hear that, as might be expected, he is the delight of his parish. . . . ."

CHAPTER V.

CAMBRIDGE.   1834.

THE question of the admission of Dissenters to the
privileges of the Universities began to force itself upon
public attention after, and partly in consequence of, the
passing of the Reform Bill.   In 1834 it came to a practical issue as far as the Universities were concerned.   On
the 21st of March in that year a petition from Cambridge*
was presented by Earl Grey to the House of Lords
in favour of the admission of Dissenters to academical
degrees.   It was signed by sixty-three resident members of
the Senate, among the number being two heads of houses,
nine professors, and eleven tutors, and among the names
those of Sedgwick, Airy, Lee, Thirlwall, Musgrave, &c.
Three days later the same petition was presented to the
House of Commons by Mr. Spring Rice.   Counter-petitions
more numerously signed were presented in the Upper
House by the Duke of Gloucester, Chancellor of the
University, and in the Lower by Mr. Goulburn, the senior
member for the University.   Considerable debate followed

* Petitions were also presented from Oxford, and pamphlets written on
the subject, by Moberly, Sowell, Dalby, &c., &c.

the presentation of these petitions.   A Bill on the subject
was introduced in the Commons by Mr. Wood, and eventu-
ally passed by a majority of 89, but was lost in the Lords
by a majority of 102.

At Cambridge one result of the struggle was the publication of a mass of remarkable controversial literature.
Dr. Turton, Regius Professor of Divinity, started it with
a pamphlet entitled " Thoughts on the Admission of Persons, without Regard to their Religious Opinions, to certain
Degrees in the Universities of England."   Its main argument was the alleged evils that would ensue upon the
intercourse of young men differing widely from each
other in theological sentiments.   This Dr. Turton endea-
voured to prove by reference to the progress of the
Theological Seminary for Nonconformists at Northampton
and (afterwards at) Daventry.   On April the 12th Mr.
Wordsworth (now Bishop of Lincoln), Fellow of Trinity,
published a letter to Lord Althorp strongly denuncia-
tory of the proposed changes.   Next, on May the 25th,
came the memorable pamphlet of Thirlwall, entitled
" A Letter to the Rev. Thomas Turton, D.D., on the
Admission of Dissenters, &c."*   In the outset he proclaimed that his reasons for writing were to justify his
signature in the face of misrepresentation, and to show the
fallacy of the comparison made by Dr. Turton.   He
asserted as an incontrovertible fact " that our colleges are
so far from being theological seminaries, that among all
the branches of learning cultivated in them there is none
which occupies a smaller share of our time and attention
than theology."   " We have no theological colleges, no
theological tutors, no theological students."   Dr. Turton
had claimed for the members of the Church of England the same privilege exercised by Nonconformists, of
academies where " those principles of religion alone are

* An answer to Dr. Turton was also published by Professor Lee.

taught which are in agreement with their own peculiar views." Thirlwall took this as the basis of his argument, and proceeded to show what the religious instruction of the colleges was, and what effect the proposed admission of Dissenters would produce.

Among the aids to religion put completely on one side —and it was this that gave so much offence—were the chapel services, the college lectures, and the intercourse between tutor and pupils. In their place, he said—

"The means by which, in my opinion—I would not say religion is communicated to our students, because, as I have already observed, they are not supposed to come to us destitute of it— but by which their religious impressions are strengthened, their religious views enlightened and enlarged, are, in the first place, their private studies, for which our libraries, peculiarly rich in theological literature, supply them with all the aids they can desire; next, the social worship, not of our chapels, but of our churches; next, the intercourse, not with the governing part of the societies to which they belong, but with companions of congenial sentiments and pursuits; and I trust I shall not be thought romantic or sentimental if I add, that the place itself, with its groves and cloisters, notwithstanding changes in our habits, which may tend to disturb or weaken its operations, has not yet lost all that influence, which was felt and acknowledged by the great spirits of other times, among whose monuments we walk, to be highly favourable to the growth of religious feelings."

The subject of the chapel services was treated in a "serious, deliberate, and decided manner,"* with the view of showing that compulsory attendance at them had a detrimental effect. It appeared to him—

"That with an immense majority of our congregation it is not a religious service at all, and that to the remaining few it is the least impressive and edifying that can well be conceived." "As to any other purposes, foreign to those of religion, which may be answered by those services, I have here no concern with them. I know it is sometimes said that the attendance at chapel

* Whewell's "Remarks," p. 4.

is essential to discipline ; but I have never been able to understand what kind of discipline is meant, whether it is a discipline
of the body, or of the mind, or of the heart and affections."
" I confess that the word discipline applied to this subject conveys to my mind no notions which I would not wish to banish ;
it reminds me either of a military parade, or of the age when we
were taught to be *good* at church."

Then taking the college lectures in divinity, he proceeded to show that in most instances they had no claim
to the title of theological lectures.   The subjects chosen
showed—

" That they are not selected for the sake of the opportunities
they may afford of teaching any peculiar principles of religion,
but for the sake of communicating certain kinds of knowledge,
which are not at all necessary to a Christian, but of which,
nevertheless, as a gentleman and a scholar, he ought not to be
destitute."

Three pages were devoted to the compulsory knowledge
of the Thirty-nine Articles at Oxford, with a piece of subtle
irony on the Bishop of Exeter's speech in the House of
Lords.   Two gentlemen of his acquaintance had been
turned back for not knowing their Articles, " and both of
them," the Bishop proceeds,—

" ' Showed the blessed effect of that regulation ; for they
returned to their colleges, and having made due proficiency in
the most important part of knowledge—the knowledge of true
religion—again presented themselves to be examined for their
degree, and were then admitted to the highest honours for literature and science which the University could bestow.'   That
the effect produced on these individuals was indeed a blessed
one no one can presume to doubt, since it is the Bishop of
Exeter who affirms it on his own personal knowledge.   But
with ordinary men circumstances more unfavourable to the investigation of religious truth, circumstances laying a more dangerous snare for the conscience, can hardly be conceived than
those which the Bishop has described, and on which he reflects
with pride and ' high gratification.' "

He lastly disposed of two of the apprehended evils—the

disturbance of the tranquillity of the young men, and the unsettlement of their religious principles by theological disputes, as "utterly chimerical;" and ended with the hope that the time might not be distant when his opposers would rejoice to find themselves deceived.

On the 25th of May Mr. Whewell, the tutor under whom Thirlwall worked, issued a pamphlet called " Remarks on some parts of Mr. Thirlwall's Letter, &c." He began by deprecating the introduction of domestic topics as extraneous to the matter of the controversy. He then passed to the defence of the daily chapel services on the ground—

"That the aim of all such ordinances and institutions is not to reject but to use external influences; not to exclude religion from every domain except its spontaneous range in our own thoughts, but to provide occasions which may bring it to our thoughts; not to draw a harsh line of distinction between religious impressions and all that can be by possibility discovered to have a mixture of earthly cares and notions, but to throw a religious character, as far as it can be done, over all the business of life."

He acknowledged the imperfection of the methods employed to bring about regular attendance, and referred pathetically to the probable increase of difficulty from the now notorious differences of opinion on the subject of those in authority. The charges brought against college lectures and the intercourse between tutor and pupils he either allowed or weakly opposed. The great subject of the admission of Dissenters he dismissed with the avowal of his partial agreement with both sides, and that his fears were for the Church at large rather than for the Universities.

The letters that follow show the sequence of events. On the 26th the Master wrote to Thirlwall inviting his resignation of the assistant tutorship. He complied almost immediately, though under protest, and on the 28th addressed the circular letter to the resident Fellows. The letter of June the 2nd to Professor Pryme explains the attendant circumstances. The Master's authority to dismiss a tutor without the sanction of the seniority was much questioned ; and Thirlwall, too, was blamed for his precipitancy in resigning without consulting his friends.

To THE RESIDENT FELLOWS OF TRINITY COLLEGE, CAMBRIDGE.

TRINITY COLLEGE, *May* 28*th*, 1834.

" I beg leave to draw your attention to the following copy of a letter which I have recently received from the Master of our college :—

' TRINITY COLLEGE, *May* 26*th*, 1834.

'DEAR SIR,

' I thank you for your attention in sending me a copy of your letter to Dr. Turton.

' With respect to the letter itself, I have read it with some attention ; and, I am sorry to say, with extreme pain and regret.   It appears to me of a character so out of harmony with the whole constitution and system of the college, that I find some difficulty in understanding how a person, with such sentiments, can reconcile it to himself to continue a member of a society founded and conducted on principles from which he differs so widely.

' But however this may be, I consider it certain that entertaining, and having publicly avowed the opinions, and made the assertions, which you there have done in connection with several very important parts of our system (for instance, the religious offices, the lectures, and the moral discipline)—opinions and assertions very erroneous, as I think, in themselves—and very unjust to the officers of the college and to the other tutors (an injustice also which extends much farther than to our own college merely), you become, I must say, in my judgment, *ipso facto* disqualified from being in any degree actively concerned in the administration of our affairs ; and I trust, therefore, you will feel no difficulty in resigning the appointment of assistant tutor, which I confided to you somewhat more than two years ago. Your continuing to retain it would, I am convinced, be very injurious to the good government, the reputation, and the prosperity of the college in general, to the interests of Mr. Whewell in particular, and to the welfare of the young men, and of many others.

'I regret exceedingly the painful step which I am obliged to take, but the sense of duty renders it indispensable.'

' I remain, my dear Sir,

' Your very faithful Friend and Servant,

' CHR. WORDSWORTH.'

" There is one passage, gentlemen, and one only, in the answer which I have sent to this letter which I think it necessary to communicate to you. It runs as follows :—
' The right which you assume of taking from me the office which I have held during the last two years in the college is, I know, considered a very disputable one by persons better versed in such matters than myself. I beg leave to state most distinctly that, in submitting to your authority, I do not mean in any manner to recognise it, and that I reserve to myself the full right of disputing it if it should be exercised in any other case.'

" I have laid thus much of this correspondence before you, gentlemen, for two reasons, one principally affecting you, the other more immediately concerning myself. The first is, that I thought it proper that you should be apprised of the power claimed by the Master over the persons engaged in the public instruction of the college, and of the manner in which it has been exercised. My second motive is, that I wish to learn from you how far you agree with the Master as to the propriety of my continuing a member of your society. Highly as I value the intercourse which I have now for many years enjoyed with you, indeed because I value it highly, I cannot consent to prolong it any further than I retain your esteem. If I find that you are generally of opinion that, after avowing the sentiments which I have published in my letter to Dr. Turton, I cannot with consistency and honour continue a member of your society, I shall be ready and desirous to quit it. I therefore most earnestly request that you will severally favour me with a private, explicit, and unreserved declaration of your opinions on a point of so much interest to myself, and which is also of some importance to the welfare of the college."

To GEORGE PRYME, Esq., M.P.*

TRINITY, *June 2nd*, 1834.

" I think it very desirable that you should be correctly informed of the circumstances under which I have been deprived of the tutorship, and I therefore enclose a copy of a printed circular, in which you will find the Master's letter to me, and a part of my answer. It appeared to me at the time, and the impression has been confirmed by every subsequent perusal of his letter, that it could bear but one meaning, and that, after having declared that I was in his judgment *ipso facto* disqualified for my office, and that my continuing to retain it would be very injurious

---

* Formerly Professor of Political Economy, and M.P. for Cambridge Borough. He was a strong advocate of the proposed changes.

to the various things and persons which he specifies—he was as much pledged to use his utmost authority to remove me, as if he had said directly, I command you to quit your office. That this was his meaning seems to me sufficiently clear from the last sentence—what else could he mean by 'the painful step which he is obliged to take?' I may also add that I showed his letter to Whewell before I answered it, and that, though he expressed great regret, he did not intimate that there could be any doubt as to our connection being at an end. In my answer I treated his language as conveying an absolute command, to which I professed to submit, not because I was satisfied as to his right, or because I deferred to his judgment, but simply because I could not resist his assumed authority without involving other persons, namely, Whewell and Perry, in the struggle; I think this was the only course I could properly take. Even if I had stood alone it would scarcely have been possible to retain such an office in spite of the Master; but connected as I was with Whewell and Perry, I felt that I had no choice left. The answers which I have received to my circular have been uniformly satisfactory on the immediate point in question, and many of them extremely gratifying to my feelings. But perhaps my greatest consolation is to find, from the wretched feebleness of the attempts which have been made to answer the statements of my pamphlet, how deeply their truth must have been felt by the persons most interested in disputing them. I shall annex a postscript to the second edition, which is now called for, in which I hope finally to dispatch my various opponents, and then to retire for ever from the field of controversy.

"As the circular was not designed for publication, I should be obliged to you to keep it private."

The Master's action, as above mentioned, was bitterly attacked, and Macaulay, writing some thousands of miles away from the scene of the contest, went so far as to charge him with "unutterable baseness and dirtiness;" * but in justice to Dr. Wordsworth, it should be said that his action was avowedly taken, not on account of the advocacy of liberal principles in the pamphlet, for in that Thirlwall had been joined by half the resident Fellows, but because of the almost contemptuous manner in which the compulsory attendance at chapel had been spoken of. Hugh James Rose, who had contributed a pamphlet to the subject, entitled "An Apology for the Study of Divinity," was commonly supposed to have been the Master's chief counsellor in the matter. He was in Cambridge at the time, probably as a guest of Dr. Wordsworth, and on Sunday, May 18th, preached a sermon before the University (afterwards published) on "The Duty of Maintaining the Truth." His text was St. Matthew x. 27, "What ye hear in the ear, that preach ye upon the housetops." That Thirlwall suspected this to have ministered courage to the Master is confirmed by the following story. While crossing the great court of Trinity, immediately after hearing from Dr. Wordsworth, he met one of the Junior Fellows, and put into his hands the fatal letter. His exclamations of surprise were met by Thirlwall with the remark, "Ah ! let this be a warning to you to preach truth, if need be, upon the housetops, but never under any circumstances to preach error."

On May 29th Mr. (afterwards Professor) Selwyn followed with a pamphlet, called " Extracts from the College Examinations in Divinity, with a Letter to the Lecturers, &c." The object of the extracts was to show that Thirlwall's estimate of the religious instruction was incorrect, and the letter contained a violent attack on him. On the 13th of

* Macaulay's Life, vol. i. p. 429.

June Thirlwall issued the second edition of his pamphlet, which had been called for, and took the opportunity of annexing to it a second "Letter." This was intended as "a vindication of some passages in the first letter," and in answer to Whewell's and Selwyn's pamphlets; to a circular issued by Mr. Evans, Tutor of Trinity; and to one issued by fifteen tutors of colleges defending their theological instruction. In it he reiterated his charges against the chapel services. He argued that the comparison drawn between them and family worship failed, except that they were alike in daily repetition, "and that the natural effect of the daily repetition on ordinary minds is to diminish their reverence both for the place and the service." He held the circulars to be in the main proofs of the correctness of his arguments, and Mr. Selwyn's pamphlet was severely dealt with. The letter closed with the statement that "he retired from this controversy with the firm resolution that nothing should tempt or provoke him to descend into it again."

This letter called forth a reply from Mr. Whewell (whose first pamphlet also ran through two editions) entitled "Additional Remarks, &c." He re-asserted his opinion of the necessity of daily worship as a religious duty. Thirlwall had appealed to the impressive influence of the "groves and cloisters," and Whewell

"Could not understand why the monuments of the same feeling in our habits and institutions should be supposed incapable of contributing to the same effect; why the pealing organ, the well-known liturgy, the long-established orderly distribution of times and offices, the collegiate congregation ever entering and issuing from the consecrated doors with the returning hour, should not also be favourable to the growth of religious thoughts; or why we should be utterly callous to those impressions, arising from such circumstances, by which strangers are often forcibly affected."

He argued that compulsion was inevitable

" if the whole scheme and character of our college administration is not to be subverted." "When men speak of our compulsory services, they are apt to forget that this compulsion acts in a penal form only upon a few persons, the most unlucky of our students in the management of their time, and a still smaller number of very indolent characters or perverse dispositions. With respect to by far the greater number, this compulsion is felt only in the shape of a steady habit and of a regular distribution of their day."

He acknowledged that they were likely to gain little practical good from the discussion,* and retired from the controversy with the hope that he might never have to resume it. Thirlwall went on the Continent in the summer, and on his return in September addressed a long letter privately to Whewell complaining rather strongly of his "Additional Remarks," and justifying his own language. Whewell replied, and the following letter marked the close of the whole matter :—

To Mr. Whewell.

Trinity, *September 23rd,* 1834.

" I cannot suffer a moment to pass without thanking you for your kind letter. I see by it that the greater part of my own was written under an erroneous impression that your language, in the opening of your second pamphlet, referred to the nature of my opinions on the chapel service, whereas I now see that it related only to the propriety of publishing them. I have only to regret that this point was not so distinctly stated as to prevent a similar confusion in the mind of your readers. But as you intimated that the difficulty which you felt was one which might be

---

* Some of the improvements advocated for the first time by Thirlwall in his pamphlets have now been long in operation. Among them are the abolition of school-boy impositions for non-attendance at chapel, the introduction of a shortened service, and a special Sunday sermon.

lessened by mutual explanation, I could hardly help supposing that it depended solely on the opinions themselves, which I thought you had misconceived. I am, however, very willing to hope that I am the only person who labours under this mistake, or, at all events, that I have attached undue importance to it.

" With regard to the propriety of my conduct in publishing my opinions, I am well aware that you are not singular in the view you take of it, for Hare has informed me that he sees it in the same light; and you may therefore easily believe that I am more inclined to doubt the correctness of my own judgment than to wonder that anyone should differ from me on this point. But after the maturest reflection I have been able to give to the subject, I find myself still unable to assent to the general principle from which he drew his conclusion, or to perceive that I violated any other restraints than those which prudence would have imposed on me.

" In the first place, the view I took of my own station was not that which you take of yours ; and, in fact, I think there is a very material distinction between them. I did not consider myself as having anything to do with the administration of the chapel discipline, and was not conscious of having neglected my duty, though I never spoke on the subject to any of our pupils during all the time I was in office, nor do I remember that anyone even hinted at an expectation that I should do so. I conceived that my official duties were confined to giving literary instruction, and that whatever other good I might do, by conversation and advice to those with whom I stood in that relation, was left to my own discretion. As to the stipulation that I should myself attend chapel, I never understood that such an attendance implied any opinion as to the beneficial effect of the institution ; and I think I was justified in this view of it by the consciousness that my opinion on the subject was previously known to the person with whom I made the stipulation. Nor could I conceive that the notoriety of such an opinion was inconsistent with holding the office, because I think I remember that I was informed, and at all events it was the case, that some of my predecessors had marked their opinion as the same with my own, by their general absence from the service. The only question, then, seems to be whether my attendance itself implied anything inconsistent with the publication of my sentiments, because it could have no meaning or purpose if those sentiments were known. I saw no inconsistency in this respect; for though it was true that I might be supposed to go to chapel for the purpose of setting an example, yet the example I wished to set was simply that of conformity to the established institutions of the college, and I do not know how I could set any other, except by decent and reverent behaviour in the place, which was of course included in the others. But I may go still further, and add that I do not see anything in the opinions I published which should have prevented those to whom they were known from believing that, though my attendance was a consequence of the office I held, it was not with me merely mechanical; and, indeed, as the stipulation was not publicly known, if there was any contrast between my behaviour and that of any of my predecessors in this respect, the natural inference would seem to be that, though I thought like them of the effect it produced on others, I felt no personal reluctance to attending myself. And—though this is nothing to the purpose—I may add that this was really the case : that I found the habit by no means disagreeable, and that as, on the one hand, if no stipulation had been made with me I believe I should have been no less regular, so, I am sure, if I had been formally released from it I should have made no other use of that liberty. I might add that even if I had been called upon to recommend regularity of attendance and becoming deportment in others, I should have felt myself able to do so notwithstanding the notoriety of my opinions, and by arguments which to my own judgment would not have been less efficacious on account of them. But I should be content to rest the question on the grounds before mentioned. I have nothing further to say in my defence, except that it ought to be remembered that, as I had not concealed my private opinion, and had communicated it on one occasion in a manner to which no one can object, so I was at last induced to publish it by an occasion which seemed to me—perhaps mistakenly—to call for the publication, and that the nature of this occasion might be admitted as an excuse for using here and there a tone which would have been improper if the publication had been purely spontaneous. And I do not think that in this I am claiming any indulgence which was not as much needed by others who have not been so severely dealt with.

"As to another point, in which your last pamphlet appeared to me to draw an inference from my words which they did not warrant, and of which I was myself quite unconscious, I am perfectly satisfied with your acknowledgment ; and here, again, I will hope that I have attached too great importance to the effect which your language may have on the reader's mind. I do not see any mode of remedying the mischief, whatever it may be, and I would much rather acquiesce in it than that the subject should be again in any way brought before the public. Beside the explanations which I desired, your letter has afforded me a still higher satisfaction in showing me that I am indebted to you for an obligation on which I shall always reflect with pleasure and gratitude, in the attempt which you made to avert the evil which my imprudence has drawn upon me. And as this is the strongest proof you could have given of the desire you felt to continue the relation in which we stood to one another, so it encourages me to hope that I may still find opportunities before I leave this place of co-operating with you, though in a different form, for the like ends."

The " tone and spirit of friendship" between the two had been preserved throughout, and shows itself strikingly in the " Letters."   Thirlwall speaks of Whewell having " rather heightened than diminished the regard which he had long entertained for him."   Whewell expresses his " strong admiration and esteem for Thirlwall's great endowments and elevated character."   It is satisfactory to know from their after intercourse and letters that this friendship remained unbroken to the end.

Thirlwall went abroad shortly after, but returned to Cambridge for the October term, in the course of which came the offer from Lord Brougham of the living of Kirby Underdale.   He accepted it, and his connection with Cambridge came to a close simultaneously with the year.

To JOHN THIRLWALL, Esq.

TRINITY COLLEGE, *December 5th*, 1834.

' " I have just received a letter from Thomas, apprising me of your kind congratulations on my recent preferment. . . . .

" I shall postpone the ceremony of institution and induction till February next, as in the meanwhile my fellowship is running on to another quarter, and it is only from the day of institution that it becomes vacant, though after that time I have still what is called a year of grace, for which I receive the usual dividends, and then my connection with the college, for such purposes, ends. I look forward with a little trepidation to the process of establishing myself in a residence at such a distance from my present habitation. The part of the country, however, is that which I have always preferred, though I have not been able to ascertain the precise nature of the situation, except that it must be a very sequestered and thinly inhabited spot. Yet I am informed that there are a number of good families in the neighbourhood. Sir Francis Wood, the chief proprietor, bears a very high character, and I was introduced in town to his son, Mr. Wood of the Treasury.* His connection with Lord Grey will be all in my favour, as I have always been on intimate terms with Lord Grey's two sons here, and may therefore calculate on a friendly reception. I am also, for sundry reasons, much better pleased that the living is in the province of York than that of Canterbury. Its value was described to me in Mr. Wood's presence as between £900 and £1,000 per annum. But the Chancellor, in the letter in which he offered it to me, put it between £800 and £900. I hope I shall not find, what very often happens, that the lowest value assigned to it has been a good deal exaggerated. However, my lot is now cast, and indeed I had no time for any minute inquiries on the subject, for before I had signified my acceptance of the living the London papers had announced the presentation. I have at least the satisfaction of knowing that it came perfectly unsought, and the terms in which the late Chancellor conveyed his offer were only too flattering. On the whole, I am very glad of such an opportunity of withdrawing from college, where, though I have many excellent friends, I cannot help feeling my position rather awkward, and could, perhaps, never get rid of some unpleasant recollections. I have thought it prudent to repress my curiosity

* The present Viscount Halifax.

K

and to defer my first visit to Kirby, until I go to take possession, which I calculate on doing the first or second week in February. The parsonage has, I find, been long inhabited by a curate of the late incumbent, from whom I received a letter this morning, requesting to be informed whether it is my intention to reside. He speaks in a way implying a strong attachment to the place, which is at least a sign that it is possible to live there with tolerable comfort, and at the same time makes me polite offers of attention whenever I feel disposed to visit it."

To T. KEIGHTLEY, Esq.

TRINITY, *December* 9th, 1834.

" I have just received the specimen sheet of your ' History of Greece,' and am therefore writing from a first but very recent impression about it. What I see appears to me to deserve almost unqualified praise. The plan seems judicious, and the style is, as it ought to be, at once easy and grave. In saying that the praise due to this specimen is *almost* unqualified, I had one or two passages in my mind, which it strikes me may be thought liable to objection, though one which but very slightly affects the value and merit of the work. In a book of this nature it appears to me better to avoid peremptory and dogmatical assertions on disputed points ; but perhaps even this is preferable to supporting a questionable opinion by a slight and inconclusive argument. An instance in which you appear to me to have been drawn by the narrowness of your limits into either one or the other of these cases occurs in the sentence about human sacrifices. The proposition is, perhaps, not even worded so distinctly as might be wished : for it is not clear whether you deny that human sacrifices were known to the Pelasgians, or only that they were common among them. I suppose the

former to be your meaning, and in that case, though I
have no doubt that you could maintain it by strong arguments, I cannot think that those which may be urged for
the antiquity of human sacrifices in Greece, reaching to an
age earlier than Homer's, deserve to be treated as utterly
empty and worthless. To me, I confess, the indications
of such a practice existing in the Pelasgian period afforded
by the rites and traditions of later times, appear greatly to
outweigh all the objections which I have hitherto seen
raised on the opposite side. Still, if you only said to your
young reader, 'Take my word for it, there were no human
sacrifices among the Pelasgians,' no great harm would be
done. But you add something which appears to be
meant for a reason, and which cannot be allowed the
slightest weight in deciding the question. The epithet
δῖοι can no more prove anything in this respect with
regard to the Pelasgians than that of κλυτός, which is
given to the cannibal Antiphates, or that of ἀγαυοί,
which is given to the Phœnicians. . . . . .

"The only school I know of about here is the Cambridge Grammar School, the Master of which, Bailey, you
have probably heard of. He was a man of considerable
scholarship, but obliged to work for the booksellers till he
obtained his present situation. I do not know him personally, but I will endeavour to find a channel for forwarding your specimen to him, which may be likely to
procure it a good reception.

"I shall certainly leave Cambridge, for when I have
taken possession of my Yorkshire living, where, as far as I
can learn, I shall find myself in a very profound seclusion,
my fellowship expires. I believe that in any case I should
not have resided here long. I feel myself here a little in
the condition of Ajax—Ἔχθει με Τροία πᾶσα καὶ πεδία
τάδε—and I therefore welcome the opportunity of a decent
retreat."

CHAPTER VI.

KIRBY UNDERDALE, 1835—1840.

Lord Brougham and Thirlwall—Commencement of the "History of Greece"
—"Lardner's Cyclopædia"—Life and Work at Kirby Underdale—Subsequent Visit—Letters on :—Kirby Underdale—His Arrival and Settlement there—Progress of the "History of Greece"—The Education
of his Nephews—The German Translation of his History—Professor
Welcker's Preface—German Reviews of the "History"—A Tour in
Germany—Visit to the Poet Tieck—His Fondness for Domestic Pets.

"WHEN Lord Melbourne's first ministry broke up, Lord
Brougham said he thought he had provided fairly for all
who had deserved well of the Whig party in the Church,
with the exception of Sedgwick and Thirlwall. The next
morning came the vacancy, by death, of a stall at Norwich, which the great geologist took and died in, and of
the living of Kirby Underdale in Yorkshire."* This
Thirlwall accepted, and the preferment came most oppor-
tunely, for as the letters show, his residence at Cambridge,
after the resignation of the tutorship, was attended with
a certain amount of unpleasantness.

The change was as great as could be imagined, from
the intellectual bustle of university life, to the quietness
of the country parish hidden amongst the Yorkshire
wolds. The change, however, was marked and turned to
account, as the former had been, by the commencement of
new literary labours. With Kirby Underdale is associated
the production of the "History of Greece," the work
upon which Thirlwall's reputation as an author rests. It

* Lord Houghton in the *Fortnightly Review*, February, 1878.

came about in this manner. "Among the early enterprises for the diffusion of the results of scientific and historical labours beyond the circle of professed scholars and men of science was a certain series known from the name of its editor (an active, pushing, able man of science) as 'Lardner's Cyclopædia.' To this series Mr. Thirlwall was invited to contribute a history of Greece. Taking the standard recognised for other subjects, what was probably expected was a popular narrative brought within the compass of two or three duodecimo volumes. To work on this scale, however, was soon found to be difficult, if not impossible, for one who in his treatment even of subordinate questions connected with his subject ever aimed at a singularly elaborate completeness."* This led to a gradual enlargement, but there "still remained the uneasy sense that he was writing for two different sets of readers."* The first volume was published in 1835, and others appeared at short and regular intervals.

The surrounding circumstances were favourable to the work. The perfect seclusion of the village, and the smallness of the population (under 300), gave opportunities of unbounded literary leisure. Personal reminiscences tell of Thirlwall's prodigious powers of work and passion for knowledge. Often sixteen hours out of the twenty-four were spent in the study and among the books which overflowed into every room of the house. Eating, walking, or riding he was never to be seen without a book. And all this went on with close parochial work. The recollection still survives of the regular services with the full and attentive congregations, including incomers from neighbouring villages ; of the frequent visits to the village school ; of the extempore prayers with his flock, of which the larger number were Dissenters ; and of the assiduous attention paid to the sick and poor.

* *Edinburgh Review*, April, 1876.

An instance of Thirlwall's kindness of heart is preserved in a story, which tells how he once sent a mother with her little daughter in his own gig to the seaside—about twenty miles from Kirby—to try whether the change of air would save the poor child from consumption.   His remarkable dignity and purity of character were fully recognised by his flock; and the impartial manner in which he kept himself aloof from the petty quarrels and scandals of the place was well expressed by an old parishioner, who reported that the rector's invariable answer to complainants was, " I never 'ears no tales."

Beside his other charges Thirlwall undertook the care and preliminary education of two little nephews, one of whom was afterwards the registrar of his diocese, and his devoted companion in the closing years of his life. Old friends and literary acquaintances, too, found their way at times to the secluded rectory.   The annual summer tours were not given up ; his place in the parish being supplied by the present Master of Trinity and other old Cambridge friends.   It was during one of these excursions that the offer of the See of St. David's came, as is described later on.

Twenty-four years after he had left Kirby, the Bishop of St. David's spent a few days there ; returning with the present rector on the conclusion of a visit to Lord Houghton at Fryston.   He was much interested in seeing the few old people left who remembered him.   One of the first objects of his visit was to go to an old tree, near which he had once buried a favourite dog, and look for some Greek letters that he had cut in the bark.

To John Thirlwall, Esq.

York, *February 17th,* 1835.

" Having taken canonical and legal possession of the

Rectory of Kirby Hundersdale, alias Underdale, in the county of York, and being on my return to Cambridge, I think it will be best before proceeding southward to give you an account of the substance of what I have seen and observed at the place of my future residence. I must premise that on my arrival at Doncaster I found a servant whom Sir Francis Wood had sent over with a gig to take me to his seat, Hickleton Hall, which is five or six miles off. I found the baronet in his hunting-dress, for he had left the fox-hounds for the purpose of receiving me. Sir Francis is a very important person to every one connected with Kirby Underdale, as you may easily suppose when I mention that out of about 5,000 acres of which the parish consists 4,600 belong to him. He also possesses about 2,000 or 3,000 in adjacent parishes. Of course nothing is done in Kirby without his leave, and the light in which he is viewed there was illustrated to me by an expression used by an old woman, who speaking of her son, said that he would no more say anything wrong when left to himself, than he would in the presence of Sir Francis Wood—or of God Almighty. It is, therefore, a piece of peculiar good fortune to find that a person of such extensive influence in my sphere possesses every quality which is likely to render our personal intercourse agreeable. He is a man of great natural intelligence and acuteness, and besides being thoroughly master of every kind of information connected with rural pursuits, possesses a great deal of a more ornamental nature, both scientific and literary. He appears, as far as I can judge from a short acquaintance, to be a person of a very benevolent disposition, and at all events received and entertained me with the greatest kindness. He showed me plans of the parish, gave me an account of the principal inhabitants, and communicated a variety of information very important for enabling me to understand the state both of persons and things in the place. He would have taken me with him to Kirby, but I was obliged to stop at York to receive institution, and I therefore left him on the second morning and arrived at York on Thursday the 12th. I was obliged to wait there for the arrival of the Canon Residentiary who was commissioned by the Archbishop to give me institution. This ceremony took place the next day, and immediately after I met with my curate, Mr. Whitelocke, who had come over on some business with his lady, and offered to take me back with him that evening. He is a son of the celebrated General Whitelocke, and has a living in Lincolnshire which he is now on the point of exchanging for one about ten miles from Kirby, and has also, I believe, a considerable private fortune. Accordingly he had come in a very handsome four-wheeled carriage, a kind of phaeton, I believe, drawn by a pair of good horses. In this I took a seat and was conveyed to the parsonage, which I found in a very different state from that which I had been led to expect. For it is still inhabited by Mr. Whitelocke, with all the furniture in *statu quo*, Mrs. Ridley having been induced to let it stay there till I came to look at it. My entry took place in the dark, yet it was soon bruited about the village, and for an hour after the parish clerk was employed in ringing all the changes he could think of on a couple of bells, one of which is a little cracked, and the whole effect so little answered to his good will that though the steeple from which the sounds issued is within a hundred yards of the house, they did not reach my ears, and I was only apprised of the honour that had been done me next morning.

To JOHN THIRLWALL, Esq.

KIRBY UNDERDALE, NEAR POCKLINGTON, *July* 10th, 1835.

" I should have written some days sooner to announce to you my arrival at my new abode, if I had not been occupied ever since, not only by a series of journeys which I was forced to take for the purpose of effecting the transport of my effects from a place about nine miles distant, to which they were carried by water, and by other pressing business incident on my entrance upon housekeeping, but likewise by a piece of duty which fell upon me most unseasonably, viz. the task of preaching a sermon at the visitation at Scarborough, which I was called upon to do just as I was on the point of leaving Cambridge. And though the time allowed for the preparation of my discourse would under any other circumstances have been amply sufficient, I found so much difficulty in obtaining the necessary intervals of leisure that I had not finished it many hours before it was to be delivered. I only mention this that you may not think that I have postponed what I an now doing to any but really unavoidable engagements.

"I left London by a Hull steam packet, which brought me and a part of my baggage, most urgently wanted after a very cold and wet voyage, without any material damage to Hull, where I found the heavy cases and hampers containing my books, wine, &c., which had been sent on from Cambridge by Lynn. After making arrangements for the conveyance of these things by a small vessel which comes up to within the above-mentioned distance of my house, I proceeded to York, and on the morning of Saturday, June 27, reached this place, which I found perfectly ready for my reception, and all my household in attendance. . . . .

" On my way from York hither I met Sir Francis Wood, who I believe had come over to meet me and had stayed till the last moment, expecting my arrival.   He has shown me a number of civilities, besides affording me much substantial accommodation in allowing me the use of land, and the loan of two horses, one of which I drove over to Scarborough in a gig which I purchased at York second-hand, but very nearly as good as new.   I have thus leisure to look out for a horse of my own, which is indispensably necessary.   I also expect soon to become owner of a cow.   After several journeys to Pocklington, near to which my things were brought by water, I succeeded in carrying them safely away in sundry waggons which I borrowed here.   I brought my shelves from Cambridge along with my books : and though they suffered some slight fractures on the way, the village joiner has put them together again very fairly, and has adapted them to the form of the house, so that they are now ready to receive books, and we are beginning to clear the encumbered floors.   I hope in a few days to have put everything in order for the present, though, as I have a considerable number of books still to come from Cambridge, I foresee I shall be extremely straitened for room. . . .

"The Archdeacon (Wrangham) was not at Scarborough : his son officiated for him.   I dined with the clergy, and was very well received, and requested to print my sermon, which I suppose I must do, though I shall have more than enough to do with the press for other purposes.   I should have been glad if I had been able to send you a copy of the first volume of my history, which, however, I dare say you have already seen.   I am now formally bound to produce four more at intervals of six months, or within three years : and the rate at which I am paid will depend on the regularity of their appearance.   Until this work is finished every moment of leisure left by my parochial duties will be fully absorbed by it; and I am afraid I shall be obliged to lead a very unsocial life. . . ."

To John Thirlwall, Esq.

Kirby Underdale, Pocklington, *December 17th*, 1835.

" I believe Thomas told you some time ago that I meant
to write to you as soon as I should have returned from my
journey to the south, and perhaps you may think that my
absence from home has been somewhat of the longest.   It
was indeed a week longer than I had hoped would have
sufficed for my business when I set out ; but I came back
last Saturday.   Yet I could not set to letter-writing sooner,
having been ever since most fully employed, and being only
just delivered of the last sheets of the second volume of
my history.   When I got to town I found that Dr. Lardner was at the other end of the kingdom, where it seems
he has been making observations and experiments upon
railroads, and flying about at prodigious velocities in steam
carriages—for he is a factotum, if ever there was one—and
the consequence was that the operations of the press did
not proceed with quite the same rapidity as in the publication of the first volume, and were not quite over when I
was obliged to turn my face northward.   This obliged me
to make two journeys to York—very unpleasant expedi-
tions, by the by, at this time of the year—to fetch and
carry parcels from and to the printer.   As the volume is
to come out the first of next month there was no time to
be lost, and I was forced to put the last hand to the proof
sheets and make the table of contents in a great hurry,
the effects of which, I am afraid, I shall discover in a long
list of errata.   This is one disagreeable consequence of my
distance from London and secluded situation.   Another
which I feel much more sensibly is the want of books of
reference.   Though my own library is tolerably well
furnished for ordinary purposes of instruction and amusement, and is probably better filled than the average of
country clergymen's libraries, still it is very far from

satisfying the wants occasioned by my present occupations, and I have continual cause to miss the advantages I enjoyed at Cambridge, where the public libraries were almost as easy of access as my own. The worst of all is that when I go to town to superintend the printing of my manuscripts, as I am then forced to leave my own books behind me, I find myself most destitute, though it is then that the use of a good library would be most important to me.

"I hope that you may find my next volume, at least, for the greater part, more readable than the last. It will not be quite so large, nor in other respects so full of matter. But as it will contain more of narration than of disquisition, if the subject is not too beaten, it will, perhaps, better suit the taste of most readers. The favourable manner in which the first volume has been received, at least so far as any opinions have been expressed about it, will, I hope, stimulate me to greater activity, that the succeeding parts may, at least, not fall off from the quality of the beginning. I should have been better pleased with the review in the *Edinburgh* if, though less complimentary, it had borne marks of being written by somebody more at home in the subject. Unfortunately, there is a great dearth at present among us in this department. I was more flattered by a letter which I found here on my return from a German professor, to whom I had sent a copy of the book, and who tells me, among many other obliging things, that if his occupations had permitted he should have gladly undertaken to translate it into German. Not, he observes, that there will be any lack of German translations, but he is afraid that they may not do justice to the original. Perhaps you will be alarmed lest so much praise should turn me giddy. But I believe that I can assure you from personal experience that it is scarcely possible for anyone to be very much elated with the success of a work which has cost him a good many years of labour and thought.

In such a case the author is too well acquainted with the real merits and defects of his own performance to depend upon the opinion of others. No praise or blame can either tickle or sting him, unless he is conscious that it is in some degree deserved, though no one can, or ought to be, insensible to the mortification of seeing his labour thrown away upon his contemporaries, even if he should hope that it may yield more fruit hereafter, nor to the satisfaction of finding his own judgment confirmed by the approbation of intelligent critics. Thus then, under favourable auspices, and with higher aim than I had conceived when I first embarked in this undertaking, I am on the point of setting about my third volume.

"To leave the 'History of Greece' in some respects in better condition than I found it, is, I think, a sufficiently rational object of ambition to justify me in dedicating to it every moment I can spare from the duties of my parish, which, though in point of obligation they will always take the precedency, from the portion of time which they occupy, may be considered as the chief recreation of my leisure. With respect to every other kind of recreation I am obliged to observe a strict economy. . . ."

To JOHN THIRLWALL, Esq.

KIRBY UNDERDALE, *May* 12*th*, 1836.

"I have just concluded the third volume of my history, half of which has been some weeks printed, and have only to look over the manuscript and to add a few notes and appendices. In the beginning of the week after next, the 23rd, I propose to go up to town to deposit it with the printer, that it may come out in its due time on the 1st July. . . . .

"I was much pleased to hear that you had been

entertained by the second volume of my history. This, I can assure you, has afforded me more gratification than the most flattering eulogies. I have some hopes that you will find the next at least equally interesting. I think it will be generally considered the best of the three. I have at least succeeded in most parts of it more to my own satisfaction than in the preceding one, and a comparison of what had been done by my predecessor in the same field leads me to believe that my labour will not have been thrown away. I had scarcely imagined myself that so much remained to be set right in this portion of the subject. Now, therefore, I may consider myself as having got through one-half of my undertaking, for the rest will require *three* volumes more. The remaining part will be the most difficult and laborious, as the sources are more scattered and require very careful investigation. I ought to have a year instead of six months for each volume. But Lardner's work keeps moving like one of his steam engines, and will not allow me to slacken my pace. Still, unless I should be hindered by some extraordinary interruptions, I hope to proceed without falling off, and I shall then be released from a task which, though pleasant, has often been somewhat fatiguing. Lardner intimated to me that he intended at some future time to republish it with some others in a larger form, which would give me an opportunity of correcting and improving it, which I shall gladly embrace. This, however, is not a thing to be talked of at present. . . . ."

To JOHN THIRLWALL, Esq.

KIRBY UNDERDALE, *May 25th,* 1836.

"You perceive by the date of this letter that I have been prevented from leaving home for the south at the time I had intended, and I believe my journey will now be postponed for a long while. I had relied on the assistance of a friend for taking my duty in my absence ; but he was engaged, and I did not receive his answer till the latter end of this week when it was too late to look out for a substitute, which is here very difficult to procure. This led me to think that it would be better to send up my manuscript to town, where I have in fact no business that absolutely requires my presence, and to stay here, and lay the foundations of a fourth volume, while the third is passing through the press. Accordingly I yesterday carried my manuscript to York, and saw it deposited in one of the London coaches, and expect in a couple of days more to hear of its arrival. I should have written to you sooner, but that after I received your letter I was occupied partly by the visit of a friend, who stayed with me during the two or three last days of the week, and partly by the final corrections of my MS.

" Having finished it the week before, I took it with me in the beginning of last week on a little excursion which I made in my gig, along the edge of our wolds to the Hamilton district, being thus enabled to devote the evenings and some portions of the day to it at the places where I stopped, and at the same time to enjoy some of the most beautiful scenery in England. . . . ."

To his little Nephew, MASTER THOMAS THIRLWALL,
St. Vincent's, West Indies.

KIRBY UNDERDALE, *June 8th*, 1836.

"I do not know how it is that you have not got an answer to the letters which you tell me you have written to Uncle Thomas and grandmamma. If they were such pretty letters as the one you wrote to me, I think you ought to have had an answer by this time. I have only

just received yours, and I am beginning to answer it
directly, that you may know how much I was pleased
with it ; so that instead of writing to you only because I
want to write to papa, I shall this time write to papa only
because I want to write to you, and papa will only get
as much of this sheet as will be left when I have said all
that I have to say to Thomas. I am very much obliged
to mamma for telling you how fond I was of you when
you were in England. I have no doubt that I shall like
you still better when I see you again. Everybody loved
you then, because you were such a quiet, good-tempered,
merry little child ; but then you could not say anything
to us, nor understand what was said to you, nor know
anything about us. When you come again I daresay you
will be as good-tempered and merry as you used to be,
and I shall be able not only to look at you, but, which is
still better, to talk with you, and to find out what a number of things you have learnt since you were here last, and
perhaps to tell you of a good many that you have still to
learn, and then I hope you may be as fond of me as I
shall be of you. I am glad to hear that you like Quebec
better than St. Vincent's, though I think it is very
likely that I should be more pleased with St. Vincent's
than with Quebec. To be sure it is not pleasant to be
almost always in a great heat, though it makes you enjoy
yourself the more whenever you can get cool. But then I
like to see the fine trees and fruits and flowers that will
only grow where the sun has great power ; and you cannot have them and the frost and snow too. Perhaps you
will want to know why I am glad to hear that you like
Quebec better than St. Vincent's. Now that is because I
think it is a proper taste for you to like a place where you
can be stirring about and doing something, if it is only
shoveling about the snow. Very hot weather is apt to
make one fond of lounging instead of either working or

playing, and so to bring on idle habits; and I suppose among the many wise sayings that you must have copied before you learnt to write as well as you do now, one has been, 'Idleness is the root of all evil,' or something like it. So you see I judge from what you say that you are an active boy, and I shall be very glad indeed to find that I have guessed right. Then all that will be wanting will be that your friends should put you in the way of being active to some good purpose. That is industry. I am sure you have spent a great many hours in writing the praises of industry in your copybooks; but you may depend upon it that you have never yet seen it praised half as much as it deserves to be, and that the longer you practice it, the more you will know its value. Another reason why I am glad you like Quebec better than St. Vincent's is, that it makes me think England will suit you very well. Though England is very different from Quebec, still it is more like that than St. Vincent's. Here, indeed, we cannot promise you so much snow as you have been used to, for our winters are often so mild that the snow in many places is not an inch deep in any part of the year. But if you do not dislike the sight of green fields you will be able to find other exercise perhaps as pleasant as shoveling about the snow; and though you will have no need to muffle yourself up to prevent yourself from being frost-bitten you will almost always find a fresh bracing air, and sometimes you may enjoy the diversion of skating. Then in the summer you may ramble about the fields at any hour of the day without being scorched or melted by the sun. I wish you could see how pretty my garden is looking just now, with its flowers and blossoms, some of them almost as fragrant as the orange flower, and as bright as the pomegranate. When you come to see me I hope that you and Johnny will help the gardener to raise some nice fruits and flowers. Then you shall take some drives in

L

the country and see some of the beauties of Yorkshire,
though not in a cariole, or with such a big dog as Watch
must be, or have been, if it was he that drew you and
Johnny. But I have a pretty little dog named Fop, who,
though he cannot draw you, will be glad to go out with
you, and to show you what a number of hares and rabbits
we have about us. I think you will say that England is
the best place after all to live in all the year round, though
we may be equally happy everywhere if we have only good
friends about us, and make ourselves beloved by them.
That is what I have no doubt you will do here when you
come, and therefore I long to see you quite as much as you
can long to see me. You must tell Johnny that I long to
see him too, and that I hope in time to have many letters
from him, as long and as well written as yours. Also,
when you see Sukey next, you must give her a kiss, and
tell her that Uncle Connop sent it to her folded up in a
letter all the way from Yorkshire.

" Now I must have done, or else I shall have no room
left for saying anything to papa. . . . ."

To his Brother, JOHN THIRLWALL, Esq., St. Vincent's.

June 8th, 1836.

" My little correspondent has not left me much paper,
but as the time when we hope to see both you and him is
now so near, there is the less need of a long letter. I
shall be very glad to have your two little fellows near me,
so that I may be able to have an eye constantly upon
them, to know how they are going on and to give them all
the assistance in my power. I trust that we shall find a
situation which will combine this advantage with every
other requisite. They cannot be in a healthier part of
England, nor in many much pleasanter. The thing which

I look forward to with the greatest pleasure is that as
they grow more capable of benefiting by what I may be
able to teach them, I shall have more leisure to dedicate
to them. At present I am pretty well occupied with the
task of producing a volume of history every half-year. My
second was published on the 1st of January, and the
third will I expect appear on the 1st of July. But I am
almost afraid that I have not yet got half through my
work. It is now too late to send you the second volume,
and indeed in this place I should not know how to do it.
But when you come you may carry the second and third
away with you. When this business is finished I hope to
enjoy a little leisure. At least, I do not mean ever again
to bind myself in the same manner. Your plan of sending the boys to a German University is perhaps a very
good one in itself, though I do not know that they would
find any greater facilities for acquiring foreign languages
except the German itself, there than here. The five which
they would probably find most useful—German, French,
Italian, Spanish, and Portuguese—I have had opportunities of speaking and hearing where they are spoken; and
I think I could put your boys in the way of mastering
them as far as is possible without travelling in those
countries. But I believe quite as much importance is
attached to the knowledge of Latin and Greek at every
German University as at our own; and I do not think
that the most perfect knowledge of every language now
spoken under the sun could compensate for the want of
them. . . . ."

To L. SCHMITZ, Esq.

KIRBY UNDERDALE, *March 12th*, 1838.

" I am obliged to trespass still a little longer on your
indulgence for the use of your MS. of ' Niebuhr.' I find

that I can read it so as scarcely ever to be in doubt about a word ; but the time it requires has been hitherto more than I have had to spare, as I have been lately fully occupied with the fifth volume of my history, which I expect to send to the press in about ten days.   But before I do so I wish, if I possibly can, to read through all that part of the MS. which relates to the same period.   I preferred taking it up after my own view of the subject should have been completely unfolded not only in thought but in words.   I wish, however, to read 'Niebuhr' not merely to satisfy my own curiosity, but, where it can be done in the compass of a short note, to communicate his opinions on doubtful or interesting points, particularly where they differ from my own, to my readers.   In the part which I have already looked into I found several passages of this nature, and have ventured to quote two or three lines here and there in a note.

"But before I send any such quotations to the press I wish to know whether I have your permission to make this use of your MS.   That you may know precisely what it is you consent to, I will add that I have no intention of quoting anywhere more than three lines.

"This question suggests another.   Have you heard whether Niebuhr's friends have any intention of printing his lectures ?   And if this is not the case, should you feel yourself at liberty to publish your 'Notes'?   I ask this not from an interest on behalf of German readers, but with a view to the English public and to yourself.   I am convinced that a translation of the volume you have lent me would be both a very useful and a saleable work."

To John Thirlwall, Esq.   .
                    Kirby Underdale, *May 23rd*, 1838.

" . . . . As I was present at the meeting of the [British]

Association at Cambridge,* I know pretty well what I might expect from it. It is no doubt a very interesting thing for scientific persons. But for me the proceedings have very little interest, and as an opportunity of seeing one's friends it is the worst in the world, everybody having business of some kind or other to occupy him. I should, therefore, not have chosen this time to visit Newcastle; but if I found myself at liberty it would suit me as well as any other to take a journey to Alnwick. I must, however, for the reasons I have assigned leave the whole matter in suspense. As soon as I am able to make any arrangement including a visit to you, I will of course send you the earliest advice. I have mentioned the fetters that confine me in the use of my leisure, I must add that my leisure itself is still very scanty. The fifth volume of my history is printed, and I believe will appear next month. But my work is not yet ended by several volumes; and the time I have to devote to it is a good deal curtailed by the demands of John's boys. . . . . ."

To L. Schmitz, Esq.

Kirby Underdale, Pocklington, den 26*ten Mai*, 1838.

"Wahrscheinlich wird es Sie, mein geschätzter Freund nicht befremden, noch auch Ihnen missfallen, dass ich um einer kleiner Uebungs willen sowohl in der Sprache als auch in den mir noch immer sehr fremden Schriftzügen, unternommen habe Ihren Brief Deutsch zu erwiedern. Gewiss darf ich mich dabei mit voller Sicherheit auf Ihre gutige Nachsicht verlassen, wenn dieser Versuch desgleichen ich zwar schon früher, aber doch sehr selten gemacht habe, noch so verfehlt auffallen sollte. Uebrigens was mir besonders dabei Muth macht ist dass ich mir keine

* In 1833 under the presidency of Professor Sedgwick.

sehr schwierige Aufgabe aufgestellt habe. Schwerlich wird es mir begegnen mich in diesen wenigen Zeilen so ganz unrichtig oder schief auszudrücken dass ich nicht was die Haupt-Sache ist meine Meinung Ihnen deutlich genug machen sollte. Ihre freundliche Anerbietung ist mir nicht nur an sich sehr erfreulich gewesen, sondern auch ganz zur rechten Zeit eingetroffen hat. Ich habe mich so eben das 5ten Bändchen meiner Griechischen Geschichte erledigt, und mir damit für einige Zeit Müsse erworben.

"Ich habe neulich einige litterarische Neuigkeiten aus Deutschland erhalten ; unter denen die Lebensnachrichten Niebuhrs nebst einer Sammlung seiner Briefer, Sie vielleicht am meisten interessiren wird. Auch denke ich nun ernstlich daran die Uebersetzung des dritten Bands der Römischen Geschichte zur Hand zu nehmen, und werde gern über einige Stellen Ihre Meinung vernehmen. So darf ich hoffen dass die Zeit Ihres Aufenthalts Ihnen nicht allzulange vorkommen wird."

[TRANSLATION.]

" Perhaps, my valued friend, it will not appear strange to you, or indeed displease you, that I have undertaken to answer your letter in German for the sake of a little practice as well in the language as also in the written characters, which are still very strange to me. Of course I can rely with perfect certainty on your kind indulgence should this attempt, too, happen to turn out a failure. But what particularly gives me courage in it is, that I have set myself no very difficult task. It will scarcely happen to me in these few lines to express myself so extremely incorrectly or awkwardly as not to make my meaning plain enough to you, which is the chief thing. Your friendly offer has not only been very delightful to me in itself, but has also come exactly at the right time. I have just got rid of the fifth volume of my Greek history, and have thereby earned leisure for some time.

"I have lately received some literary novelties from Germany; amongst them 'Niebuhr's Memoirs,' along with a collection of his letters, will perhaps interest you the most. I am also thinking seriously of taking in hand the third volume of the Roman history, and would gladly take your opinion on some points. So I venture to hope that the time of your stay will not seem to you too long."

To L. Schmitz, Esq.

Kirby Underdale, *August* 1, 1838.

"Your packet seems to have arrived here only a few hours after I had set out on a little excursion from which I have but just returned. I am much obliged to you for the loan of Matthias, and will send you the second volume of 'Niebuhr's Letters' as soon as I shall have received and read it. I have not yet heard that it is published.

"As to the lectures I am inclined to take Dr. Arnold's view. I cannot pretend to say what impression might be made on the German public by the original if it were published just as it is in the manuscript, with only verbal corrections; but I am strongly of opinion that in England a strictly faithful translation would be generally much more acceptable than any attempt to give the work an appearance of finish. I think people here would like best to have it rough as it came from the master's hand, and that they would be attracted by the very thing which you fear might repel most readers. The only freedom which I should venture to take would be to supply or correct whatever was grammatically defective or inaccurate so as to obscure the meaning. But I think the safest way, if you conclude your bargain with Messrs. Taylor and

Watson, would be to send a specimen of the translation to Mr. Taylor, whose judgment you might rely on more safely than mine. I agree with you as to the propriety of the plan you propose to adopt for the publication of the lectures on Roman History."

[The next four letters refer to the German translation of Thirlwall's History. Two volumes were published at Bonn, the first translated by L. Haymann, with a preface by Professor Welcker, and the second by Dr. Schmitz.]

To L. SCHMITZ, Esq.

KIRBY UNDERDALE, *December 27th*, 1838.

"It gives the most lively pleasure to hear that you have undertaken the translation of my work. Whatever assistance I can give to you, you may depend on receiving. I hope you will let me know, whenever you meet with any passage about which you either feel any doubt as to the meaning, or see any objection to its accuracy. It is probable enough that when I look through the second and following volumes, which I will do for the purpose, I may find occasion for some corrections or additions. I now remember one or two passages in the second volume which will require some.

"I have written to London to order the first volume of the translation. When I get it I will detain it no longer than just to read the preface, and some specimens of the execution, and with them immediately forward it to you.

"I have hardly words to express my sense of Professor Welcker's generosity. Much as I had heard of the nobleness of his character, this instance of it has surprised me, at least as much I can assure you as it has gratified me. For though I am fully sensible of the advantage I personally derive from it, I feel that I have unwittingly done a great deal of mischief by giving occasion to the sacrifice of so much valuable time.

"If you should be writing to him again, pray tell him from me that I shall hope to have an opportunity of thanking him in person for this and his other favours."

To LEONARD SCHMITZ, Esq.

YORK, *April* 13*th*, 1839.

"It has happened very unluckily that I have been detained in York ever since last Tuesday, in constant expectation of receiving a parcel from London containing the last sheets of the sixth volume of my 'History,' which I was told is to be published on the first of next month.   I am at present quite unable to conjecture the cause of the delay which has cost me so much time. . . . . .

"If Friday the 26th will suit you I will wait for you at the 'George'; and I will bring with me a few notes to my second volume.   I have been so fully occupied during the last three months with that which is now in the press that I have not had time to look through the second; but purpose doing so in the course of next week.   If I do not hear from you next week I shall take it for granted that you accept my proposal.

"The first volume of the Translation seems not to have been yet published."

To LEONARD SCHMITZ, Esq.

KIRBY UNDERDALE, *May* 10*th*, 1839.

". . . . I shall inclose some additional notes and corrections for the second volume.   You will see that my first volume fills a decent octavo. The publisher of course would not be able to sell one much thicker at the same price; and perhaps it would be expedient for the sake of uniformity, and also with a view to the sale, that the average bulk should not much exceed five hundred pages.   If you make your second volume include Chapter 18 it will be of about that size, and this will be a natural and proper termination.   I will send you at another time any corrections that may occur to me in Chapters 17 and 18.   The delicate kindness which breathes through Welcker's Preface shows that his character is as noble and amiable as his genius and learning are admirable.   If the first volume finds a tolerable sale, notwithstanding such a formidable host of errata, I shall have good hopes for the success of the whole.

"I go up to London about the 27th of this month, and shall be kept there until the end of June.   And I shall be obliged to be there again before August 5th to take part in another examination.   In the interval I shall probably go over to the Continent, and perhaps to Bonn.   If it was in my power during that time to be of any use to you by correcting the proofs of the Translation, this would determine my plans.   Pray let me know, as soon as you have received the parcel, whether I can be of any service to you in this way."

To LEONARD SCHMITZ, Esq.

KIRBY UNDERDALE, *January 28th,* 1840.

". . . . I have read the article in Gersdorf.   It certainly does not impress me with a favourable opinion of the writer's judgment or learning.   I should not quarrel with him for thinking that my work was not indispensable for any German scholar.   I never imagined that it was.   It was designed simply for the use of the English public; and I have reason to be abundantly satisfied with the testimonies of approbation which it has received both in public and private from very competent judges here.

"But yet it is remarkable that everything which the Reviewer has said to depreciate its value might be perfectly true, and, notwithstanding, the book might be extremely useful even to a German student.

"Whoever is acquainted with the immense mass of German literature on the subjects contained in the first volume, and with the conflicting views it exhibits, might think it something highly desirable to see the *results* of those voluminous *inquiries* presented to him in a small compass. But the Reviewer has committed the ludicrous mistake of supposing that these *results*, which after all can only be the judgment which I have formed on the disputed questions, are something apparent in the books themselves, and that I had nothing to do but to copy them into mine. I wonder how many persons would come to the same conclusion as to *results gained* by Hermann and Creuzer in their correspondence on the Greek mythology. The charge of *prolixity* rather surprised me. One would think that in a volume embracing so many important subjects the only fault of this kind could be the neglect of due proportion in the distribution of the space ; and this, if it existed, might have been proved in a few lines by a reference to the Table of Contents. It is certainly suspicious when a Reviewer makes his readers take his bare assertion, when the proof might be so easily given. So as to my alleged incapacity for distinguishing fable and history—an example or two would have filled very little room, and might have satisfied the reader as to the critic's superior judgment.

"There is one little circumstance which inclines me to believe that you are not much mistaken in your conjecture as to the manner in which the article has been composed. Who would not think that Fatalism—which happens indeed to be mentioned in the Table of Contents, though it is dismissed in four or five sentences—was one of the subjects on which I had chiefly dilated in the section on religion, and that Naturcultus and Zeus included all the rest ?

" Still I regret the effect which this notice may have on the sale of the Translation. The only person who has reason to be pleased is Haymann ; for it is clear that in the Reviewer's judgment the Translation, though not quite perfect, is in its kind better than the original. The next volume will, I hope, appear in the course of the Spring. Its progress has been retarded by a number of unexpected interruptions, but I am now hard at work.   I rejoice to hear that you are so far on your way with ' Niebuhr.' "

To JOHN THIRLWALL, Esq.
12, SUFFOLK STREET, PALL MALL EAST, *June 24th*, 1839.

" . . . . I have been now some weeks in London engaged in an examination of candidates for degrees in the new University of London. . . . .

" It will be necessary for me to be in London again by the 5th of August for another examination, which will terminate my official duties. This being the case, I intend to take advantage of the opportunity for an excursion on the Continent, and if all be well shall embark to-morrow night in a steamboat for Hamburg, and after a short stay at Berlin, and Dresden, shall return by the Rhine. Though the chief object of my excursion is of course to see Germany, and some of its celebrated men : it happens that it will also enable me to transact some business relating to the German translation of my ' History ' which is of some importance, and could not be so well settled without my presence at Bonn where the publisher lives. . . . ."

[With reference to a tour in Germany.]

To JOHN THIRLWALL, Esq.

KIRBY UNDERDALE, *August* 22*nd*, 1839.

" . . . . At Berlin I had a great number of letters to the most eminent among the learned men of the University, and was very hospitably received, and besides gratifying my curiosity with their conversation and lectures, formed some very pleasing and valuable acquaintances. Niebuhr's son, who had just gone through his examination as a student of civil law, and is about to become a professor at another University, paid me several visits, and showed me great attention. I saw the German translation of the first volume of my History in a bookseller's window. . . . . .

" My pleasantest recollections of Dresden are of the three evenings which I spent at the house of the poet Tieck, who received me with great kindness, and spoke much better than it deserved of the translation which I made many years back of two of his little tales. . . . .

" I went down the Rhine by steam to Bonn, where I stayed two or three days, which passed most pleasantly in the society of the Professors, by whom I was received with even greater hospitality and more marked attention than at Berlin. . . . ."

[The following letter contains an indication of the extraordinary fondness which Thirlwall, like Southey, had for cats, and which was also extended to dogs and poultry.]

To REV. W. H. THOMPSON, Trinity College, Cambridge.

KIRBY UNDERDALE, *May*, 1840.

" Many thanks for your good offices. You may tell Mr. Cooper* that my present intention is to leave home

---

* Formerly Fellow of Trinity, now Vicar of Kendal and Archdeacon of Westmoreland.

in the last week of July, and to return in the first of
September, so that his labours will include five Sundays.
Beg him to invite a friend as often as he can get one to
stay with him.   It will be quite a relief to my servants,
who so seldom see a strange face in the house.   Considering the uncertainty of all things here below, I think it
will be desirable that he should let me have his address,
if he is to be away from Cambridge during June and July,
that we may fix the day of his coming. . . . .

"I hope his hostility to dogs is merely official,* or if in
any degree personal, that it is compensated by a partiality
for cats.   Since you were here I have added another dog—
it is a little one—to my establishment, and receive much
pleasure from his gambols with my youngest cat, a present
from the Admiral.   The old one has had a paralytic
stroke, and is only kept alive by the most delicate atten-
tions.   I think she will hardly last out till Cooper's arrival,
and if she goes before I will keep her place vacant till I
return."

* As Dean of his College.

CHAPTER VII.

St. David's, 1840—1860.

" Lord Melbourne seems to have taken a considerable interest in Thirlwall, from an early period of his career, of which the object was entirely unconscious. In 1837, at the time of the nomination of Dr. Stanley to Norwich, he had carefully read the translation of Schleiermacher's Essay on St. Luke, with the introduction which opened out what was then a new view of the composition of the Gospels, and had referred it to the Bishops of Ely (Dr. Allen) and Chichester (Dr. Otter), who expressed a want of confidence in its orthodoxy." *   Thirlwall's promotion was consequently delayed (according to another account) from the twofold desire of not causing a rupture upon a Church question, and of not forcing the King's conscience by an unwelcome nomination. In July, 1840, "the death of Bishop Jenkinson drew upon Melbourne once more the convergent fire of clerical importunities ; but to none was the offer of St. David's crozier sent, of the many who relied on parlia-

* Lord Houghton in the *Fortnightly Review*, February, 1878.

mentary influence or family claims—and to none did it occasion more surprise than to the unambitious object of the premier's choice." Thirlwall was away at the time on a five weeks' ramble, and his place at Kirby was supplied by Mr. (now Archdeacon) Cooper.

"It thus fell out that when a letter franked by the First Minister reached the rectory, the owner was absent, and his servants knew not where he was to be found. One of his intimates, Mr. T. A. Barnes, undertook to find him, but for some days searched in vain. At length as he passed after nightfall a village inn, his eyes rested on a shadow on the window-blind, cast by a strong light within. He could not be mistaken. 'My man at last,' he said; and entering, presented the letter which made his unexpectant friend a spiritual peer. Thirlwall's first impulse was to refuse. He was anxious to complete his History of Greece, and was meditating a visit to the land of art and song during the autumn. It is said to have taken all the power of suasion by his friends to make him agree to be a bishop. His hesitation somehow became known, and it tended to confirm the conviction that he who was least anxious for promotion was most deserving of it. He called at South Street as he had been asked to do; and on finding that the minister had not yet risen, was about to leave his card, when he was told that directions had been given that he was to be shown in whenever he happened to come. Melbourne was in bed surrounded with letters and newspapers.

"'Very glad to see you; sit down, sit down; hope you are come to say you accept. I only wish you to understand that I don't intend if I know it to make a heterodox bishop. I don't like heterodox bishops. As men they may be very good anywhere else, but I don't think they have any business on the bench. I take great interest, he continued, in theological questions, pointing to a pile of folio editions of the Fathers. They are excellent reading, and very amusing; some time or other we must have a talk about them. I sent your edition of Schleiermacher to Lambeth, and asked the Primate to tell me candidly what he thought of it; and look, here are his notes in the margin; pretty copious, you see. He does not concur in all your opinions, but he says there is nothing heterodox in your book.'

" This was peculiarly gratifying to the visitor, for Archbishop Howley was a great scholar and a great Churchman; and hated with all his heart the multiplication of Whig suffragans in his province; but he was a just man, and bore his testimony according to the faith that was in him. Briefly and without blandishment, Thirlwall responded to the appeal thus made to his sense of religious honour. He valued highly the confidence implied in being unexpectedly sought out to fill the vacant See, and nothing could be more alien to his feelings than any reservation of conscience or thought of insincerity in accepting it. Melbourne was satisfied that he had chosen the right sort of man; and after an episcopate of four and thirty years the public judgment has notably ratified his judgment."*

The news of the Rector's elevation caused great commotion at Kirby Underdale. The servants were much attached to their master, and a good deal excited at the prospect of receiving him back as a Bishop. Mr. Cooper, his *locum tenens*, was consulted as to the proper mode of showing him respect on his arrival. When, however, the event occurred, the programme, whatever it was, was entirely disconcerted by the riotous welcome of two or three dogs, who covered the Bishop with their caresses and effectually prevented him from holding any communication with his human friends until he had with some

* The above graphic account is taken from Torrens's " Memoirs of Viscount Melbourne," vol. ii. pp. 330—332.

difficulty extricated himself from their embraces. He thoroughly enjoyed the humour of the situation.* It is almost needless to add that servants and domestic pets alike accompanied their master and his vast library to the distant home in Wales. The Bishop was soon settled in his new sphere of labour. Whatever may have been the motives which originally led Thirlwall to seek orders in the Church, there cannot be the slightest question as to the marked piety and activity of his episcopal career. "His sense of duty at once constrained him to throw his vast linguistic power into the homely and perhaps ungrateful task of learning, as no English Bishop since the conquest had ever learnt, the language of his Cambrian diocese."† Within six months of his appointment he was preaching and performing service in Welsh, with a correctness and purity of accent that made the people insist on claiming him as one of their own race. The vigour and thoroughness with which he threw himself into his work extorted praise even from those who were most opposed to him. The History of Greece still remained to be finished, and the eighth and last volume was brought out in 1847. Before that, however, he had embraced an offered opportunity, long-wished for, and between the years 1845 and 1852 published an improved edition of the "History."

This is the last great literary achievement of Bishop Thirlwall that remains to be chronicled. A natural feeling of wonder and regret arises that this should be the case ; that the vast stores of classical and theological learning accumulated in his mind should never have been applied to the production of some work that would have made his name a household word to English students for all ages. It may almost be said that some of his ecclesiastical con-

* Letter from Archdeacon Cooper.
† Dean Stanley's Introduction to Bishop Thirlwall's "Letters to a Friend."

temporaries, confessedly inferior to him in the extent of their acquirements, have achieved that reputation. The reason for this barrenness of production can never exactly be known. It was not, at any rate, from any disinclination to print, for publications on various subjects—in the shape of sermons, pamphlets, and letters—often issued from his pen. The choicer part of them, including the invaluable Charges, " which stand out among the episcopal utterances of the century like Turnus among the Rutuli—*toto vertice supra*,"* are to be found collected in the three volumes of " Remains," edited by Dean Perowne.

The life at Abergwili was marked by the same characteristics as that at Kirby Underdale, except that it was so frequently broken in upon by the exigencies of diocesan work, or by the necessary attendance in Parliament or Convocation. Letters and friends alike tell of the Bishop's devotion to his books, the greater part of the day being spent in " Chaos," as he familiarly and aptly termed his study. Every table and chair in it, with the single exception of the one in which he sat, were hidden beneath piles of books and papers ; and, as at Kirby, nearly every room of the house was brought into requisition for the storage of his library. When away from home on confirmation tours he generally used a commodiously-built carriage, with one seat for himself, and another opposite him for a vast assortment of books which he carried about, and which consisted largely of the most recently issued works of Germany and France. His fondness for domestic pets has been already alluded to, and he might be seen after a meal going round the table and sweeping the broken fragments of bread into his napkin to carry off to his favourites. Later on, when his nephew's family formed part of the home circle, his affection for children showed itself in a marked manner. He entered heartily into their enjoy-

* Letter from the Dean of Lincoln.

ments, and his whole being changed and lighted up when he was with them. A story is told of the keenness with which the Bishop shared in a school entertainment given in the neighbouring village, and of the charming address that he gave to the school children. Boys, he told them, were like tops. There were some tops that gave no trouble, but only needed to be set spinning and they would go; these were like good boys. But there were other tops which could only be kept going by constant whipping; these were the naughty boys, whom nothing but the rod would keep to their work. To those who did not know him, his demeanour might seem stern and his speech sometimes severe, but this severity and sternness were only brought to bear upon duplicity and pretence of knowledge where there was ignorance, which were heinous faults in his eyes. On the other hand there must be many who can bear witness to the consideration, gentleness, and sympathy shown to those who needed encouragement and help; and in times of difficulty or trouble Bishop Thirlwall proved a friend whose counsel, wisdom, and affection could always be relied upon.

[The following letter, which was the first written by the Bishop in his official capacity, was addressed to a clergyman in his diocese, who had refused the Holy Communion to some persons on the ground of their attendance at a theatre. It is thoroughly characteristic of the wise freedom and liberality with which the Bishop uniformly dealt with controversial matters.]

40, St. James's Place, August 10th, 1840.

"Rev. Sir,

"I have received some papers from his Grace the Archbishop of Canterbury, from which it appears that you have refused to administer the Sacrament of the Holy Communion to some of your parishioners on the ground that they had attended the theatre. They conceived that you had overstepped the limits of your ministerial authority, and applied first to their late Diocesan, and during his illness to the Archbishop for his interposition. The See having become vacant, his Grace thought proper to reserve the business for the decision of the next Bishop of St. David's, and it therefore now becomes my duty to deliver my opinion on the subject. I cannot but regret that the first occasion on which I am called upon to exercise my pastoral authority in the diocese committed to my care should be one which compels me to differ very widely in my judgment from one of my clergy. I am, however, much consoled by the reflection that the case is one in which a difference of opinion is consistent with the highest respect for the motives of those from whom we differ.

" I have no doubt that, in the course you have taken, you have been guided by the purest intentions and the most earnest desire of discharging your duty; but I am no less decidedly of opinion that you have been transported by your praiseworthy zeal beyond the bounds of Christian prudence, and that you have assumed a kind of jurisdiction which does not belong to you. I must own that in this point of view expressions which I perceive in the letters of the complaining parties, alluding to the arbitrary power exercised in former times by the Romish clergy, appear to me not wholly without foundation. I conceive that you have not the right which you have practically claimed, of affixing your own private interpretation to the language in which the Church describes the class of persons who are to be excluded from participation in her means of grace.

" You must, I conceive, be aware that your proceeding in this case is an innovation on the practice which has

been commonly received in our Church : that it has not
been customary to exclude persons who attend the theatre
from the Holy Communion ; and, consequently, that you
are setting up your own judgment in opposition to that of
the great majority, at least, of your brethren in the
ministry.

" I beseech you to consider whether such an innovation
is consistent with Christian humility in one of the inferior
ministers of the Church ; whether its principle is in harmony with the spirit of charity in which the Church loves
to deal with her children ; whether its tendency can be to
promote unity, peace, and concord, or to excite heart-
burnings, schism, contempt of legitimate ecclesiastical
authority, and, in a word, to diminish your ministerial
influence.

" I would hope, that on maturer reflection, you will see
that you have gone too far, and that you will have the
good sense and generosity, or, more properly speaking,
Christian discretion and humility enough to change your
line of proceeding, and to confine yourself, for the purpose
you have in view, to the legitimate course of argument and
exhortation.   Though I have myself no doubt on this
question, I am happy to know that my view of the case
coincides with that of his Grace the Archbishop of Canterbury.   I have no doubt that you will readily defer to the
judgment of your ecclesiastical superiors on a point of this
kind, especially as it appears that you are officiating for
another person, by whom it is not even clear that you are
authorized to proceed as you have done ; and I shall be
glad to hear that you have admitted the persons whom
you rejected, on the ground of their attendance at the
theatre, to the Holy Communion.

" I am, Reverend Sir,

" Yours very faithfully,

" C. St. David's."

[In reference to a proposed memorial to Bishop Farrer, a former Bishop of St. David's.]

To T. FARRAR, Esq.

ABERGWILI, *September* 11*th*, 1840.

". . . . With regard to the subject of your application I regret that, highly as I respect the motives, both personal and public, by which you appear to be animated, I do not feel myself at liberty to accede to your request. I entertain strong doubts as to the wisdom of erecting new monuments at this day to revive the remembrance of scenes of bigotry and cruelty which were the curse and the disgrace of former generations. We know that the intolerance which gave rise to the persecution in which so many excellent men, the ornaments of our Church, perished, was not peculiar to any religious party, either abroad or in this country. I consider it, in fact, as belonging to the imperfection of our nature; as a tendency which may be restrained by good social institutions, and may be entirely overcome in individuals by an enlightened spirit of Christian charity, but which exists and shows itself in various forms in our own day, quite as much as at any former time. It may, therefore, in my opinion, be very useful to preserve faithful records of the excesses into which men have been carried by this malignant principle, provided it be not done so as to throw the reproach of them upon any particular sect or party. Still, I do not mean that this ought to prevent us from paying a tribute of respect to persons of eminent piety and virtue, because they happened to be sufferers in a religious persecution. But on the other hand, I do not think a crown of martyrdom in itself a sufficient title to public honours. My belief is that many have received that crown, as well as others, who did not deserve it.

"With regard to Bishop Farrer, I must own that my

knowledge of his character is confined to some very slight biographical notices which I have seen of him; but they lead me to question the expediency of bringing him forward into public view as a martyr in whom the Church of England glories. It seems to me sufficient that his sufferings should induce us to throw a veil over his errors and frailties. If, however, his life and character have been misrepresented by the authors who have described them, I should think that the best monument that could be raised to his memory by the piety of his descendants would be a more correct account of him, which might do justice to his merit. But until that be more clearly established, I feel persuaded that such a monument as you propose would neither promote the diffusion of Christian charity nor reflect honour on the Church of England."

To W. J. BAYNE, Esq.

ABERGWILI, *October* 27*th*, 1840.

"For your kind invitation accept my sincere thanks. But as the hypothesis on which it was founded is erroneous, and I have no immediate intention of going to Cambridge for a degree, having already received one through the special favour of his Grace of Canterbury, it must remain uncertain whether I see you next in Cambridge or in London, but with a preponderance of probability in favour of the last-mentioned place of meeting, there being it seems little hope that you will this year be tempted to visit the banks of the Towey which, however, I can assure you are well worth seeing, as I trust you will convince not only yourself, but Mrs. Bayne and my little godson before another summer is over.

"Do you know that if I were to go to Cambridge I should not be able to accept your proffered hospitality, the Master of Trinity having bespoken me as a guest at the Lodge?

"I am at present occupied in all my spare intervals with the arrangement of my books, which, I am happy to say, have all arrived safe, and rejoice at the sight of the accommodation provided for them after the very rough lodging they have been put to for many a year past."

To his Brother, the Rev. T. THIRLWALL.

ST. DAVID's, *January 2nd*, 1841.

" . . . . Few occurrences worth recording took place in my history since I wrote last until I left Abergwili. In the number I may reckon that on Sunday, the 6th of last month, I read the Morning Service, including the Thanksgiving for the Queen, in Welsh and administered the Sacrament in the same tongue to above 100 communicants. Another event of some importance, though one in which I was merely passive, was the discovery that the dry rot had made its way into the house, and an architect whom I sent for from Haverfordwest spent two days in tracking its progress, opening floors, panels, &c. I have preserved some enormous specimens of the fungus. I have reason to believe that the evil has been thoroughly investigated, and that it will be effectually removed, and its return prevented. I think I mentioned the honour which the *Société d'Afrique* had proposed to confer on me. I received an early answer to my letter from Paris, complimenting me, with the assurance that I am there regarded as one of 'les illustrations de la Grande Bretagne,' and accompanied with a diploma, by which I am elevated to the rank of (not a Vice-President, but) a president of the society, in which dignity my name is united with those of a prince, a duke, two grandees of Spain, a marshal of France, and other great personages.   Nearly about the same time I received a Welsh letter from the secretary of the London Cymrygyddion Society, informing me that the society, hearing of my progress in Welsh, proposed to elect me one of its honorary members.   The letter alluded to my speech at Abergavenny, laying rather too much stress on one passage.   I accepted the compliment in a guarded reply, which corrected the mistake. I just have seen in a newspaper that the two letters were read at their annual meeting in London, and that my health was drunk with great applause. . . . .

"On the 24th I received an address of congratulation and apology from the Committee of the St. David's and Dewisland Auxiliary Bible Society, expressing their satisfaction at my arrival and their regret that (being it seems Dissenters, not keeping Christmas Day), they had, according to custom, fixed a meeting on the 25th of December, a custom which, if they had known sooner of my intention to be here on that day, they would have departed from out of respect for me ; but had now made arrangements which they could not alter.

"The Deanery, of which I am enjoying the use, is a tolerably comfortable, roomy house, on the south side of the valley.   The view from the back rooms presents a little garden, the ruined ivy-grown walls of the Close, the continuation of the valley with its little brook, some pastures above, with black cattle, some white cottages, and in the distance rocky cliffs, and the Isle of Ramsey. The sea is not visible, though only a mile off, and at times perfectly audible. . . . .

"On Christmas Day I preached in the afternoon to a crowded choir.   In the morning the Welsh and English services with a Welsh sermon lasted four hours.   The next Sunday one of the Welsh Prebendaries being absent on account of a domestic affliction, I undertook the Welsh

service in the nave.   It happened to be the morning
when an English sermon was expected, and I preached
also.   I was told next day that the people insist on
it that I must be a Welshman by birth, "for I read better
than the clergy."   I believe it possible that my pronunciation may be more correct than that of many who officiate
here. . . . . "

[In reference to a pamphlet on the Athanasian Creed.]

To Rev. F. MARTIN.*

ABERGWILI, *November 8th*, 1841.

"I have received the pamphlet you were good enough
to send me, and only waited to read it before I thanked
you for it.   It has afforded me much pleasure.   Several
nice points appear to be very happily stated.   With regard
to what you call the 'contemptible legend,'† which I think
hardly deserves so harsh a term, and might be considered
as a natural and popular mode of conveying the general
and well-founded belief as to the apostolic character of the
creed ;—but with regard to this legend you seem to be in
several respects under an erroneous impression.   I infer
from your note that you have not an edition of St. Austin
at hand.   You would have seen that the sermon which
contains the legend is not one of the discourses (Libri)
'De Symbolo ad Catechumenos,' but one of the 'Sermons
De Tempore,' viz., cxv. 'De Traditione Symboli.'   Bingham (Book x. c. iii. p. 72), treats it as spurious.   I do not
know whether with sufficient reason.   I should think it
difficult to detect in it any marks of a later age.   In fact
the only ground that I can find in it for doubting whether

---

* Formerly Rector of South Somercotes, and Examining Chaplain to
Bishop Thirlwall.

† *I.e.* that the Apostles each contributed one of the Articles of the Creed.

it might have been St. Austin's, is that the explanation of
the article 'Sedet ad dexteram Dei patris' is a little
different from that which is given in the treatise 'De
Fidei Symbolo,' and in another sermon (c. xix), 'De
Symbolo.'   In these the article is explained to signify a
share in the divine blessedness.   In sermon cxv. 'Sedere
ad dexteram Dei patris dicitur, non ut dicatur major, sed
ut ostendatur *æqualis*.'   But these explanations are, if
not fundamentally identical, at least not inconsistent.
Nevertheless I do not believe that the legend contained in
the sermon was delivered by St. Austin.   But there
appear to me very strong reasons for considering it as an
interpolation.   Not only might it be omitted without
leaving the slightest appearance of a void, but it is positively
at variance with the statement which immediately precedes
it, and which, therefore, might have been expected to
introduce it.   The name *symbolum* is explained as equivalent to the Latin *collatio*.   Then follows 'Collatio ideo
quia collata in unum totius Catholicæ legis fides symboli
colligitur brevitate, cujus textum vobis modo deo annuente
dicemus;' that is, it is a brief compendium of Catholic
doctrine.   And then comes immediately, 'Petrus dixit,'
and so on to 'Matthias complevit vitam æternam, Amen.'
Now, whoever was the author of the sermon, if he meant
to have detailed the legend he would surely have referred
his interpretation of *collatio* to it.   But this is not all.
The author proceeds, apparently quite unconscious of what
he has been telling his hearers, and after a solemn appeal
to them, goes on : 'Ideo, carissimi, hujus mysterii sacra-
mentum, sicut fide concepimus et corde credimus, perfectis
vocibus declaremus. Credo in deum patrem omnipotentem
et reliqua sicut supra.' This '*et sicut supra*' of course I
take to be also an interpolation, consequent upon the first.
When we consider that the sermons were taken down by
the hearers, it seems easy enough to conceive how such an

interpolation might be introduced. But that the preacher should have recited the creed twice seems utterly incredible. But with regard to the legend itself you seem not to be aware that Austin—supposing him the author of the sermon as it is—would not be the earliest authority for the legend. It is related by Rufinus in his 'Expositio in Symbolum Apostolorum,' with the introductory assertion 'Tradunt majores nostri : ' which seems to prove at least that the tradition had become current early in the fourth century. It would spring up naturally when the title *symbolum apostolorum* had come into general use, even without that confusion between σύμβολον and συμβολή which you conjecture, and which Austin and Rufinus ('Symbolum Græce et *indicium* dici potest et *collatio* hoc est quod plures in unum conferunt') attest ; indeed, it seems very doubtful whether the name συμβολή *could* have been applied to the creed with reference to such a legend : it would then rather have been called συμβολαί, according to the analogy of δειπνεῖν ἀπὸ συμβολῶν.

"I do not think the illustration you give from Boswell's Johnson goes far to solve the difficulty [caused by the supposed inequality of reward.] It would only do so on the supposition that the subjects of each rank were unable to conceive a state of happiness superior to their own. Yet the schoolmen do not seem to have gone farther, though they take a somewhat different view. At least Aquinas, after observing 'non est nisi unum summum bonum scilicet Deus cujus fruitione homines sunt beati,' reconciles the equality of reward signified in Matthew xx. 10, with the gradation expressed in John xiv. 2 by the remark, 'Unitas denarii significat unitatem beatitudinis *ex parte objecti*, sed diversitas mansionum significat diversitatem beatitudinis *secundum diversum gradum fruitionis.*' This, as I said, leaves the main difficulty untouched. But it is solved by Dante in a beautiful passage, to which you might

have referred in your note. The question is there raised
('Paradiso' III.) 'Voi, che siete qui felici, desiderate voi
più alto loco?' and the answer states,

> ' Frate, la nostra volontà quieta
> Virtù de *carità*, che fa volerne
> Sol quel ch'avemo, e d'altro non ci asseta.
> Se disiassimo esser più superne
> Foran discordi gli nostri disiri
> Dal voler di colui che qui ne cerne;
> *   *   *   *   *
> *E formale ad esto beato esse*
> *Tenersi dentro alla divina voglia.*
> *   *   *   *   *
> Sì che, come noi sem di soglia in soglia
> Per questo regno, a tutto il regno piace
> Com' allo Rò che'n suo voler ne invoglia
> *In la sua volontade e nostra pace.'*

The poet concludes :—

> ' Chiaro mi fu allor, com' ogni dove
> In ciolo ò Paradiso, e si la grazia
> Del sommo ben d'un modo non vi piove.'

"Your quotation from Bp. Copleston does not seem to
me to show any material difference between the Romanists
and the Reformers on the head of predestination. With
both it has respect to a foreseen quality. The difference
described seems to belong to the head of Justification by
Faith. Another minute remark and I have done. In a
note you seem to have confounded two verbs of totally
distinct origin.* The Anglo-Saxon *helan* is still represented
by the modern German *hehlen*, to conceal. But the verb
hylle in the 'Morte d'Arthur' seems to correspond exactly
to *huellen*, to wrap.

"'Brown-Willis' I have already, and unless I saw
Thorpe's catalogue could not judge whether the MS.
additions are worth the money.

"I received your 'Illustrations' some time ago, and am
sorry to find that I have not before thanked you for it. It

---

* Referring to the derivation of the word *Hell.*

is a book which I shall have great pleasure in recommending to students. . . ."

To Rev. F. Martin.

ABERGWILI, *December 4th*, 1841.

". . . . I cannot help regretting that Lachmann's beautiful and valuable Paper should never yet have been translated into English. May I not add, that there is no English theological journal connected with the Church which does not *studiously* keep its readers in the dark as to everything that is said and done in German theology. For English readers that Paper ought to have a peculiar interest, besides the new light which it throws on Biblical criticism, on account of the view taken in it of Bentley's character as a Biblical critic. We often talk of the Papal Indices Expurgatorii with a mixture of contempt and indignation. They are, indeed, poor things compared with our methods of compassing the same object, while we are able to talk big about light and freedom. . . . ."

[In reference to the Rev. Isaac Williams.]

To Rev. J. Hughes.

ABERGWILI, *December 14th*, 1841.

" I received a letter last night from Mr. Williams, enclosing a correspondence which has lately taken place between you and him on the subject of the sermons to be preached at the approaching consecration of Llangorwen Church, and I take the earliest opportunity of correcting a mistake into which you appear to have been led by the ambiguous expression used by Mr. Williams in his note to you, where he states that it is at my *particular* desire that his brother is to preach at the consecration, and equally an arrangement of mine that you should preach in the afternoon. I observe that in your answer you suppose, very naturally, that I had appointed Mr. Isaac Williams to preach on this occasion. The fact, however, is that the whole arrangement was, in the first instance, proposed by Mr. Williams, and that I simply assented to it. Mr. Williams afterwards consulted me on the expediency of having both the services in Welsh; and when I expressed my readiness to perform the consecration in that language, he inquired whether I would also preach in it. This I declined to undertake, and at the same time mentioned that even if I had thought myself qualified to do so I should have been very unwilling to forego the pleasure of hearing his brother, and that I also considered it very desirable that the other sermon should be preached by you.

"I think it also proper to state that my acquaintance with Oxford is so very slight that I have never known anything of Mr. Isaac Williams but by reputation, and that of the most general kind. It has been very recently, since I was at Aberystwith, that I have learnt that he is a distinguished member of the party to which Dr. Pusey's name has been attached; and it was only last night, through your letter, that I found he was a writer in the Oxford Tracts. In a word, I have never, to this moment, read a line or sentence which I knew to be his. You may, perhaps, be the more surprised at this, as his name has lately acquired great notoriety through the contest for the vacant professorship of poetry. But the fact is I am not a great reader of newspapers, and having been very much by myself for the last six weeks, and a good deal occupied, I have hardly looked into one during that time.

"It is now too late to consider whether any other arrangement as to the services might have been more desirable, as I certainly should have done if I had been sooner aware of the possibility that they might become an occasion of controversy. I hope, however, that no startling or ambiguous peculiarity of doctrine will be brought forward in the morning sermon. But in any case I think you will fully have discharged your duty if, in yours, you confine yourself to the statement of what appears to you important and seasonable truth, without any controversial reference or allusion to the morning sermon, which I should particularly deprecate on such an occasion ; and, indeed, as in all probability very few of your hearers will have been able to understand the English sermon, such a proceeding could hardly answer any useful purpose."

To JOHN THIRLWALL, Esq.

LONDON, *July 8th*, 1842.

" I enclose a sermon which I preached some time ago in London, and which has been published, or at least printed, at the expense as well as at the request of the governors of the hospital. . . . .

" I came up from Wales about ten days ago for sundry purposes which I could accomplish within a short time. One—indeed the main one—was that I might see my mother, who, when I saw her in April, seemed to be rather losing strength. I went down to Ickleford the day after my arrival in London, and had the pleasure of finding her quite as well in every respect as I had left her. . From Ickleford I proceeded to Cambridge, where the Master of Trinity had invited me to become his guest during the installation [of the Duke of Northumberland as Chancellor of the University]. I was not able to stay there long enough to partake of the festivities, but enjoyed much pleasure in the revival of old associations connected with the place. I remained there until Monday morning, attended the Duke of Northumberland's levee, and witnessed the arrival of the Duke of Wellington, to whom I resigned the room I had occupied in the lodge. I then set off for Ickleford, where I remained till the next day, when I returned to London. . . .

"You will probably hear of some of my proceedings in the course of the summer through the Welsh newspapers."

To JOHN THIRLWALL, Esq.

ST. DAVID'S, *November 9th,* 1842.

"I send you with this a sermon which has been published at the request and expense of the society in behalf of which it was preached.* I wish it had been in my power to add a copy of my Charge, which has now been some weeks in the press but seems to proceed very slowly. As I had only one copy of it I did not like to trust it to the chances of the road to London, and also thought that time would be saved in the correction of the press if it were printed in my neighbourhood. I should not have done so if I had been aware of the immense difference between the rate of movement in town and country printing offices. I have this year paid my annual visit to the cathedral earlier than usual, on account of some circumstances which would have rendered it inconvenient to be away from Abergwili at Christmas. I have some thoughts of taking this opportunity to make some excursions into distant parts of Pembrokeshire to inspect the condition of the churches, about which it is not easy to obtain satisfactory information without personal inspection. There are, however, considerable difficulties at this time of year opposed to such visitations, in the shortness of the days, the state of the roads, and the extreme scarcity of places affording any kind of accommodation. Gentlemen's seats

---

* For the Society for the Propagation of the Gospel at Haverfordwest, October 12th, 1842.

are either scattered at great distances from one another, or lie in groups in a few of the more favoured spots. Even in summer, the country, though often very fertile, presents few attractions, being almost wholly bare of wood, and with little variety of features, except in the vicinity of the Precelly Mountain (as it is rather flatteringly termed), which stretches for some distance towards the borders of Cardiganshire. Elsewhere the only natural objects that relieve the general monotony of the landscape are the projections of naked rock, which rise every here and there out of the plain sometimes in rather picturesque forms. Though the cottages of the peasantry look very wretched, I find that the owners are in general by no means badly off. They have the advantage of the peculiar kind of fuel called *culm*, a preparation of coal-dust and earth in balls or bars, which, when once heated, last a very long while, and diffuse a uniform warmth, to which, by the way, it is said the Pembrokeshire hot-houses owe their celebrity. The preparation is very cheap, and is used by some gentlemen in their houses. The poor people live hardly, but contrive to save a little, and very often become owners of a few fields; and as this improvement in their station produces no change in their habits, they are as small farmers in less jeopardy from the vicissitudes of seasons and fluctuation of prices than others who make a better show. But even in the cabins of the labourers you seldom look in without seeing a pig or some fowls, which, though not cleanly, are profitable inmates. . . . ."

To Dr. Whewell, Master of Trinity.

[In reference to the proposed union of the two North Wales bishoprics on the creation of the See of Manchester.]

St. David's, *November 18th*, 1842.

"The subject on which you desire to know my opinion is one on which I have for some time past made up my mind as decidedly as it is possible for me to do with the information I at present possess on it : and I have no reason to think that my view of it would be changed by any facts which have yet come to my knowledge. I need not, therefore, take time to deliberate on my answer to your inquiry, and do not hesitate to say at once that in my judgment the proposed union of the two North Wales Bishoprics is a measure utterly unnecessary, impolitic, unjust, and pernicious. The case seems to me so clear that one is almost ashamed to assign reasons : it is usurping the province of the opposite party, with whom the onus undoubtedly lies. A glance at a map must, one would think, satisfy every one, that if a Bishop is anything more than a purely ornamental part of the hierarchy, each of the dioceses which it is proposed to unite is amply sufficient to afford occupation for one, and, consequently, that either the pastor or the flock, or, more probably, both, must suffer if his duties are doubled. A very slight acquaintance with the state of the Church in Wales seems likewise sufficient to convince any one that no dioceses in the kingdom can so ill afford to lose any part of their ecclesiastical revenues. That there are no peculiar circumstances to weaken the force of these observations when applied to Bangor and St. Asaph, seems sufficiently proved by the unanimous opposition which the Bishops of those Sees have made to the projected union. All this is so plain and trite that it is almost a waste of paper to mention it, and yet, until these objections are met and disposed of, it seems superfluous to touch on any other topics, which the case furnishes in abundance : as the application of the alienated funds ; the unpopularity of the measure ; its permanent effect on the feelings of a very sensitive people, who already are extremely dissatisfied with the treatment they have suffered in Church matters. The more obvious question is, what argument, what plea, what ground, either of justice or policy, is alleged on the other side to counter-balance any one, and that the slightest, of these which are apparently decisive against the measure. I can only say that I have never yet heard more than one, which is compounded of the supposed necessity for giving the new Bishop a seat in the House of Lords, and the supposed impossibility of increasing the number of the episcopal seats. If there is any other reason assigned or assignable, I am open to conviction, and willing to weigh it when presented to me. But my judgment on this single one which I am acquainted with is, that it merely aggravates the wrong, the mischief, and the folly, which it is put forward to shield, by its transparent and therefore irritating futility. For it seems to me equivalent to a declaration that in the opinion of those who allege it, the interests of the Church, and the feelings of the people, in North Wales, are of so little importance that they may properly be sacrificed, not to the welfare of an English diocese, not to any object of political expediency, however paltry, but to a point of politico-ecclesiastical etiquette, or to a notion of symmetry, or to some episcopal arcanum of danger to be apprehended from the example of an English Bishop who should not be a Lord of Parliament. Even with regard to this point, I think the plea, miserable as it is, raises an argument of at least equal weight on the other side. For I think the Welsh might contend with quite as much reason that, if there is any advantage to be derived from the representation of the Church in Parliament, they have not now more than their fair share of episcopal representatives. The expedient for meeting the difficulty appears to me really preposterous: a sacrifice of the greater to the infinitely less—something as if, supposing the number of Bishop's wigs to be limited, it had been thought better to reduce the number of heads than to let one of them appear in its own hair. But I am growing unepiscopal, and giving you more than you wanted, which was I believe rather my opinion than my arguments.

"To slide into other subjects—my ill-fated Charge, about which I have heard many inquiries, has fallen into the hands of a Welsh printer, whom I employed partly from a desire to encourage native art, and partly to secure my single MS. from the chances of a journey to London. He received it very nearly five weeks ago, with assurances that he would proceed with it at the most rapid rate, and this morning I received the fifth half-sheet, being, I believe, less than half : so that, even if he continues to move with the same super-Celtic velocity, it will hardly see the light before Christmas—some time after it has been forgotten that I ever delivered one.

" The beauty of the summer made me the more regret that I did not see you at Abergwili ; but I hope it is the beginning of a fair cycle, and that you will pay me a visit in the course of the next. I wish you, or Thorp,* were here now. We are on the point of converting the south transept of the Cathedral—which is now a heap of rubbish—into a parish church, which is sadly needed. We want to combine utility and beauty as much as possible ; but I am afraid shall commit a great many blunders, as it seems as if there were few people here who understand more about the matter than myself.

" I had a letter yesterday from Milnes, dated *Athens*, *Oct.* 19. He had been making a pilgrimage to Delphi—on his way, I believe, to Jerusalem and Mecca—for he concludes with the words, 'I hope to be at Constantinople next week, at Jerusalem in December, and at Cairo in

* Formerly tutor of Trinity, and afterwards Archdeacon of Bristol.

January.' I hope he will return safe to receive the honours of a Hadji, with a load of cockleshells, relics, and sonnets."

To Dr. Schmitz.

AbergwILI, *December* 17*th*, 1842.

"I have received a copy of your translation of 'Niebuhr' as well as the volume which you committed to my nephew. I congratulate you on the completion of your laborious undertaking, and hope you will be abundantly rewarded by its success.

"I am sorry to have been obliged to inform Mr. Lewis that I can promise nothing at present for your Journal, as it is absolutely necessary that I should devote whatever leisure I can find to the completion of my 'History,' which is urgently called for by the publishers. . . . ."

To Dr. Schmitz.

Ickleford, Hitchin, *February* 20*th*, 1843.

"I return the proof-sheet. I received it at the time when I was called away from London by a domestic affliction,* and have perhaps been prevented by the same cause from giving it all the attention which I might otherwise have paid to it. But I wish you to observe that, as I had not the original to compare with the translation, the alterations I have made must only be considered as suggestions for your consideration, indicating that I found something which struck me as obscure or harsh, and which I thought might perhaps be advantageously corrected in the way I have proposed. In some passages which I have marked

* The death of his mother, on February 13th, 1843, in her eighty-eighth year.

with a note of interrogation in the margin, I could not
go so far, not being able to guess what the precise meaning is. I am only sure that something is wanting to make
it intelligible to common readers. On the whole, your
translation appears to me surprisingly good. I had not
seen or heard of Poppo's remarks on my 'History.' I did
not even know that he had completed his edition of
Thucydides, of which I have only so much as included
the first book of his Commentary.

[The following are extracts from the journal of an episcopal tour made in 1843. Reference is made to the Rebecca
Riots, which came to a head in that year, and still, at times,
break out in minor forms. Outrages were committed by
bodies of men in disguise, known as Rebecca's men, the
leader usually being in female attire. The toll-gates were
the main object of their attacks, and their name was taken
from a curious application of Genesis xxiv. 60 :—]

To JOHN THIRLWALL, Esq.

ABERGWILI, *September 1st*, 1843.

" . . . . As you used to be amused by my accounts of
my travels, perhaps you may derive some entertainment
from a narrative of a little excursion—partly of business
and partly of recreation—from which I returned a few days
ago. The main object of my journey was to minister confirmation in the parish of Kerry, in Montgomeryshire, the
remotest of all from my residence, and which, from peculiar
causes which need not be explained, I had been compelled
to omit on my confirmation circuit. I set out with my
friend Mr. Melville on Tuesday, the 15th ult., a little after
noon. . . . . .
" All the great features of the country, the direc-

tion of the hills, and the course of the rivers, to a considerable extent, were exhibited to us as we crossed the common of Llandrindod Wells, a place of great resort on account of its mineral springs and pure air. The living is worth a little less than £50 per annum, on which, with the addition of a curacy worth perhaps £30 more, the incumbent has contrived to bring up a numerous family. He is past eighty, indeed, I believe, very near ninety but regularly performs his duty, walking on Sundays ten or twelve miles to one of his churches. The living of which he had been curate is in my patronage, and became vacant a few months ago, when I gave it to him ; perhaps unnecessarily, as I have been told that he had saved a good deal of money out of his previous income. It was, however, the great object of his ambition ; and lo! scarcely has he attained it, when, for the first time, he is taken seriously ill, and not expected to recover! With him, whenever he goes, will disappear one of the few remaining specimens of the old school of Welsh clergymen. . . . . .

"We drove to Kerry, where I was entertained at the parsonage, which is a very good house, having been enlarged and put into good repair by Dr. Ollivant just before he was appointed to the Divinity Professorship at Cambridge. Its situation, commanding a rich valley, bounded by high hills, is uncommonly beautiful, and I should have been very loth to exchange it, as he has done, for a parish in Huntingdonshire. His place is filled for the present by two curates, one of whom was my host, both very zealous and active men, yet hardly equal to the labour arising from the great extent of the parish. The next day I confirmed at the church, an old and not very sightly building, even if it had not been disfigured as it is by some hideous galleries. As I returned through the churchyard I was greeted very respectfully by a person whose dress seemed to indicate that he was a functionary of the Church. I learnt that he was the sexton, but that he also discharges another very useful office, which, as far as I know, is peculiar to Kerry. It appears that it is by ancient custom a part of his duty to perambulate the church during service time, with a bell in his hand, to look carefully into every pew, and whenever he finds any one dozing to ring the bell. He discharges this duty, it is said, with great vigilance, intrepidity, and impartiality, and consequently with the happiest effect on the congregation, for, as everybody is certain that if he or she gives way to drowsiness the fact will be forthwith made known through the whole church by a peal which will direct all eyes to the sleeper, the fear of such a visitation is almost always sufficient to keep every one on the alert. . . . ."

To John Thirlwall, Esq.

Abergwili, *September* 16*th*, 1843.

" . . . . Soon after this we descended to a little hamlet, called Pont-Rhyd-fendigaid, which, being interpreted, is, Bridge of the blessed Ford. Here I halted, having both business to transact and curiosity to satisfy. I wanted to inspect the grammar school of Ystrad Meurig, of which, as bishop of the diocese, I am visitor, which lies about three miles from Pont-Rhyd-fendigaid. . . . .

" I set out, accompanied by a lad whom we engaged to guide us. . . . .

" To beguile the time I amused myself with a pretty long conversation with our guide, from whom, as I found he had been educated at Ystrad Meurig Free School, I hoped to get some useful information. He had left school, he told me, upwards of a year, and since worked on his father's farm ; but retained a little smattering of Latin and Greek. Unluckily his knowledge of

English was also very imperfect, and it was sometimes necessary to resort to his mother-tongue in order to make sure of his meaning. On our way we met the master of the school, the Rev. Mr. Morris, who, having heard of my arrival at Pont-Rhyd-fendigaid, had come over from Ystrad Meurig with a couple of horses, one of which he offered for my use. But I was so wet that I preferred continuing on my legs. Mr. Morris then guided us to the remains of the Abbey, which are confined to the arch of the west entrance and a part of the contiguous wall. The arch is circular, with some remarkable ornaments, and of good masonry. I then walked to Ystrad Meurig. . . . .

" I inspected the school buildings, which had been represented to me as neglected. The scholars I could not see, as it was vacation time. The schoolroom stands in the churchyard, and is a much larger and better-looking edifice than the church, being built of very good stone. At one end is a smaller room, containing a library in excellent oak book-cases. I did not find, in the aspect either of the books or the building, much ground for complaint ; but all that I saw and heard rendered it clear that the school, though well endowed, can never again become what it was previous to the establishment of the College at Lampeter, when a great number of the Welsh clergy received their whole education at Ystrad Meurig. After having rested a few minutes at Mr. Morris's house, we returned to Pont-Rhyd-fendigaid. I gained one piece of experience by this excursion. It turned out, on inquiry from Mr. Morris, that either through ignorance, stupidity, or wantonness, our Welsh guide had deceived me in every particular that he had stated with regard to the school. . . . .

" The well-known road to Abergwili presented only one object to attract any particular attention, and that a very melancholy one : a turnpike and toll-house close to Abergwili, recently demolished by Rebecca. One or two articles of furniture were still remaining in a corner of the ruins. Such is the spirit of the times, that after the destruction of the house, the collector, who also carried on the business of a bookbinder at Carmarthen, could not prevail on any of his neighbours to help him to remove his furniture. At last a stranger consented to let him have the use of his cart for that purpose. But when they arrived at Carmarthen a mob assembled round the cart, cut the traces, threw the furniture into the street, and were with difficulty withheld from maltreating the owner of the cart. Not content with this, they broke open the collector's house, and scattered the books which they found there about the street. No advice of the disturbance reached either the police or the military until the mischief was done and the mob had dispersed. This was bad; but since that the appearance of things has been growing worse and worse. You may judge of it by one specimen. A few days ago Rebecca's emissaries set fire to the cottage of a poor old woman who received the toll at a gate. None of her neighbours would help her to put out the fire, though she assured them 'it was not much.' But hearing her say this, the incendiaries returned to complete their work. It seems that she then gave them to understand that she knew them, upon which they instantly lodged the contents of several guns in her head, and she expired almost immediately. A coroner's inquest sat on her body, which presented a shocking spectacle, the head being dreadfully shattered. The verdict they returned was to the effect that she died a natural death, through a suffusion of blood in the chest. It was previously believed that no Welsh jury would venture to give a verdict unfavourable to Rebecca, and now the fact is placed beyond a doubt. There is on the one side perfect impunity from the law, on the other no protection from outrage. In fact, nobody who has anything to lose considers either his property or his life as secure. A gentleman of large property, and till lately (as well on account of his Liberal politics as of the great number of people he employs, whose welfare and comfort have been the objects of his unremitting attention) possessing, perhaps, greater influence than any other in the county, has found it necessary to send away his wife and family, remaining himself for the protection of his property, which has been repeatedly attacked by incendiary fires. Another less gallantly leaves his mansion, which stands in a retired situation about five or six miles from Carmarthen, to sleep every night in the town, fearing personal violence in consequence of the threats which he has received. There has been much speculation about the causes of this deplorable state of things, and a general disposition to refer it to certain alleged abuses. But I believe I may venture to say, on the concurrent authority of all the persons I have met with who possess the best means of information, that the real cause is very different. Abuses there certainly have been in the management of the turnpike trusts, and perhaps in other matters, as the administration of the new Poor Law. But it is clear that they have been nothing more than the occasion or often the pretext of the outbreak, and in a different state of things would hardly have excited anything but a slight feeling of discontent, which would probably in the end have found some lawful and peaceable way of venting itself. The real cause of the present evil is to be sought in the weather of the years 1839—1840, in the first of which the crops in this part of Wales were utterly destroyed, and in the second very nearly so, by the rain and floods. The farmers, originally poor, have never recovered from this blow; their distress has rendered them almost reckless and desperate. Believing themselves aggrieved in some points, they resort to illegal combinations at first with a specific object, but now,

it would seem, with a general indefinite view of mending
their condition by means of a system of intimidation,
which up to this moment they have pursued, notwithstanding the presence of a large military force, with com
plete success. . . . . ."

[In reference to the term commented on in the next
letter, it may be noticed that Carlyle, writing in the *Edinburgh Review* in 1827 (No. XCI.), on Richter's "Life," and
alluding to his "Introduction to Æsthetics," added a foot-
note explaining the doubtful phrase. "Æsthetics," the
note says, "was a word invented by Baumgarten (some
eighty years ago) to express generally the *Science of the
Fine Arts*, and now in universal use among the Germans.
Perhaps we also might as well adopt it, at least if any
such *science* should ever arise among us." He lived to see
the science arise and the word adopted.]

To Rev. T. Belcombe.

Tenby, *April* 18*th*, 1844.

" . . . . The term *æsthetic* in the sense in which it is
used in the *Quarterly Review* was imported from Germany. The Germans—like ourselves—were in want of a
general term to express what relates to the sense of beauty.
We took the name of one of the senses—taste—and gave
it an enlarged signification comprehending the perception
of beauty, by whatever means introduced into the mind.
One inconvenience of this term is that we have only the
substantive *taste*, but no adjective expressing that which
relates to it, for *tasteful* has, of course, quite a different
meaning. The Germans, on the other hand, took an
adjective from the Greek, properly signifying what relates
to perception in general, but they limited it in use to that

perception of the beautiful which is grounded upon, or at least capable of, scientific investigation. From this adjective (æsthetic) they form the noun *æsthetik*, the science of the æsthetical, answering pretty nearly to what we mean by a theory of taste or of the beautiful. I think it has been proposed to substitute the term *calesthetic*, which would certainly describe the thing more distinctly. Hence you will see that the writer in the *Quarterly* meant to say, in the passage which you quote, that Hume was almost the first of our historians whose work did not merely convey historical information, but might gratify the æsthetical faculty—'the sense of the beautiful'—as a work of art. But I think he has expressed himself awkwardly and improperly when he talks of an æsthetic sense of the term historical literature. He might have said, in an æsthetical point of view."

To JOHN THIRLWALL, Esq.

ST. DAVID'S, *October 2nd*, 1844.

" With this I send a sermon of mine,[*] which has just been published, with some other matters of little interest except to Church people in this diocese, but which may on that account have somewhat more for you. I arrived here but a few days ago, and intend to stay the best part of this month—thus gaining the advantage of longer days and fairer weather than can be expected at the seasons which I have on former occasions chosen for my temporary residence. I was here about a month ago for a few hours to open a part of the cathedral which has been fitted up for the parochial service with a Welsh sermon ; and since then I have been making another little tour in North Wales, partly over ground which I travelled over last year,

[*] Preached for the S.P.C.K. on their anniversary.

but taking a somewhat wider compass. I proceeded from Haverfordwest—where, in conjunction with Bishop Coleridge, I assisted with a sermon at the reopening of the principal church—to Cardigan, where I was able to relieve the vicar by preaching for him, twice in English and once in Welsh, and administering the sacrament in each language. . . . .

" I arrived at Aberystwyth, where I found the Bishops of London and Winchester at the same hotel. The former had come from Chester through Bangor, and was going to return to Chester by another road. On Sunday I preached in Welsh and English. Monday was chiefly occupied with receiving visits, and in the evening I dined with the Bishop of Winchester and Mrs. Sumner at Nanteos, the seat of Colonel Powell, the Lord-Lieutenant. The next night I slept at Lampeter, in the house of Mr. Browne,* one of the tutors of the college, and on Wednesday I arrived at Abergwili. The following Saturday I again started for Nevern, in Cardiganshire, where I had engaged to preach the next Sunday. . . . . .

" On Monday the people at Nevern were so much pleased with my two Welsh sermons that a strong wish was expressed to see one of them in print. . . . . .

" Before I leave Pembrokeshire for Abergwili I meditate an excursion into that corner of the country which forms the south side of St. Bride's Bay. I shall then in the course of this year have traversed the diocese at almost every considerable part."

To Dr. Schmitz.

Abergwili, *December 24th,* 1845.

" I most heartily wish you joy on your success. The announcement in your letter was a most agreeable surprise

---

* The present Bishop of Winchester.

to me, as I had not even heard of the vacancy. It certainly is a rather remarkable circumstance that in the modern Athens one great school should have been committed to the government of a Welshman,* and the other to that of a German. But I think on the whole this *Xenodokia* does credit to the people of Edinburgh, and I have no doubt that it will redound to their advantage even more in the last instance than in the former. You will probably soon become acquainted with your rival of the Academy. . . . . I have always hoped to be able to pay another visit to Edinburgh, and it will certainly be an additional inducement to do so that I shall now find you there in so honourable and important a station. That you may long fill it with ever-increasing satisfaction to yourself and to the public is my sincere wish."

[The following letter refers to the publication of the improved edition of his "History," and also to the appearance of Grote's "History of Greece." In connection with the latter, the generous language used here is in accordance with all Thirlwall's utterances on the same subject. In the "Life of Grote" (p. 173) a beautiful letter is published from the Bishop, congratulating Grote on his work and acknowledging its superiority. Grote answered in a corresponding spirit, and explained his reasons for taking up the work. Thirlwall expressed himself even more warmly and generously on another occasion in a speech at Charterhouse.]

* The late Ven. T. Williams, M.A., Archdeacon of Cardigan, and Principal of the Academy at Edinburgh.

To Dr. Schmitz.

Christie's Hotel, April 9th, 1846.

"Since your migration to Edinburgh the second volume of my 'History' has appeared, and you ought to have received a copy some time ago, but I scrupled about sending one by an ordinary conveyance to so great a distance. Having just come to London, I should be glad to know whether you can point out any less expensive means of forwarding parcels to you. I shall hope at the same time to hear how you like your new situation and prospects, and in what condition you have found the High School. The Rector of the Academy complains that the religious discords with which he is surrounded render his position so disagreeable that he is anxious to retire from it. I hope you have not experienced any annoyance from the like cause.

"You have, no doubt, been enjoying, as I have, Grote's 'History.' High as my expectations were of it, it has very much surpassed them all, and affords an earnest of something which has never been done for the subject either in our own or any other literature. It has afforded me some gratification to find that in the flood of new light which he has poured upon it his views do not appear greatly to diverge from mine on more than a few important points, and those of a special nature not involving any general principles. For though I am not yet satisfied with the limits he prescribes in his first volume to the investigations which occupy a part of mine, I think it would be found on a further analysis that the difference between us is not very material."

[In reference to Hegel's Philosophy.]

To Dr. Whewell, Master of Trinity.

Aberowili, Carmarthen, October 31st, 1849.

"Pray accept my best thanks for your Memoir on

'Hegel's Criticism of Newton's Principia,' which I found here a day or two ago on my return after a short absence. I have read it with some pleasure, but without the smallest surprise, as it only tends to confirm an opinion which I have long entertained. My own examination of certain portions of Hegel's works, which I had occasion to study attentively, has impressed me with the deepest conviction that he is, to say the least, one of the most impudent of all literary quacks, and I feel sure that there is no part of his so-called philosophy which, if carefully examined by a competent and impartial judge, would not lead him to a like conclusion. It may be said that one is not entitled to speak of Hegel in this way without having made one's self master —if that be possible—of all his writings. But I do not believe that any genuine philosopher ever wrote a volume, or even a page, of what a well-informed contemporary could consider as arrant nonsense. Whether Hegel's volumes, after the subtraction of their common-place, contain anything else, is more than I am, or probably ever shall be, able to say. I have so much faith in the force of truth as to believe that sooner or later Hegel's name will only be redeemed from universal contempt by the recollection of the immense mischief he has done. It is certainly a very remarkable phenomenon, and one which will well deserve to occupy a large place in a future history of European philosophy and literature in the nineteenth century, that such a man should have exercised so great an influence over the mind of Germany, and should have been an object of at least professed veneration to so many of its most eminent men in various departments of literature. But I should be curious to know whether this high opinion of his merits is shared by a single German, whom you would recognise as a competent judge of a scientific subject, such as those stated in your Memoir. This of course, as involving a negative, it might be difficult to ascertain. But you probably know what your scientific German acquaintance think, and how they feel on this subject, and whether any of them is a professor of Hegel-worship. If you have any doubt on the point, it would certainly be worth while to circulate your Memoir for the sake of drawing out their opinions. On the metaphysicians and literators I do not suppose that it would produce the slightest impression. They will no doubt continue to believe that each of the passages you quote contains a treasure of wisdom, only lying too deep to be explored by a Stock-Engländer."

[On the same subject.]

To DR. WHEWELL, Master of Trinity.

ABERGWILI, CARMARTHEN, *November 9th*, 1849.

" Many thanks for your most welcome present of your work on Induction and the Second Memoir, both of which I have read with great interest. The former brought back to my mind several passages by which I had been much perplexed and dissatisfied in the midst of the pleasure and admiration with which I had gone through Mill's book some three years ago. It is not for me to pronounce between two such thinkers, at least till I have seen a rejoinder to the reply ; but I certainly have a very strong impression that your main position cannot be shaken.

" The additional Note to the two Memoirs marks, I think very justly, Hegel's place in the history of German philosophy, and shows that he has no claim to the merit either of original speculation or of a healthy development and judicious modification of previous systems. The master thought of his philosophy belongs to Schelling ; all that is his own is the rashness and violence with which he has carried it out into detail, by a perpetual perversion of facts and juggle of words. When we are inquiring how it has happened that he has nevertheless established such a powerful sway over German literature, it must not be forgotten that his ascendency has been and is, to a considerable extent, maintained by a kind of influence quite independent of the innate attractiveness of his philosophy. There can, I think, be no question that he owes it in a great measure to the authority of the Berlin *Jahrbücher*, the principal organ of his school. A profession, if not of Hegelianism, at least of reverence for the name of Hegel, seems to form the common bond which unites the contributors together. Many, probably, add the weight of their reputation to it who have little faith in his doctrines. And it is a serious matter for a writer whose prospects, perhaps, mainly depend on the success of his book, to brave the risk of being either ignored or crushed by the leading Review. This, however, only goes some way towards accounting for the continuance of the prestige which surrounds the name of Hegel. It certainly does not explain that state of the German mind which enables a portion of the reading public to enjoy works professedly treating on scientific subjects, in which the authors have given the reins to their fancy in such conjectures and analogies as those of which I find specimens adduced in Cotta's ' Letters on Humboldt's Kosmos '—particularly from Carus. It is really, after all, an inestimable blessing to live in an intellectual atmosphere, in which such monstrosities either could never come to light or must instantly die, even though it may not be quite so genial as that in which they flourish. I hope that the changes which are now going on in our academical system will yield more and more of the good without any admixture of the evil. But when we consider what we have escaped we can hardly regard our national *vis inertiæ* as a subject of unmixed regret. . . . ."

To Dr. L. Schmitz.

ABERGWILI, CARMARTHEN, *November 6th*, 1850.

" . . . . I shall look forward with interest to your 'Abridgment,' * though I cannot but deeply regret that its appearance should have preceded the completion of the second edition of my 'History,' and particularly of the volume on which I am now engaged. But my life is a constant struggle against time."

To Dr. Schmitz.

ABERGWILI, CARMARTHEN, *December 4th*, 1850.

" I have been so much occupied since I received your last letter, particularly with the new Appendix to the 'History of Modern Rome,' that I have been obliged to defer answering it. And I have been all the while in a puzzle, trying in vain to recollect whether I had previously received a letter from you in the course of the last two years. But not only can I find no trace of any such letters in my memory, but, what is more material, I have not been able to discover either your little 'History of Rome' or the second edition of Niebuhr's Lectures among my books, nor do I recollect having ever seen either of them. As I have the first edition of the latter work it might have been possible that I should have put the second into some secluded nook of my library, where it still eludes my search. But as to the 'History of Rome,' I think it is quite impossible that I should not at least have looked into it enough to remember having seen it. It seems clear, therefore, that somehow or other both letters and books must have miscarried. But I can assure you that, though I was unconscious of having received your intended presents, nothing

* Dr. Schmitz published a small History of Greece, "mainly based upon that of Connop Thirlwall."

that I may have written in my last letter was meant to convey an intimation that I felt myself to have been neglected by you, as I have never had any such impression on my mind. It would only have concerned me very much if, having received such presents, I had omitted to acknowledge the receipt. And the fact that you have received no such acknowledgment very strongly confirms my belief that I never knew it to have been due. I am very glad the circumstances have led to this explanation, in which I am the party most interested. . . . ."

[In reference to the proposed revision of the Bible.]

To GEORGE BROOM, Esq., Llanelly.

December 28th, 1850.

" I have attentively considered the important subject of your letter. But I find, on mature reflection, that I cannot altogether assent to the view of the subject on which your proposal for a new version of the Scriptures appears to rest. I am quite aware that the present authorised version is susceptible of great improvement ; and I should be glad to see a new version which should embody all the surest corrections which have been hitherto proposed, as well as any others which competent judges might deem requisite. Whether it would be proper immediately to substitute such a version for the one now in use would be quite another question. But I more than doubt whether a new version, constructed on the principle of modernising or popularising the style, would be desirable for any purpose. I cannot conceive that such an alteration would make the Scriptures more generally intelligible. The obscurity of the received version arises, I apprehend, either from that of the original text, or from

mistranslation.   The latter cause may be removed, so far
as it has been ascertained, by simple correction.   But I do
not believe that any obscurity arises from the slight tinge
of antiquity which pervades the whole ; and I should fear
that to efface this, by clothing the same thoughts in modern
and popular language, would be likely to deprive the
Bible of a great part of its charm and influence with ordinary readers.   Whatever farther elucidation of its contents
they may require would, I apprehend, be better sought
from paraphrases, commentaries, sermons, and other helps;
and, indeed, I do not think it possible that any mere
version, whatever may be its style, should ever supply the
place of such assistance.   I think the Dissenters have
acted in a spirit of Christian wisdom, as well as charity,
in abstaining from the introduction of any new version for
public use, as I am persuaded that they could have done
nothing which the Church of Rome would have witnessed
with greater pleasure or turned to better account for its
own ends."

[The following letter refers to a point in the memorable
attack of Sir B. Hall on the Bishop in the House of Commons.   The occasion was a debate on July 1st, 1851, on
a motion for Church Extension.   The Bishop was warmly
defended by his friend and pupil Mr. Monckton Milnes
(Lord Houghton), and by Mr. Morris, M.P. for Carmarthen.
The latter spoke of " the manner in which his lordship
performed the duties of his high office, his unbounded
charities, his attention to everything that could contribute
to the advantage of his diocese," as forming a " striking
contrast to his predecessors."   The Bishop himself answered
the attack and exposed its inaccuracies in his Charge

in 1851. *See* the " Remains," vol. i. pp. 141—151, and
194—196.]

To Rev. J. Evans.

ABERGWILI, *August 4th*, 1851.

" I am much obliged to you for the information contained
in your letter, and particularly for the part relating to the
Archdeacons. I do not know whether you will be surprised to hear that the sole foundation for the assertion
that my ' Archdeacons had been prevented or forbidden to
act,' was a letter written by me to the Archdeacon of Cardigan in 1843, when he was Principal of the Academy at
Edinburgh, in which, while I expressed the great ' pleasure that it would give me to see him entering on the
discharge of his archidiaconal functions,' I stated—as I
had then recently heard from Mr. Burder—that there was
reason to doubt whether, although he had the power, he
would be at liberty legally to exercise it until the mode of
holding his court should have been regulated by provisions
which had not then been yet enacted, and ' whether he
had any of the machinery indispensable for the purpose.'
This is the only communication I ever made to the Archdeacon of Cardigan on the subject either by word or
writing ; and at the time that Sir B. Hall made his statement in the House he had in his possession a letter from
the Archdeacon in which this fact was stated. What may
have previously passed between them in conversation I
cannot say, as while the Archdeacon declares—in a private
letter to me—that he spoke only of himself, Sir B. Hall
not only said but has now printed that the assertion
related to all the Archdeacons. That in either case the
House of Commons was grossly imposed upon is very clear,
and will, I hope, in time be more generally known.

" I do not know whether I am to infer from your letter
that your church has been reopened for Divine service."

To HIS NEPHEW, JOHN THIRLWALL, Esq.
WARREN'S HOTEL, REGENT STREET, *November 4th*, 1852.

" All's right. I crossed the Bridge in safety, and of course arrived here without any disaster. My journey was not marked by any very memorable passages. At Swansea another traveller entered the carriage, but was called back by a friend at the door, where the following dialogue took place :—

' *Q.* Do you know who you have got with you in the carriage ?

' *A.* A low negative growl.

' *Q.* The Bishop of St. David's ! ! ! ! ! !'

The announcement was made in a voice which would have been perfectly audible from one end of our long drawing-room to the other. My companion evidently appreciated the revelation, though rather with the air of a man who thought it need not have been quite so loud. But he had hardly time enough to satiate himself with the contemplation of my features, as he was obliged to get out at Neath. Then at last the time came for the inevitable friend. He appeared in the person of Inspector Jellinger Symons, with whom I had a discussion on the character and origin of the word *off* in the phrase ' I am badly *off.*' He had been puzzling the workhouse school children with the question, but candidly admitted that he could not answer it himself. This lasted us to Cardiff, where he got out, and I had then my book to myself until dark.

" Only one thing beside occurred worth mentioning, as it illustrates Dickens's power of attraction. At Didcot we stopped a few minutes, and received offers of literary supplies. A neighbour called for a ' Bleak House,' which was produced, but at first refused because uncut, the bidder having no paper knife. The vendor, however, ran to a

stall and returned with the number in a state for immediate consumption. The purchaser immediately set to,
but I suppose in a critical chapter found the envious light
failing him. I, who sat close to the windows, had long
given up my book, though of much larger print. He continued to catch at every gleam of light that permitted
him to read another line. I would have offered him my
place, but thought that the sooner he closed the book the
better it would be for his poor eyes. While I was waiting
with painful curiosity to see when he would acknowledge
that his visual powers were unequal to their task, he suddenly raised his eyes to the faint glimmer of the lamps on
the opposite side, and instantly sprang up on the seat
which was unoccupied, and holding his book close to
the glass, remained perched there until we reached Pad-
dington. The most remarkable thing was that when we
stopped he observed to me that we had come uncommonly fast—'had never gone a better pace.' I civilly
assented, though I had not been struck with any sensation
indicating the fact. He was totally unconscious that it
was the 'Bleak House' that had made the time pass so
quick ! . . . .

"Foreign News.—I heard from J. Symons that Thackeray, whom I fully expected to see in town, has set sail for
America, leaving his novel * behind him, which I shall
probably take back with me. . . . .

"Do not mope while I am away. If you feel your-
selves growing melancholy there is an excellent work
which you will find in my library, and may read of an
evening—it was translated by King Alfred for the purpose
—it is called ' Boethius on the Consolation of Philosophy.'
Give my love to the partner of your solitude, and tell her
to keep up her spirits.

"I am going to hear the Queen's Speech. She has one

* " Esmond " was published in 1852.

of her fine days, and I must start early to be in advance of the crowd, and shall have to kill an hour or so in the library of the House of Lords."

[The next letter is one addressed to Lord Arthur Hervey in reference to his work on "The Genealogies of our Lord, &c."]

ABERGWILI, CARMARTHEN, *January 4th*, 1854.

"It is high time that I should thank you for the pleasure and benefit which I have derived from the perusal of your work on the Genealogies. I think there can be but one opinion as to its usefulness and the excellent spirit of judicious and candid criticism which runs through it, though there will no doubt be a good deal of variance as to some of the principles which you have laid down, and still more as to the application of them to particular controverted points. For my own part I can say that I met with nothing material to disturb my acquiescence in your general conclusions before the chapter on the chronology of the Book of Judges, to me the most interesting in the work. If everything there was not equally satisfactory to my mind, this may have been a perhaps inevitable consequence of the peculiar difficulties which beset that part of your subject, so as to render a completely convincing solution apparently hopeless. I assent to your general principle that the genealogies are a surer guide than the corresponding Numbers, and I have no doubt that the period indicated by those which we find in the present text for the time of the Judges is much too long. I would say farther that the numbers which seem most open to suspicion are the large round numbers, 40, 40, 40, and 2 × 40, which are suspicious as well on account of their roundness and their identity as on account of the character of the number itself, more frequently adopted than any other where the exactly real one was unknown. That several of the events which are recorded in the Book of Judges as having happened successively were really contemporaneous is certainly a tempting hypothesis; but I think it is clear that the author of the book was quite unconscious of such a synchronism; and as he appears from i. 21 to have compiled it early in the reign of David, your own hypothesis as to the comparative shortness of the interval by which he was removed from the time of the transactions related considerably increases the difficulty of the synchronistic view. In a short notice of your work which I find in the 'Journal of Sacred Literature' for this month, which I have received this morning, the critic dissents from your opinion that 'there are cases where conjectural emendation carries as full conviction of its truth as the authority of the most accurate MS. can do,' and thinks that 'in the absence of authorities derived from ancient versions and MSS., or certain deductions from the grammatical structure of the text itself, conjectural emendations are unwarrantable and inadmissible.' I so far agree with this view that I would never admit a conjectural emendation without some such external support into the text of Scripture. But, on the other hand, I would not deny that cases such as you describe are to be found. Only I would observe that the remark, however true in the abstract, can hardly apply to a number forming part of an intricate and questionable chronological system. And I cannot agree with you that there is any sufficient reason for suspecting corruption in the text of 1 Kings vi. 1. I do not think it at all evident that the variation in the Septuagint gives evidence of various readings, but that it may very well have been grounded, like the statement of St. Paul in the Acts, on a different calculation. And it appears to me that these three statements mutually confirm one another as to the integrity of the text, though they may not establish the certainty of the number, even so far as they agree. Still less can I admit the change which you propose in Judges xi. 26, as an example of a certain conjectural emendation. On the contrary, I feel no doubt of the correctness of the present reading. I would speak with great diffidence as to the grammatical argument grounded on the absence of the demonstrative זֶה. But I cannot help thinking that you have considerably overstated its force. I cannot say whether another instance of its omission is to be found where it might have been properly inserted. But I observe that Gesenius in his Thesaurus s. v. only says, '*Sæpe* numeralibus præmittitur, max. tempus indicantibus.' And in his small lexicon, '*Aeusserst haüfig* vor Zahlen und Zeitangaben um ihnen Nachdruck zu geben.' I conceive that, however unusual the omission may be, it could never amount to a grammatical solecism, and therefore cannot of itself warrant your emendation. Putting this, then, out of the question, I conceive that the context requires the reading 'years' and not 'cities.' It is clear that the number of cities included in the conquered territory was quite superfluous to the argument, while that of the years during which it had been occupied was most material. No doubt this does not appear when verses 25, 26 are read together as you cite them; but, on the contrary, the mention of the three hundred years is absurd when it is supposed that in both those verses 'the appeal is simply and only to the precedent of Balak.' I apprehend that this is the case only with regard to verse 25, and that verse 26 contains a fresh and different argument —an *argumentum ad hominem.* First, the King of the Ammonites cannot pretend to be a better man than Balak, who forbore from all attempting to dislodge the Israelites from the land conquered from him by the Amorites. But again, though the Israelites had occupied it for three hundred years, the children of Ammon had not heretofore tried to wrest it from them, and so had tacitly let in a prescription against themselves. If the time mentioned at the end of verse 26 was not the period of three hundred years, but the time of Balak as you suppose, I do not understand how Jephthah could put such a question, which would be in substance this : ‘ Why did not you, King of the Ammonites, who surely will not pretend to be a better man than Balak, wrest this country from us at the time when Balak let us alone ? ’ It seems to me that the appeal to the precedent of Balak in verse 25, and the personal comparison there drawn between him and the Ammonite king, exclude the possibility of a reference to him and his time in verse 26. I might also add that for the time of Balak the infinitive שבת, signifying a continued abode, seems strangely chosen, and that we should have expected רשת ‘ when Israel took possession,’ whereas, with reference to the period of three hundred years, the former word is perfectly appropriate. It has, I suppose, been often observed that the three hundred years need not be considered as complete. I am not sure whether this may help to account for the omission of זֶה, which, perhaps, might seem too emphatic if the number stated greatly exceeded the period which had really elapsed to the time of the speaker.”

[On the same.]

To LORD ARTHUR HERVEY.

ABERGWILI, CARMARTHEN, *January 19th*, 1854.

“ I have been prevented by absence from home and by other engagements from immediately turning my attention to the subject of your letter ; but it is certainly interesting and important enough amply to repay the trouble of inquiry, and I am much obliged to you for the additional help with which you have furnished me by your answer to my remarks. The result of the farther consideration which I have given to it has been to modify my opinion in some respects, particularly with regard to the importance to be attached to certain points on which I was led to lay what now appears to me undue stress; but, on the whole, it has left me more clearly convinced than before that your emendation of Judges xi. 26 is perfectly needless, except in the interest of your chronological system; and I feel no doubt that the present text contains the original reading.

"I believe it will be most convenient to take your arguments in the order in which they stand in your letter. 1. I agree with you that the force of זֶה before periods of time exactly answers to our use of 'these,' and therefore it could hardly be omitted in such a sentence as this: 'We have been dwelling in the land three hundred years.' But it appears to me that the case is very different in an *oratio obliqua*, such as that of the text: 'While Israel dwelt . . . . three hundred years.' Here I do not think there is anything startling in the omission, much less that it can be considered as ungrammatical.

"2. I see no more difficulty in giving to בְּ the force of 'within' when it is coupled with the words עֵת הַהִיא than when the length of the time is specified. Gesenius (Thes.) gives as its third meaning *intra*: 'sæpe de tempore (Jes. xvi. 14) intra tres annos' (where, by the way, it is followed by a זֶה, as in our text), &c. It seems clear that as עֵת may signify either a moment or a period of time, its sense can only be determined by the context.

"3. The punctuation or division of the sentences between verses 25, 26 is a question of very considerable moment; but I do not think it is in the slightest degree affected by the presence of the וְ, which you seem to regard as an insurmountable obstacle to placing a note of interrogation at the end of verse 25. Nothing, I believe, is more common than for וֹ to appear in the Hebrew, where in English it might seem 'redundant,' and look as if it 'would not construe.' I have already noticed an instance in Isaiah xvi. 14. Another occurs in Isaiah vi. 1, where our translation gives an unmeaning 'also.' A third you will find at verse 17 of this very chapter of Judges, and after a בּ, which is rendered 'when.' I need not tell you that though וֹ has not the thousand and one meanings devised for it by the indefatigable Noldius, it is not always a copulative; and I believe that though there are many places where it may seem 'redundant,' there are few in which it 'will not construe.' In our verse, supposing the sentence to begin with the verse, I think וּמַדּוּעַ may be properly rendered, 'Why, pray.' As to the division of verses 25, 26 there is a great variance among the versions. The LXX. and the Vulgate make 25 run into 26, as the English. But among seven continental versions which I have examined I find only one which does so—Luther's. All the rest place a note of interrogation at the end of verse 25, except the Swedish, which converts the interrogation into the negative implied in it, and puts a full stop. Oddly enough it afterwards puts a note of interrogation in verse 26 in both the places in which it occurs in the English version. Again, of the four Celtic versions the Manx is the only one which follows the English punctuation. The Irish, Gaelic, and Welsh begin a fresh question with verse 26. From them down to the latest German commentator, Bertheau, I do not find that anybody has felt that the more ordinary distribution of the words involves any grammatical difficulty. It offers two not inconsiderable advantages: one, that of gaining two arguments in the room of one; the other, that of accounting in the most satisfactory manner for the change of number from the singular to the plural, for which, according to your reading, no reason appears. But although your proposed emendation is quite irreconcilable with the separation of 25 with 26, I now see what I had before overlooked—that your emendation is not required even when the two verses are thrown into one. It is only necessary, and not difficult, to suppose that the speaker, though he began with the mention of Balak, yet as he went on took the Moabites into his view, and so was induced to advert to the length of possession which had been undisturbed on the part of Moab. This appears to have been Luther's conception, as indicated by his rendering, 'Meinest du dass du besser Recht habest, denn Balak, der Sohn Zipors, der Moabiter König? Hat derselbe auch je gerechtet oder gestritten wider Israel, obwohl Israel nun drei hundert Jahre gewohnt hat in Hesbon,' &c. But I will now follow the course of your remarks on the context. You meet my objection, that 'the number of the conquered cities was superfluous' (I should rather have said irrelevant) to the argument, with the answer that it was mentioned from the same motive that led the speaker to 'heap up the mention of Heshbon and her towns, and Aroer and her towns, and all the cities which belong to the coast of Arnon.' But this 'heaping up' is simply a description of the conquered territory, 'all the coasts of the Amorites from Arnon even unto Jabbok,' and was not at all likely to suggest the summing up of their number. On the other hand, it would be surprising if the whole number of these cities was stated here but nowhere else in the Bible, though Deuteronomy iii. 8—10 would have been a fitter place for it. The absence of any other allusion to the aggregate number at least raises a strong presumption that it was not so familiar to men's minds as to follow naturally after a detailed description of the several groups of cities. But I think you encumber your own argument with a very grave and yet needless difficulty when you suppose these three hundred cities to have included those of Og. In that case the statement would be glaringly incorrect and a gratuitous misrepresentation. The question, as distinctly stated by the King of the Ammonites, was not about the right to the dominions of Og, but to the country between the Arnon and the Jabbok; and if the Israelites meant to speak of all their conquests east of Jordan they would have added the cities of Argob or Bashan to the list before they gave the sum total. But here all the difficulty arises out of your own unnecessary supposition. We know nothing whatever of the real aggregate, for 'the rule of multiplication' certainly does not bring it out without some most arbitrary postulates; but it is quite credible that between the Arnon and the Jabbok there may have been somewhere about three hundred $\pi \acute{o} \lambda \epsilon \iota s$ and $\pi o \lambda \acute{\iota} \chi \nu \iota a$. It is not, therefore, to the supposed number, but to any statement of the whole number in such a context, that I object. Your next remark, that 'the historical sense of verse 25 is quite incomplete without the additions of verse 26,' seems to me to miss the point; for if the sense is incomplete without those additions, it is not completed by them. They do not make the question, 'Did Balak strive,' &c., more intelligible to any one who was not acquainted with the history which we gather from Numbers xxi., that Sihon had conquered the country from the Moabites; but the knowledge of that history being assumed, the meaning of the question in verse 25 is perfectly clear without the additions of verse 26. The *time* when Balak might and should have fought against Israel could not need to be more exactly determined, in answer to the King of the Ammonites, after what had been said in verses 13—15. But I really do not see how Numbers xxi. 25 bears upon this point, nor can I admit any of your other inferences from it. In the first place, I am not satisfied that the verb יָשַׁב has a different sense in that verse from that which I suppose it to have in the infinitive in our verse. I believe that in the former it describes not merely the definite act of settling, but the subsequent state of continued habitation. This would be quite conformable to the use of the word in the literal sense in Psalm cx. 1: 'Sit thou upon my right hand until,' &c. But still less can I assent to your remark about the whole Israelitish nation *dwelling* in the newly conquered territory of Sihon and Og in any other sense than as it might be said to *dwell* in the land inhabited by any one of its tribes. Even if it should appear (and until I have leisure to go through all the columns under the word in Fuerst I would not speak positively on this point) that יָשַׁב is ever applied in the metaphorical sense to the simple act of settling or taking possession, it would not follow that when it describes a state, as you suppose it to do in Judges xi. 26, it could not be applied to the temporary sojourn of the whole nation in a particular part of its territory, as distinct from the permanent occupation of the tribes to which that part was allotted. I conceive that this last is the idea which it would inevitably convey. According, therefore, to either punctuation, I should still interpret בְּשֶׁבֶת as referring to the whole period of possession, and take it to be properly rendered not *when*, but *while* Israel dwelt. These are the main grounds on which I plead for the present reading; but I do not pretend that they are more than sufficient for the purpose of defence—that if your conjecture had been the reading of all the MSS. they would have warranted the substitution of that which we now have there, or that if the authorities had been divided they would remove all doubt as to the true reading. Your remark as to the 'diffuseness of Jephthah's message' and the 'obscure conciseness' of the mode in which the argument from long quiet position is expressed, seems to me too subjective to require or admit of any reply, except that I have not received such an impression from the words, and that I do not find any trace of it elsewhere. With regard to 1 Kings vi. 1, I do not see how the variation of the LXX. from the Hebrew text, whatever may have been its origin, is 'favourable to your view' that the number as to which the texts agree, both with one another and with the statement adopted by St. Paul, is corrupt. I find no reason for supposing that in this passage 'numbers were inserted where none were originally found;' for even if that hypothesis was adopted to account for the variation it would not affect the number, as to which there is a perfect agreement, and therefore does not, I think, 'leave us free to discard' that number along with the others. On the contrary, these variations seem to me to corroborate the authority of the *text* in the point of agreement; but it is quite another question whether all the numbers are merely the result of a fallible calculation, and therefore leave us free to discard them from our systems of chronology. Finally, with regard to conjectural emendations of the text of Scripture, it seems to me that we are perfectly agreed. And I am not sure that the critic in the 'J. S. L.' differs from either of us in principle. But as to myself, I readily admit that a conjectural emendation of the sacred text may possess the utmost degree of probability short of absolute objective certainty; but that, nevertheless, without 'external support,' *i.e.* authority of MSS., or at least of ancient versions, all alike are inadmissible into the text, and this for the simple reason that no human judgment can be allowed to measure the degree of probability required for such a purpose, and that to break through that rule would be to open a door for endless innovations.

" P.S. On looking through what I had written I perceive

that I have expressed myself too strongly on the parenthetical remark that 'your emendation is quite irreconcilable with the separation of 25 from 26.' With your interpretation of בְּשֶׁבֶת, though all the description of the locality in verse 26 would be completely superfluous—as the *time* referred to is distinctly marked in the preceding verses—and therefore would weaken the force of the question, still there would be nothing illogical in it, only a fault in rhetoric."

[On the same.]

To LORD ARTHUR HERVEY.

ABERGWILI, CARMARTHEN, *January* 28*th*, 1854.

"I am inclined to believe that your last proposal for the solution of our difficulty will prove the most satisfactory. Perhaps I have said more on the grammatical points than my scanty knowledge of Hebrew warrants. And my only excuse is, that it seemed in some measure sanctioned by the silence of the best scholars, who do not appear to have stumbled at the disputed reading or its consequences.

" With regard to the 'historical completeness' of verse 25 I seem not to have expressed myself clearly. I only meant to say that the question would have been complete and intelligible if it ended with the verse. But I did not deny that it joined on most naturally with the following words, all but the contested 'three hundred years,' and I admit that the awkwardness of beginning a fresh question with verse 26 is almost intolerable—in other words, the separation of the two verses from one another is hardly tenable. Again, if this is abandoned, the reading 'years' can, perhaps, only be defended on the supposition that the speaker had a past period in his mind, except for the instant that he was led to advert to its length. But it may be fairly questioned whether it is not easier to suppose an interpolation. On all this, however, it will best become me to wait until the question has been discussed by persons more competent to deal with it.

" With regard, however, to the force of יֵשֶׁב, I must for the present retain my opinion, which seems to need a little further explanation. I do not deny that the word is used of a temporary sojourn—as in Deuteronomy i. 6 ' of the encampment in Horeb,' and iii. 29, ' in the valley over against Beth Peor." But I conceive that in this sense the host of Israel might indeed be said to *dwell* (שָׁבַת) east of Jordan, but not in the *cities* enumerated in our text. These, I apprehend, were only occupied by the tribes to which they were assigned by Moses, whose wives and children contrived to dwell there (יָשְׁבוּ Deuteronomy iii. 19) when the warriors went over Jordan with their brethren. But the rest of Israel would not, I should think, have been dispersed among these cities, but have remained as before in one encampment, to which alone I take Numbers xxii. 1 to refer.

"I shall be very glad to hear of any fresh light that may be thrown on this perplexing question."

To Mrs. Bayne.

[On her going to Italy.]

Abergwili, Carmarthen, *July* 18*th*, 1857.

" . . . . The falls that you have to see are those of Terni, by far the most beautiful in Italy, and I believe in the world : for Niagara only surpasses them in grandeur. Whatever else you omit be sure that you see them, and, if possible, both from the top and the foot. There is a goatherd's hut at the top, where I passed a night, and where you might lodge deliciously, carrying your provisions and furniture with you. If you can only see one view let it be that from above. From below you see nothing but the Fall : from above you have the most magnificent of prospects into the bargain. No danger.

"I am quite grieved that the only persons I know at Rome, even by name, are the Pope and Cardinal Antonelli, to whom you will of course be introduced by Mrs. Jameson. You will naturally expect to see the Pope all scarlet. Instead of that, you will find him white as a lamb from head to foot.

" I need not say how glad I shall be to receive a letter from Lucerne, and how heartily I hope that all may prosper.

"My time, before and after my Visitation, will be broken up into little excursions for the opening of churches. I expect that the twelfth opening will take place on St. Martin's day, he being the patron Saint of Langharne, which celebrates his feast with great solemnity. Is not that charming ?

" Give my love to Bella and Willy. Mi farebbe molto piacere ricevere da lei o da lui un piccolo biglietto scritto nella bella lingua Toscana."

[The following letter was written to a young lady, aged fifteen, who had, during a visit to Rome, sent him a letter in Italian :—]

ALLA SIGNORINA ISABELLA BAYNE.

ABERGWILI, 17 Aprile, 1858.

" Con vivissimo piacere ho ricevuto la sua pregiatissima lettera, non solamente come saggio del progresso che ha fatto nella bella lingua Italiana, ma anche, e molto più, come segno della sua amorevole ricordanza di un vecchio e lontano amico.   Non so se troppo mi lusingo, ma non vorrei esser disingannato di una illusione così piacevole, credendo che sia questa la prima lettera Italiana che ha inviata in Inghilterra : e, come tale, ne fo grandissima stima, e la guarderò sempre al par di una reliquia.   E veracemente è cosa da lodare la rapidità colla quale le è riuscito impadronirsi a tal segno di una lingua straniera, specialmente quando ci rammentiamo quanto è stato ristretto il tempo che ha potuto consagrare a così fatti studii, per cagione della sua lunga e noiosissima infermità.   Ora finalmente è giunto il buon tempo.   E, se è vero, lo che dice il gran poeta, " Nessun maggior dolore che ricordarsi del tempo felice nella miseria," sarà altretanto vero " nessun maggior piacere che ricordarsi del tempo cattivo nella felicità."

" Oh ! quante belle cose ha vedute, e sta vedendo, e per vedere ! Ma che gran galantuomo e Pio Nono, che ha voluto creare tanti Cardinali, come a bella posta per divertimento delle donne Inglesi! Adesso non le manca che una sola cosa : cioè, che potesse vedere questi Cardinali mettersi a creare un nuovo Papa. Ma sicuramente Ella non vorebbe godere questo trastullo alla spese di Pio Nono, che ha fatto tanto per trattenerla, e poi le ha gettato la sua Benedizione.

" Io però non mi lascio abbagliare da quel lusso di seta, di ricamo, di gioelli—e che so io? Ma il vedere svillupparsi la primavera Italiana 'la bella stagione' al dir del Tasso, 'tra'l fin d'Aprile e'l cominciar di Maggio.' Oh questo si, che è una delizia, da destare qualche invidia in chi la conosce, e non ispera di goderla mai più.   E pure anche qui vi sono erba e fiori, e'l verdeggiar dei prati, e'l germogliar degli alberi, e'l canto degli uccelli, che al di là de'i Monti di rado si senta.

" Dice un proverbio Italiano, 'Vedi Napoli, e poi mori.' Io no.   'Ma, Vedi Napoli, e poi rivedi l'Inghilterra.'   Io sò bene che, in paragone di una Benedizione Papale, poco pesa quella di un semplice vescovo. Nientedimeno le mando la mia, con una preghiera, che esce dal fondo del cuore, che piaccia a Dio restituirla, e tutta la brigata, salva e sana, lieta e allegra, alla patria e al suo amico fidele."

[TRANSLATION.]

" I have received your much-prized letter with keenest pleasure, not only as a specimen of the progress you have made in the beautiful Italian language, but also and much more as a sign of your affectionate remembrance of ·an old and distant friend. I do not know whether I flatter myself too much—but I should not wish to be disabused of such an agreeable illusion—in believing that this is the first Italian letter you have sent to England, and as such I hold it in great esteem, and I shall always keep it as a relic. And really the rapidity with which you have succeeded in mastering a foreign language to such a point is worthy of praise, especially when one remembers how restricted the time has been which you could devote to such studies by reason of your long and very troublesome sickness. Now at last the good time has come, and if that is true which the great poet says, ' In misery there is no greater grief than to remember one's happy time,' it must be equally true, ' in our happiness there is no greater pleasure than to remember our hard times.'

" Oh! what beautiful things you have seen, and are seeing, and have yet to see! But what a fine gentleman is Pius the Ninth, who has been good enough to create so many Cardinals as if for the sole purpose of entertaining some English ladies! There is only one thing lacking, which is, that you might see those Cardinals set to work to create a new Pope. But surely you would not wish to enjoy this treat at the expense of Pius IX., who has done so much to entertain you and has thrown you his blessing. I do not, however, allow myself to be dazzled by this pomp, silk, embroidery, and jewels—and what not? But to see the Italian spring develop, ' the beautiful time,' as Tasso calls it, ' through the end of April and the beginning of May'—oh, this is indeed a delight, the enjoyment of which I envy in those who have it, and I never expect to enjoy it again. And yet here also are grass, and flowers, and the verdure of the meadows, and the budding of the trees, and the singing of the birds, which there, among the mountains, is rarely heard.

"An Italian proverb says, 'See Naples, and then die ;' but I, on the contrary, say, 'See Naples, and then see England again.' I know well that in comparison with the Papal benediction that of a mere Bishop weighs little. Nevertheless I send you mine, with a prayer that proceeds from the bottom of my heart, that God may be pleased to restore you and all your party, safe and sound, happy and bright, to your fatherland and to your faithful friend."

[An account of a tour in Holland with the acquisition
of the knowledge of Dutch.]

To Mrs. Bayne.

Te's Gravenhage, 22 *Julij*, 1859.

" Ik neem de pen op, myne waarde vriendin, om aan uwen wenschen te voldoen. You desired, I think, that I should write to you in Dutch, but you did not expressly require that the whole letter should be in that language, and I shall find it on the whole more convenient to finish it in English. We had a very prosperous and, on the whole, pleasant voyage to Rotterdam, shortened by a favouring breeze, so that, when I came on deck between two and three in the morning of the 20th, I found we were already on the bar, with a Dutch pilot on board, only waiting for more water to tide us over the low line of the coast in sight, summer lightning playing beyond a mass of dark cloud in the west, while eastward the most glorious preparations were making for the sunrise. The passage up the river was enlivened by a succession of Dutch pictures ; villages, farmhouses, creeks lined with shipping, and long lines of trees so cut as to put one very much in mind of the Roman aqueducts. In short, having loosened our moorings at St. Katherine's Dock at eleven the day before, we stepped ashore at Rotterdam at five A.M.

(Alhier moest ik ophouden, om onze reis voort te zetten—nu zijn wij te *Leiden*, 23 Julij.)

" My journey to Holland has, hitherto, been very pleasant to myself. I had the good luck to meet with a Dutch Jew on board, and milked him to a very considerable extent on the pronunciation of the language, and find that I can now both make myself understood and understand pretty well what is said to me. Yesterday we made a delightful excursion to Delft in the *Trekschuit*—the Dutch gondola gliding softly through the midst of rich pastures and woods, studded with pleasant villas. But what would you have said to being conducted over a fine old church, Calvinized with tiers of naked deal pews, by a clerk who not only kept on his cap, but was all the time smoking his cigar ! Nu moest ik ophouden voor deeze maal, en blijve altoos de uwe C. St. D."

[On the same.]

To MRS. BAYNE.

ABERGWILI, CARMARTHEN, *August 8th*, 1859.

" We returned to London about noon on Friday, when I found the accumulated letters of the preceding three weeks, with which I am still struggling, though they served to keep me awake after a night spent between reading and dozing in the crowded cabin of the Rotterdam steamer, where I sat at the table as in my study, amidst sights and sounds of unspeakable anguish, strongly contrasting with the peace and stillness of the outward voyage.

" I am now in a condition to communicate the grand total of my impressions. They are altogether pleasant. I do not think I ever made a more satisfactory and successful trip with reference to the objects I had in view. Our movements were entirely confined to Holland. We described a little circle, all by rail, including Hague, Leyden, Haarlem, and Amsterdam, and devoted the last two days before the return to Rotterdam, to Arnheim and its environs, stopping for an hour each at Utrecht and Gouda. I believe that I have-carried away a pretty lively and complete idea of Dutch town and country and of the sounds of the language, and am looking for a nice little assortment of Dutch classics selected at Amsterdam. Though, as I said, with the help of my Jew, I could have made my way by myself—especially after I had taken four lessons at Amsterdam—our progress was much facilitated by a Dutch courier, whom we engaged for the journey at Rotterdam, who spoke English fluently, and made himself very useful as a cicerone, and in all manner of ways. All experience, however, has its shady side. I found myself, as you did in Italy, to some degree what the Dutch call *te leur gesteld* (try to pronounce that). . . . . .

" I did not go to Holland—as I might have gone to Belgium—to see churches : rather to see congregations and hear sermons. It was an agreeable surprise to find one church—at Gouda—so little disfigured by the internal boarding that one could easily fancy what it was at the time that it received its splendid painted windows—each the gift of some king or grandee—which have been permitted to remain. Walls and pillars are everywhere beautifully whitewashed; of late years a good many curious frescoes have been discovered under this coating; but the utmost that has been done in any case has been to take a copy in time to prevent the next congregation from being shocked by the profane lines and colours, which were forthwith reinvested with their simple covering. I think I noticed the conduct of the verger at Delft. You must not suppose that there was anything singular in it. On the other hand, there is no smoking during divine service —a piece of self-denial in a Dutch congregation hardly to be overrated. The men, however, mostly keep on their hats—and of course remain sitting—throughout, except during a prayer. They then rise and uncover; but the women continue seated without any intermission. We were, however, very much struck with the congregational singing—generally to a fine organ—in which everybody seemed to join. I also thought it a good practice that, when the preacher has concluded the first part of his discourse, a verse or two of an appropriate hymn is sung before he enters on the second. After all, not the least considerable part of my gain has been the heightening of my enjoyment of everything English by the contrast with that which I left behind. A fortnight is well spent in Holland, even if it was for the sake of that alone.

" We are at present in a spell of rain, very much needed for the refreshing of the ground and the replenishing of our almost exsiccated pools, which, when I left, were nearly in the condition of the Thames. But the change is less propitious for the interest of the harvest, and especially for the excursions of the Cambrian archæologists, over whom I am to preside next week at Cardigan."

[On the same.]

To HIS SISTER-IN-LAW, MRS. THIRLWALL.

ABERGWILI PALACE, *August 9th*, 1859.

" . . . . I think you have done wisely in devoting the larger part of your time to Bangor rather than to Aberystwith, where there is nothing to be seen that will bear a comparison with the manifold beautiful scenes in the neighbourhood of Bangor. It is the place where I first enjoyed the sense of sublimity in nature (having, as I suppose you know, spent there the long vacation before I took my degree). And, though I have since enjoyed the same sense in a far higher degree among similar objects on an immensely greater scale, I am sure that no difference of degree can impart a pleasure equal to that which arises from the freshness of the peculiar sensation when it is new. I am only sorry that you do. not know what Bangor was then—alas ! nearly half a century ago. It is true, there was then neither Tubular nor Menai Bridge, only a ferry boat, sometimes affording a very rough and rather hazardous passage ; nor were there any artificial walks along the shore of the Menai. But Bangor itself was so much more enjoyable then than it is now. . . . . .

" How odd, that while you have been leaving your low ground in Hertfordshire to refresh yourself with the sight of mountains and precipices, and torrents and waterfalls, I should have been quitting my hilly region to enjoy the sight of a country in great part below the level of the sea, land nowhere rising much above the height of a sand-down, and intersected by lazy streams and almost stagnant canals. The pleasure of contrast, however, is at least as great in the one case as in the other ; and I certainly do not enjoy my hills the less on my return to them. My chief object, however, was not so much the sight of Dutch nature—if it can be said that there is such a thing—but of Dutch men and their works. And very glad I am to have seen those famous and curious old places—Rotterdam and Delft, and the Hague, and Leyden, and Amsterdam, and Utrecht, and Gouda, and Brock village, and Peter the Great's house at Zaandam. Not that everything came quite up to my expectations. I had formed a somewhat exaggerated idea of Dutch neatness and cleanliness. Leyden on the whole answered it best. But still everywhere there was something peculiar which you can see nowhere else. The ordinary street in a Dutch town is a picture—often, indeed, represented in the paintings of the Dutch school —but not otherwise to be seen in any other part of Europe. . . . .

" The churches are curious in themselves, and so far as they have not been disfigured by the boarding and white-wash mostly very handsome : and certainly not regarded with any superstitious respect. We were rather scan-dalised when we were shown over one at Delft, by a verger who not only kept on his cap, but was smoking his cigar all the time. And we found that we were singular and attracted some attention when we took off our hats. There is a good deal that is peculiar in the form of the Dutch service, in that which may be called the National Church. It is begun with singing. Then the precentor, or clerk, at a low desk below the pulpit, reads a chapter in the Bible, to which little attention seems to be paid. Before he has finished, the minister, in the old Geneva or Puritan costume, mounts the pulpit, always overshadowed by an enormous sounding-board, hangs his bonnet on the nail, and offers (in goodly contrast to the Scotch practice) private prayer. And then he begins the proper service with a short formulary, gives out a Psalm, then makes a short prayer, and, having moistened his lips with a glass of water, which is always placed by his side, begins the sermon. At the end of the first part he generally gives

out a verse or two of an appropriate hymn, and sits down.
After the hymn he resumes his discourse, which is followed
by more singing, a short prayer, and the blessing ('The
grace of our Lord,' &c.).   After that, perhaps, he baptizes
several children, addressing questions and exhortations to
the parents from above, and then descending to perform
the rite, unless another minister is there for that purpose.
During all these operations, from beginning to end, the
female part of the congregation remains seated.   The men
also sit with their hats on, during both singing and
sermon.   But for the prayer they rise and uncover their
heads.   The service altogether is agreeably varied, no part
lasting over long.   And the singing, which is generally
accompanied by a fine organ, is shared by the whole congregation : the music to each psalm and hymn being
printed with it in everybody's book.   This was the part
which we most admired, not without regret there is so
little like it in our churches. . . . ."

To Miss Bayne.

Abergwili, Carmarthen, *December 6th*, 1859.

" I am happy to be able to enrich your collection with
some more Sibylline leaves. . . . .

" You are very likely still haunted with the belief that
Cobden has been giving alarming evidence before the
Defence Committee.   The fact is directly the reverse.   He
has been laid up at Paris with indisposition, which prevented him from attending a meeting of the Finance
Reform Association at Liverpool.   But he wrote a letter,
which was read at the meeting, and which must relieve us
from all our uneasiness.   He says that he has been living
at Paris quite unmolested, and that, so long as he does
not himself assault any one, he has no fear of any ill-

treatment, and therefore he cannot conceive how people on this side the Channel can imagine there is any danger. Pray communicate this to any of your friends who may take a gloomy view of public affairs, and rejoice to think that, if you only visit Paris without being mobbed, you have the authority of that great statesman to assure you that the country is safe. . . . . .

" I wish there was a cat-post. I could send you a lovely tabby. He was brought to me by Tom from Nantmel, having received his education from the daughter of a neighbouring squire, who taught him among other things to scramble up your back and perch upon your shoulder. This enables him, if you are writing, to check any rash movement of your pen, and, if you are at dinner, to inter- cept any morsel which seems to him likely to go the wrong way. Though his name is Lion, he is the most good- natured and friendly creature in the world. But his young life has been embittered by the implacable animosity of an elder Tabitha, who had been long in possession of my part of the house, and declares herself resolved to main- tain her exclusive right. L. consequently divides his time between the kitchen, where I believe he is a favourite, and the open air, where he pursues the sports of the field with great ardour, and I seldom see him except on my visits to the water-side. Perhaps with these tastes and habits he might hardly take to a London life."

CHAPTER VIII.

ST. DAVID'S.   1860—1869.

[The reference in the following letter is to a paper on
the " Submersion of Ancient Cities," since reprinted in the
"Remains," vol. iii. p. 189.]

To Thomas Keightley, Esq.

Abergwili Palace, *March 22nd*, 1860.

"I am much obliged to you for your remarks on my
paper.   My reason for assuming that the legend of Cantrif
and Gwaelod is generally known was that it is the subject
of Peacock's humorous tale, called, I think, ' The Fortunes
of Elphin.'   The Breton legend had not come in my way.
Those which I have given might, I have no doubt, be
greatly multiplied.   The Dead Sea, though in one respect
the most striking of all examples, is so distinguished from
all the cases I have cited by the character of its waters,
that it would not have served my main purpose.   I have
not yet seen Masson's ' Life of Milton.'   I was less attracted
by its promise of fulness than deterred by its bulk.   He
is the editor of *Macmillan's Magazine*, which I take in

"

and have mostly read with pleasure. But the only contribution of his which I have seen was not written in a very captivating style.

" The aspect of public affairs is certainly very far from satisfactory either abroad or at home. Yet in some re-respects it is to my eye less threatening than it appeared six months ago. I am on the whole thankful for the annexation of Savoy, which seems to me to lessen the danger which would otherwise have been likely to arise from the commercial treaty, and which was probably one of the objects of that treaty on the French side, viz. false security. I think it will at least keep Europe and England awake, and counteract the efforts which Bright and Cobden will be making to disarm us. How far the purely commercial results of the treaty will be beneficial remains to be seen. The evil and mistake of it is that it is not a treaty with France but with Louis Napoleon, which as long as he is in power will probably neutralise all the good effect that might otherwise ensue from the extension of commercial intercourse. As to domestic affairs, though I fully expect a great deficit next year, and think it likely that Gladstone will be disappointed in many of his calculations both as to incoming and outgoing (especially as to the expense of the war if it is to go on with China), still I should not venture from that to draw any inference as to the probable effect of the financial scheme."

[In reference to a Dutch work called "De Pastorij te Mastland," by C. E. von Koetsveld, translated and published by Mr. Keightley, on the recommendation of the Bishop. The preface contained a letter from him highly commending the story. Further allusion is made to it in "Bishop Thirlwall's Letters to a Friend," p. 288.]

To THOMAS KEIGHTLEY, Esq.

ABERGWILI PALACE, *October 29th*, 1860.

"I have received your 'Manse of Mastland,' and am much obliged to you for so pretty a book. I shall very likely be tempted to refresh my memory of the original by reading it through. In the meanwhile I have read, beside the preface, the first chapter, to form an opinion on the quality of the translation. As designed for readers who know nothing else of the original, I find it perfectly flowing and easy, so that any one not otherwise informed might read it without suspecting that it was a translation. I heartily hope that it will be duly appreciated, especially in religious circles, where, if it once gains admission, it can hardly fail to obtain a large circulation.

"With all my prepossessions in favour of Dutch literature, I cannot help fearing that if any of your readers should be tempted to study it, by the account you give of the euphony of the language, some of them might be a little disappointed and surprised. I own that the sound of their *g* in general, but especially that of *gl* and *gr*, did strike me, and would, I think, most English ears, as rather 'rugged,' independently of the difficulty they occasion to English organs of pronunciation. Have you any authority for your derivation of *Mastland?* I do not understand, if it comes from Maas, either how one of the *a*'s could be lost or the *t* come to be inserted."

[On Dutch sounds.]

To THOMAS KEIGHTLEY, Esq.

ABERGWILI PALACE, *November 13th*, 1860.

"I cannot help thinking that while the statement you quote from your grammar itself needs limitation, your assertion goes considerably beyond it. If your authors had said that there is no Dutch guttural which is not agreeable to ears which are used to it, and coupled with organs of speech to which it is natural and easy, I should not have questioned that proposition. All I say is, that every guttural is more or less hard to ordinary English ears. And this would be not the less true if there were many who, like yourself, liked a rough sound, as more vigorous and masculine. But I do not find that your grammar itself warrants the preference you give to the Dutch over the other Teutonic dialects. To that I think it could only be entitled if the strongest guttural is the softest and sweetest. You quite misunderstand me in supposing that I had any doubt of χ being a guttural. My question is as you say only as to its degree of intensity. I always pronounce it, whether before a vowel or a consonant, as we all used to do at the Charterhouse, exactly as if it was k. This very fact seems to me to confirm my opinion as to the effect of a guttural on unsophisticated English ears.

" A Welsh boy reads his Greek, no doubt, much more like what was spoken, always rendering the χ by his native *ch*. The substitution of the k in its room would to him, I have no doubt, be intensely disagreeable ; but just because the k *is* the softer sound. That our language in its development has shed some of its graces, which would have rendered it better adapted to poetry than it is, I have no doubt. But perhaps it would be worse than useless, it would be ungrateful, to regret this loss. For it was the price—which could not have been paid if it had not been necessary—at which the language has acquired the perfection of those qualities by which it earned the highest eulogy it ever received, that which was solemnly pronounced by Jacob Grimm.*

* " Ueber den Ursprung der Sprache," Berlin, 1823, p. 50 ; quoted in Trench's "English, Past and Present."

"I think the most determined hater of slavery might admit that it would have been desirable for all parties if the emancipation of the West India negroes had been more gradual: if, for instance, all had been raised to a state of serfdom, and only permitted to rise out of it separately into a still qualified freedom, to be earned by individual exertions. But I am not sure that, if the consequences of the more rapid process could have been clearly foreseen, it could have been delayed, or that the danger was sufficient to justify the continuance of an institution so unjust and demoralising. The slaves of the Southern States are to be pitied; but they are hardly so much degraded and brutalised as the masters who roast them alive, while Methodist preachers protest against the inadequacy of so lenient a chastisement, and call out for red-hot pincers and slow dismemberment."

[On the same.]

To THOMAS KEIGHTLEY, Esq.

ABERGWILI PALACE, *November 30th*, 1860.

"I believe that in the majority of cases the cause of doctors disagreeing is that they do not understand one another; and that as soon as they did it would appear that there was no real disagreement between them. There is none whatever between Atrou and me as far as I know. I do not find from your report that he has affirmed that every sound in the Dutch language is agreeable to me; and I am sure that I never asserted that any sound in it was disagreeable to him. Even between yourself and me I am not sure that there is any real difference, only you have rather perplexed the question by substituting the terms agreeable and disagreeable for those which you used in your preface with regard to Dutch sounds. If the question

had been simply about what was agreeable or disagreeable
perhaps I should have thought of another instance as
coming under the second head more decidedly than the
gutturals, viz. *uu*—but I should not have called this or
any vowel *harsh*.   I have, however, pointed to the fact
that there is a division of sounds into harsh and soft, and
that by universal consent gutturals are referred to the
former class.

" The authority of an educated native is supreme as to
the matter of fact, what a certain sound in his own language *is ;* but as to its quality, of agreeable or disagreeable,
he is the least trustworthy of all witnesses—except as to
his own sensations.

" Your remarks on the Welsh, Spanish, and English
ejaculations appear to me to miss the point.   I should
myself be as much offended as you can be by the substitution of *k* for the guttural in Welsh, German, Spanish,
or any other language.   That has nothing to do with
the quality of the sound.   *Ojala* is to my ear also more
musical than Oh me! but not on account of the guttural, rather in spite of it, for exactly the same reason that
oi mé is so.   I do not consider the Welsh *ll* as *harsh*,
and to me it was never *disagreeable*.   But I am persuaded
that the difficulty of pronouncing the sound is no test of
either quality.   You misunderstood what I said as to
here, and I suppose I misunderstood you.   I was not
speaking of the vowel, but of the consonant, supposing
that you gave a vibration to the *r*, which is foreign to
English pronunciation.   I cannot admit the authority of
Milton in such a case as of the smallest weight.   No
genius can warrant any man in the insufferable presumption of pretending to pronounce better than the whole
people.   Moreover I must say that I think his ear must
have been capricious as well as fastidious.   His aversion to
the sound of *sh* was a mere idiosyncrasy.   No doubt it

might be repeated too often in one line or sentence. That, however, would be the fault of the writer rather than of the language. It is, as you have observed, a conspicuous element in the Portuguese, which Cervantes somewhere praises enthusiastically as the sweetest of all languages, conscious, as I think, that this was not the prominent quality of the Castilian, and probably just on account of the guttural. I have no doubt that the sibilants, and particularly that which answers to *sh*, temper the harsher sounds of the Sanskrit. I had the curiosity to count how many times the *sh* occurs in the extract which Bopp gives in his grammar from the Nalus, which, as it contains thirty slokas, is just about the length of Tennyson's ' Ulysses.' I found there were thirty-three ; but I did not count the other sibilant which seems to be distinguishable from it, though nearly approaching to it. Wilson says it is pronounced softly, as *sh* in *shun*. But I am vexed to find that I could not distinguish this sound from *sh* in any other combination. Your ear is no doubt much finer than mine.

" I quite agree with you as to the ' privilege ' of reading Shakespeare and Milton, but I should value it as much if I was dumb.

The celebrated volume of " Essays and Reviews " was published in the spring of 1860. Early in 1861 appeared the famous " Encyclical Letter," signed by every member of the then bench of bishops, addressed to a Buckinghamshire clergyman (the present Dean Fremantle), and containing a vague censure of the volume. The authorship of the " Encyclical " was unknown, and the absolute unanimity of the Episcopal bench was believed only to have been brought about by the personal efforts and influence of a prominent member of the Episcopate, since dead. The action of one or two of the bishops, notably Bishop Thirlwall, was much questioned.[*]

One curious feature of the controversy was the publication of a pamphlet entitled "Essays and Reviews Anticipated," the authorship of which has been attributed to George Eliot. It consisted of copious extracts from a work published in the year 1825, and attributed to the Bishop of St. David's (Schleiermacher's "St. Luke"). The preface to it contained an attack ending with the words, "His lordship has been so fortunate as to discover a royal road to orthodox faith, a solution of every difficulty, a confutation of every heresy, but, unhappily, this royal road opens its magnificent portals only to twenty-six individuals out of twenty millions." This little work was reviewed by the *Spectator*, and called forth an answer from the Bishop in that paper (April 20th, 1861). After boldly maintaining his own early teaching he added, "I am not aware of having refused to others the license which I ever claimed for myself. And, if it please God, I shall never consent to the narrowing by a hair's breadth that latitude of opinion which the Church has hitherto conceded to her ministers." The Bishop's charge of 1863 was also partly devoted to a defence of his action.[†]

To THOMAS KEIGHTLEY, Esq.

1, REGENT STREET, February 27th, 1861.

"If it is vanity to be gratified by what the Germans call 'Anerkennung,' I am not the person who has a right

* See Dean Stanley's article in the *Edinburgh Review* for April, 1861, since republished, with modifications, in his "Essays on Church and State."
† See "Thirlwall's Remains," vol. ii.

to exclaim against it; for it is a feeling of which I am fully conscious.

"I do not appear to myself to read much. The time I can give to general reading is very scanty. If I read more than most others who are in a similar position, it is only because I do not stand in the same need of intervals of exercise and relaxation. I can read literally from morning till night, without any interruption but that of professional business. Eating, walking, or driving, I have always a book in my hand. As to writing, the case with me is quite the reverse. In general I find it extremely disagreeable, and it is only in the morning, that is before dinner, that I can bring myself to do it without a violent and painful effort. Scraps of broken time, which I can employ in reading, are to me entirely lost for the purpose of writing anything but a letter. I see that the letter which you wish I had not signed has been censured in several quarters. It is, however, a comfort to me to observe that the censure has either been accompanied by no reason at all, or by such as to me seem utterly devoid of common sense. The *Spectator* calls it an 'extraordinary document,' and so it undoubtedly is, inasmuch as it partakes of the nature of the book which occasioned it. The *Times* calls it libellous; the *Globe* considers it as a violation of the Protestant principle of 'private judgment,' as it certainly is if that principle gives a clergyman the right of preaching Deism or Atheism, while he continues to minister in the Church of England. The latest objection is grounded on the Bishop of Carlisle's nepotism.

"What yours is I can only conjecture from your remarks on the book. If they really contain it, I think it must be grounded on a misconception. I am not aware that the Bishops, when they were addressed on the subject, had more than three courses open to them: 1. They might have declined to express any opinion. 2. They might have expressed an opinion favourable to the book. 3. They might have done as they have done—declared it in their judgment irreconcilable with the doctrines of their Church. I can hardly suppose that you would have thought it better that they should have adopted either course one or two. If your only objection is to the terms employed, that seems to me so unimportant as not to be worth discussing. You rather seem to intimate that, if parts of the book are open to 'little exception,' it aught not to be condemned because other parts are open to much.

"But surely that is neither the usual nor the right way of dealing with any work. The character of every work must be estimated, not by that which it does not say, but by that which it does. It would be a strange plea for any author charged with pernicious doctrine to set up that there are some chapters in it perfectly harmless.

" If the work, though the production of several writers, is treated as one whole, whose fault is that but theirs, who have sent it into the world as one volume, and have allowed it to pass through several editions without a word from any of them to signify that there is anything in it which any one of them does not think consistent with the profession of a clergyman, while atheistical lecturers are using it as a text book ? You yourself call their conduct 'impudent,' but if it is that, it must also be something worse. I was reading the other day old Chubb's 'True Gospel of Jesus Christ.' The whole substance of it might have been inserted in the volume without additional scandal, and would not have been thought the most heterodox portion of it. He seems to me to come nearest to R. Williams. The chief difference between them is, that Chubb speaks plainly and bluntly, and does not affect to use the technical terms of a theology which he regrets, and that he was not a clergyman."

[The following letter, referring to the same subject, is inserted here, though nine years later in date, because of the obvious and striking reference to the Bishop himself :—]

To the DEAN OF WESTMINSTER.

BEAUMARIS, *July* 11*th*, 1870.

"This morning has brought me another most welcome and valuable present in your 'Volume of Essays,'* all full of interest to every one who takes any in the recent phases of Church history, and some peculiarly to myself. In looking back on that of 'Essays and Reviews,' I cannot help lamenting that the secret history of the Episcopal Letter will never be known beyond a very small circle of persons, among whom I know only of one who would wish it to have been divulged.

"I have also received a bundle of protests on the report, though not including my paper on the Athanasian Creed.

"I could have joined with great willingness in the Bishop of Gloucester's expression of regret at the retention of the Ornaments Rubric."

[In reference to a tour in France.]

To MRS. BAYNE.

CLERMONT, *September* 27*th*, 1862.

"Though I am only at the second stage of my journey (from Paris) I am going to send you a few lines, thinking that you would rather have a short circumstantial story than a longer but less detailed sketch of my movements. It seems wonderful that having last Sunday held my ordination at Abergwili, I should now be writing from the

* "Essays on Church and State."

capital of Auvergne under the shadow of the Puy de
Dôme.   I broke the journey from Paris to Clermont for
the sake of seeing Bourges, where I arrived a little before
four p.m., and immediately sallied out to visit the glorious
cathedral.   The architecture quite justifies its celebrity,
though the exterior is not equal to Rheims, nor the in-
terior to Amiens.   I was rather sorry to find it entirely
silent, and almost empty—only two or three people setting some of the furniture in order—and having completed my inspection, strolled round the adjacent public
walk at the back of the archeveché.   By-the-bye the
Archbishop is also a Cardinal, and the entrance of the
palace is adorned with a sculptured hat, as well as
guarded by a Zouave.   This walk abuts on the ancient
wall, and there is some Roman work visible at one point
of it.   After I had surveyed all this to my heart's content, I set my face toward mine inn, having only one
other lion to kill, the Hôtel de Ville, which was likely
just to fill up the interval before dinner.   Returning to
take a parting look at the front of the cathedral, I found
a crowd, chiefly of women, standing on the top of the
perron, and evidently waiting for something or somebody.
The great bell of the cathedral was also sounding a very
deep note, and I joined the expectant throng.   Presently, out of the lane through which I had passed, which
joins the archeveché to the cathedral, sounds of ecclesiastical melody began to issue, proceeding from a procession which was advancing towards us.   It was headed by
two Suisses, followed by two mace-bearers, and an army
of priests in two columns.   Then, conspicuous above the
rest, appeared the golden mitre of the Cardinal Archbishop, preceded by four persons bearing—1st, his silver
cross; 2nd, his *mitra preciosa*; 3rdly, his crozier; 4th,
a book (it is to be hoped the Gospels).   On each side of
him was an ecclesiastic, opening his cope so as to leave

him at liberty to hold out his hand for the benediction.
As he approached the foot of the *perron* he stopped for
that purpose, and afforded me an opportunity of examining his features. His complexion was singularly dark,
face not unhandsome, and the expression, whether natural
or assumed, one of intense devotion.* I have seen such
in many pictures of saints. You know my weakness for
ecclesiastical ceremonies, and how sure I was to follow in
his wake. At about half-way down the nave he stopped
in front of a pulpit, which was presently mounted by a
dignitary who, after receiving his benediction, proceeded
to edify us with a sermon on the dignity of the priesthood. I took a chair within little more than one inter-
columnar space, and though at the side, heard tolerably
well. One of the most expressive passages was that in
which he expressed his fear lest he should fail to do
justice to so great a theme, and his wish that, rather
than prejudice it in the minds of his hearers, he might
draw his last breath at their feet! Yet it did not seem
as if the sacerdotal dignity could have been much lowered
through the inadequacy of his conception of it. For he
not only exalted it above that of angels and of the blessed
Virgin herself, pointing out that the priest "engendra le
Fils de Dieu"—not in his state of humiliation, but in
one as free from all mortal soil as that in which he
existed before his incarnation—but, with regard to the
rest of mankind, above Le Père Éternel himself. How,
will you ask, was that? Well, it was so. In the case of
"imperfect contrition" (one of pretty frequent occurrence)
God says to the sinner, "Thou art impure, an abomination
in my sight, I cannot admit thee into my presence,"
&c. "Le prêtre lui dit, ne t'inquiète pas : je le forcerai
de te presser sur son sein." This I suppose was nearly
the climax, and the preacher came down, not struck by

* Mgr. de la Tour d'Auvergne.

a thunderbolt.   The procession then proceeded to the high altar, which by this time was blazing with lights, and the archbishop took a seat immediately in front of it, and every one of the many hundred of priests went up, prostrated himself before him, and received a kiss. I also had advanced ; one of the Suisses passed close by me and relaxed into a smile, as who should say, ' You ought not by rights to be there ; but I suppose you never saw such a sight before.'   This encouraged me to ask him what it was all about, and he informed me that it was preparatory to a ' retraite pastorale.'   It occurred to me that a ' retraite ' might be a very wholesome thing for the clergy of my own diocese, but I congratulated myself that it was no part of my duty to kiss them all. The whole ended with the sacramental benediction, and the procession returned in the same order to the palace. It had lasted two hours, and I did not get back to my inn much before eight p.m.   I observed that the streets were lined with gazers, as if hoping to catch some air of sanctity from us who had beheld the ceremony.   I was curious to know the name of the preacher, and found that it was an Abbé Corsini who had come from Boulogne."

To L. Schmitz, Esq.

[On the death of his son.]

March 3rd, 1863.

" I have hardly courage to address you while the terrible blow you have suffered is so recent, and yet it is the time when a word of condolence is most seasonable, little as it can do to soothe so keen a pang.   You will at least be sure that it comes from one who really in a measure shares your grief, as retaining a lively recollection of him whom you have lost as he appeared in his amiable

and hopeful boyhood.   How gladly would I add a word
of consolation.   But I feel that there is something presumptuous in the attempt.   I can only point to that which
springs out of the depth of the sorrow itself, that there
would have been less cause for it if its object had not, as
far as Providence permitted, fulfilled all the hopes which
your affection had ever formed for him; if his career, within
its appointed limits, had been less successful, less complete.   That is indeed a thought which at first may rather
aggravate the bitterness of the bereavement, but yet it
contains the germ of the most solid and abiding comfort.
It may or may not be a blessing to die full of days.   It
can be so only so far as all have been well spent, and leave
none but happy and honourable memories behind.   But
where that is the case, how little does the highest value of
life depend upon its length ?   He was all you could wish ;
that is the best thing, which can never be taken from you ;
he might have been so longer, but he could not have been
so more."

[The two following letters are placed together, as they
both refer to Thackeray.   They show the friendship that
existed between the Bishop and the great novelist.   Bishop
Thirlwall presided at the anniversary of the Royal Literary
Fund in 1860, and referred to Thackeray in the following
terms :—

"Think of our admirable friend Mr. Thackeray.   I am
sorry I cannot ask you to look at him.   We must all
deplore his absence on this occasion; but see, what an
immense amount of ecclesiastical patronage he has at his
disposal !   What a number of sees *in partibus* are in his
exclusive nomination.   I have never been ambitious of

being translated to any of them, but I believe there are few clergymen to whom it can be a matter of indifference what position they occupy in Mr. Thackeray's books."]

To W. M. THACKERAY, Esq.

1, REGENT STREET, *May* 19*th*, 1860.

"I am almost ashamed of receiving so gratifying a letter from you on so slight an occasion. It must be difficult to attend a dinner of the Literary Fund without thinking of you, whether present or absent, still more to say anything about the influence of literature without alluding to you. I was glad of the opportunity of giving even a partial utterance to that which must have been in everyone's mind. It is an unexpected pleasure to me to find that it has directly or indirectly yielded any to you."

[On the Death of Thackeray.]

To MRS. BAYNE.

ABERGWILI PALACE, *December* 26*th*, 1863.

"Your letter, which I read before I had opened the *Times*, caused me the most painful surprise I have felt for a long time. As you spoke of Thackeray's 'serious illness' I hoped that he was now out of danger, and I could hardly believe my eyes when I found that it had ended fatally. It is a very great public and private loss. I hope you will get the *Times* of yesterday, which has a very good article on the subject, doing justice both to his mind and character. I, as you know, always thought his character was most noble, and his heart full of kindness. I see it is stated that he was much annoyed by what always seemed to me the dulness of the people who, unable to appreciate his humour, talked of him as 'cynical.' I believe that nobody loved more everything and everybody that was worth loving. But what would have been the value or merit of such love if he had not keenly perceived and felt the difference between that which was to be loved and that which was to be hated, or had shut his eyes to the dark side of the world? Since the death of the Prince Consort no event has thrown a greater gloom over the season."

[The two next letters refer to the visit of Prince Arthur to Tenby in August, 1865, on the occasion of the inauguration of the Welsh memorial to the Prince Consort. Prince Arthur unveiled the colossal statue of his father, erected on an elevated position overlooking the sea.]

To MRS. BAYNE.

ABERGWILI, *August 8th*, 1865.

"I must entertain you with a few personalities inaccessible to the newspapers. I was of the dinner-party, and sat on the Prince's right. I found him a very pleasant, frank, and intelligent boy, in that respect a year or two in advance of his age (fifteen). He told me he had been at Jerusalem. It seems that his time was very narrowly limited, but he gave me some account of what he saw on his way home. During dinner we were regaled with the music of a Welsh harper, and when we had returned to the drawing-room he was brought in with a young Welsh girl in the perfection of Welsh costume, and looking as if she had been just taken out of a bandbox. She sang two Welsh songs, and the performance concluded with the 'Men of Harlech.' In the proceedings of the next day there were three things to be done, most indispensable for the occasion: an address to be read, a prayer to be offered, and a speech to be made on proposing the memory of the Prince Consort.   I had reason to be more than satisfied with the manner in which my speech was received.   The Prince told me I had made 'a beautiful speech.'   But what was most to the purpose Sir C. Phipps, who sat by me on the other side, observed, 'You understood him,' adding, as to himself rather than to me, ' which very few do ; ' and half-an-hour afterwards, as we were returning from the room, he said he was sure that the Queen would be gratified by my speech.   This was my motive for revising the report ; and I sent a copy yesterday to Osborne directed to Sir C. Phipps.   But I am not sure whether it will arrive before she sets out for Germany.

" More Welsh was visible on banners and triumphal arches than has been heard in Tenby probably for centuries. It was no doubt intended to represent rather what ought to be than what is.   The Prince asked me to explain two which were conspicuous at the other end of the room.   I forget what was that on our right.   But as I proceeded to translate the other, ' Long life to——' he broke in with his very natural guess, ' the Prince of Wales,' which I was obliged to correct, as that which really followed was ' the Welsh language.' . . . ."

To MRS. BAYNE.

ABERGWILI PALACE, *August 23rd*, 1865.

" The honours of my fortunate Tenby speech have now culminated in a letter from the Queen, forwarded to me by Sir C. Phipps, thanking me for the copy I sent, and asking for some more.   It is not only full of the most obliging expressions that it was possible to use, among which is that of her ' satisfaction that *one* for whom her dear husband entertained so great a respect should have so well understood that *perfect* character ; ' but is written throughout as if to a friend to whom she could freely communicate her thoughts and feelings. Etiquette obliges her, I believe, in writing to any but royal personages to use the third person. But otherwise the whole tone is one of the most amiable warmth and open-heartedness, of which I could hardly give an idea without transcribing more than I should like to do : as the expression of her maternal hopes for the son for whom she thinks it a happy circumstance that he should make his first appearance in public life on such an occasion. The conclusion was to me very touching : informing me that she 'writes from the lovely spot (the Rosenau) where her dear husband was born, and which. he dearly loved.' I shall keep it in my writing-desk, that, whenever we meet, I may be able to let you have a sight of it."

To the Rev. J. J. STEWART PEROWNE.

[On his review of Dr. Pusey's " Lectures on Daniel," in the first number of the *Contemporary.*]

ABERGWILI PALACE, *December 12th,* 1865.

" I am very much obliged to you for the sight of your review, which I have read with much pleasure. Your judgment of the general character of Dr. Pusey's book appears to me very just, and at least very mild. Between ourselves, I find it very difficult to resist the impression that such resolute and passionate one-sidedness in a man of such extensive learning must be a reaction against inward misgivings kept under, as suggestions of the Evil one, by a violent effort of the will. His notice of Schleiermacher, however, is creditable to him, and leads one to hope that he would not now recall anything he had said of S. in former times.

" I must confine myself to a very few remarks which

occurred to me on the topics which you have selected. I
entirely agree with you in rejecting the opinion that the
Canon was closed by Nehemiah. The latest discussion of
the question by Kuenen in the third vol. of his Introduction must, I think, satisfy every candid reader that this
opinion is untenable, and bring him to K.'s conclusion,
that no precise date can be assigned to the event. If the
book was a production of the Maccabean age I should
consider its ultimate reception into the Canon as not merely
easy but inevitable. Whatever difficulty there is in the
matter seems to me to lie in that which must have preceded the reception, viz. its general acceptance as a work
of the old prophet. It seems strange that it should have
occurred to no one to ask how it happened that it had
never been heard of before. And I am not aware that its
genuineness was ever disputed among the Jews. But I
also think that in speaking of the closing of the Canon we
should bear in mind a distinction which I have not seen
noticed, but which appears to me of some importance. It
is, that the Canon might be said to be closed in one respect,
while it was still open in another; closed so far as to exclude
any new insertion, but yet so far open as not to preclude
doubt and controversy about some of its contents. The
Canon of the New Testament has been long closed in the
first sense, but is still open in the second. I do not mean
that the universal unquestioning belief in the genuineness
of the book, if it made its appearance four centuries after its
fictitious date, is absolutely inexplicable, but I think it is
nearly the whole of the real difficulty on this head.

"With regard to the Greek words, I quite agree with
you that there is not the slightest improbability in the
supposition that Greek musical instruments were imported
into Babylon and there called by their Greek names ; and
your remarks seem to take off the edge of the objection
that the same names are not found in the contemporary

Hebrew literature. Only about the word *sumphonya* there remains a difficulty. I cannot believe it to be anything but *συμφωνία*. And then I do not know how to account for it, unless some Greek maestro had enriched Nebuchadnezzar's band with a new instrument which combined several in one.

"I also agree with you that the Aryan words tell most strongly against the later authorship. But I am not quite satisfied with your explanation of the manner in which they were introduced at Babylon. You will see that I have pencilled a note of interrogation in the margin. And I mean it to ask whether it is indeed certain that *Babylon was taken by the Medes** before Nebuchadnezzar came to the throne, or, indeed, before Cyrus. The history of this period has been very carefully investigated by Marcus v. Niebuhr 'Geschichte Assur's und Babel's,' and his reading of it is, that Nabopalassar (whose name remains to be inserted) revolted from Nineveh and contracted an alliance (cemented by the marriage) with Cyaxares— possibly even consented to become his vassal, in a sense like that in which the Pasha of Egypt acknowledges the sovereignty of the Sultan, and 'joined the Medes in their attack on the city,'—not of Babylon, but of Nineveh. According to Niebuhr, if Iranian terms were naturalized at Babylon by the presence of an Iranian court it could only have been that of Cyrus. How far it is conceivable that the mere political connection between the two States might be attended with the same result I do not venture to say. But it certainly seems less difficult to imagine than how such terms could have entered into the vocabulary of a Palestinian Jew under Ant. Epiphanes.

"It is remarkable that M. Niebuhr maintains the perfect accuracy of the statements as to the succession to

---

* [This was merely a slip, and was afterwards corrected. I had written Babylon inadvertently instead of Nineveh.—J. J. S. P.]

the throne of Babylon—Belshazzar and Darius the Mede
—which have been thought to betray the hand of an ill-
informed or careless romance writer. If it should turn out
—as he believes himself to have shown—that they are in
accordance with facts ascertained by independent evidence,
they will certainly constitute another strong argument in
favour of the antiquity of the book. They imply an
accuracy of information which would be incredible in an
author touching only incidentally on the subject in the
Maccabean times. On the other hand, no part of Dr.
Pusey's argument appears to me less satisfactory than that
in which he attempts to meet the objections grounded on
the minuteness of the details in the eleventh chapter. It
ought not to be denied that *such* a forestalling of history
by prophecy is absolutely unique in the Old Testament,
and I believe that the fact will always be felt by intelligent
readers as a very serious difficulty; that which weighs
most of all against the genuineness of the book. And it is
one that can be but partially lightened by speculations on
the design of Providence in such a singular departure
from its ordinary ways. Your suggestion does not
appear to me quite adequate to the end. Admitting that
the Jews needed a warning such as you describe, I do not
see that the purpose of the warning required a development of the vision in c. 8 (which would seem of itself a
sufficient admonition) into such minute particulars. But
this is a part of the question in which large room must be
allowed for differences of subjective views, to which no
fixed standard can be applied. Your reflections on the
expansiveness of the prophetical word appear to me very
just and valuable. Prideaux was not far from the same
view when he observed, ' as much of these prophecies as
related to the profanation and persecution which Antiochus
Epiphanes brought upon the Jewish Church was all
typically fulfilled in them (the wars of Syria and Egypt),

but they were to have their ultimate and thorough completion only in those profanations and persecutions which
Antichrist was to bring upon the Church of Christ in after-
times.'

"The hypothesis, which is by some proclaimed as a fact
admitting of no reasonable doubt, and imposed upon our
assent under penalties of moral excommunication, appears
to me to fail, not only as raising difficulties on particular
points for which it provides no solution, but inasmuch as
it does not cover the problem which it attempts to solve.
It supposes the book to have been written for the purpose
of cheering the Jews through their struggle with the
heathen tyrant. And no doubt there is much in it that
is well suited to that purpose—as it would equally have
been if the whole is genuine—but there is also much in
which I can perceive no reference to that object : as c. 2,
c. 4, and if there is any in c. 9 it is very remote and
obscure, while it is very difficult to imagine *that* chapter
the fabrication of one who had nothing in view but a
moral lesson. Yet I should not expect every one who
rejects this hypothesis to feel himself obliged to return to
the traditional belief. I cannot help thinking it possible
that the book may have had a history not exactly agreeing
with that which is affirmed on either side of the controversy,
and which, if we did but know it, would clear up the whole
mystery."

To the REV. W. H. THOMPSON, D.D.

[On his being made Master of Trinity College, Cambridge.]

ABERGWILI PALACE, *March* 14*th*, 1866.

"Pray accept my most hearty congratulations on your
elevation to one of the noblest positions in which it is
possible for a man to be placed. I had wished it so much
that I felt the sort of hopelessness with which one always

looks for a piece of personal good fortune, though in this case it was the common weal that was at stake."

[On the proposed increase of the Episcopate.]

To LORD ARTHUR HERVEY.

ABERGWILI PALACE, *June* 13*th*, 1866.

"Many thanks for your letter on the increase of the Episcopate, which I have read with much interest. But I cannot help lamenting that a Bishop should not be able to delegate his authority for specific purposes without an episcopal consecration of his delegate. I know that some will be shocked at the thought; but I do not believe that it is at variance with any sound principle, and I think it would be found convenient in practice."

[On the same.]

TO LORD ARTHUR HERVEY.

ABERGWILI PALACE, *June* 18*th*, 1866.

"I was so fully aware of the difficulty which any one would find in reconciling a large section of the Church to a delegation of episcopal authority to presbyters, that I did not mean my remark to be taken for anything more than the expression of an opinion and a wish. I may, however, observe that your own plan seems to me no less open to objections of a technical kind, as well as to others, on ground of policy, which would not affect my suggestion. Surely the cumulation or amalgamation of the archidiaconal and episcopal office, by which the Archdeacon would be merged in the Bishop, would be a very startling innovation in our hierarchy.

"Your plan, however, has an entirely different object from mine. You propose to make a permanent provision for the execution of every part of the Bishop's functions in

every possible contingency. This is so far an advantage.
But on the other side is the inconvenience that there may
be a number of Bishops in every diocese, who in that capacity have nothing to do, and may never be called upon to
perform a single episcopal act. What I suggested was,
that the assistance should be not provided before the
emergency arose, but called forth to meet it, and that not
only the vicarious function, but the vicarious character,
should cease with the need. There are, I think, some
analogies which show that there is nothing very monstrous
in such a delegation of episcopal authority. I might
point to the practice by which a barrister often takes the
place of the judge in circuit. But there is another example
which would, perhaps, have more weight with sticklers for
episcopal privileges. They cannot consider the distance
between Bishop and Presbyter as wider than that which
the Pope asserts to separate him from every inferior
member of his own hierarchy. Yet his Cardinal Legate *a
latere* was invested with the plenitude of Papal authority,
and this, you know, was the cause through which the
appointment of such a representative fell into disuse, as
the exercise of such powers was found to clash with the
civil government. The Archdeacon is already the Bishop's
alter ego, visits in the Bishop's stead, is not merely his
eyeglass, but his *eye*. How strange that he should be
incompetent to execute the Bishop's commission to confirm
and ordain!”

[In reference to “ Guesses at Truth,” a new edition with
a Prefatory Memoir by Professor Plumptre.]

To the Rev. E. H. Plumptre.

Abergwili Palace, *December* 11*th*, 1866.

“ I have deferred thanking you for your kind present
until I had read the Memoir, which has of course for me a

peculiarly deep though melancholy interest.　As a record it contains every fact that can now concern the general reader, and reflects a true and lively image of the man. The volume on the whole is that by means of which, above every other, it will be known what Hare was.　You have attributed to me a happiness which I never enjoyed.　I was never at Hyde Hall, and I believe never saw Sir John Malcolm, though I remember the time when he seemed to occupy more of Hare's thoughts than any other of his friends.

"The statement that the undergraduates who heard the sermon 'The Children of Light,' proved that the 'Fellows and Tutors' had not given them sufficient credit for patience, requires some modification.　I was present, and I remember that, as the expectation of the close was deferred, the impatience of the undergraduates manifested itself unmistakably by a loud scraping, never probably heard before or since at a University sermon.　But I should not be at all surprised if several of the scrapers joined in the request for the printing of the sermon.

"The incident you relate reminds me of something which I always thought beautifully characteristic of Hare.　I suppose there never was a man who less shrank from speaking out on every occasion which seemed to him to call for the proclamation of the truth, whatever offence it might give ; and I remember one on which he provoked very bitter resentment by remarks which he made to one of two intimate friends (who he said was the person to whom it was right to make the communication), about some evil habit which he had heard imputed to the other.

"Yet I used to hear him lament as one of his chief failings, the timidity which so often kept him silent when it was his duty to speak.　Perhaps it may be inferred that his *parrhesia* cost him at least as great an effort as it would have done others who condemned it as indiscreet."

[The following letter refers to the " conscience clause " in the educational code, which the Bishop had fully discussed and defended in his charge of 1866. (See Thirlwall's " Remains," vol. ii. 104—120) :—]

To LORD ARTHUR HERVEY.

ABERGWILI PALACE, *January 15th*, 1867.

" I have read your kind letter with the attention due to everything that comes from you, but I cannot help thinking that you have misconceived the nature of the question. My answer is simply in the nature of a demurrer. It appears to me that everything you say might be admitted, without in the least shaking the truth of the proposition to which you object. I have asserted that a certain ' principle ' ' lies at the root of the conscience clause,' in other words, is implied in it. How do you meet this assertion ? Not, as far as I can see, by attempting to show that the conscience clause is not rooted or grounded in that principle, but that the principle is wrong and mischievous, and not within the intention of the legislature. That may be so or not, but it does not affect the truth of my assertion. It would not do so even if the legislature should decide according to your view of the subject, and declare the conscience clause illegal. Such a decision would not even alter my opinion with regard to the quality of the principle and the clause, which, in the present circumstances of education, and considering the ground on which the clause has been opposed by Archdeacon Denison, without any disavowal of his views on the part of those who reject the clause, I consider as just and necessary.

" I need hardly therefore say that I can perceive no ' flaw ' in my *argument*—if a single proposition may be properly called by that name. But in fact my argument consists in an examination of the reasons alleged against the adoption of the clause ; and I am not aware of having omitted to notice any that were or could be known to me. But the sphere of possibility is so vast and so obscure that no cautious man would venture exactly to define what does or does not lie within it. I could not presume to say with regard to the dangers which you apprehend from the admission of the clause that they are impossible. I only hold that they are exceedingly improbable. I consider the anticipated action of the Liberation Society in so very small a matter a mere bugbear, and I cannot help suspecting that you have unconsciously proceeded on a supposition that the operation of the clause extends to a greater number of cases than actually come within it. The dissenting minister is a spectre raised, I believe for the first time, by you. But even if he were to appear in flesh and blood he would not bear witness against the conscience clause, from which he has certainly received no mission, but would prove the unsettled state of the question. I believe it to be a sad mistake to suppose that the abolition of the conscience clause would effect a settlement, and not on the contrary accompany or introduce a radical change, which the opponents of the clause will think the greater evil of the two, and which will be in a great measure the result of their opposition to it."

[In reference to a sermon * on "Holy Scripture—The witness to the revelation of God in all facts;" and to No. 12 of "Tracts for Priests and People," bearing on the same subject.]

To the Hon. and Rev. W. H. LYTTELTON.

ABERGWILI PALACE, *January 22nd*, 1867.

"I received your packet the day after your kind letter, and heartily thank you for both. I have been long in

* This sermon was published at the request of the present Lord Derby.

possession of the tract, as I took in the whole series, and read each as it appeared. I can assure you that no other name than that of the author was needed to induce me to read it with keen attention. I have found it not only attractive and interesting but highly suggestive, which is, perhaps, the greatest merit of any discourse on such a subject. I would not say that it is too bold to call the Bible 'The Biography of God,' with such limitations as you add to the phrase. But I prefer the description in a later page—'a record of the divine education of mankind.' But I think even this description needs a further limitation, and that the education of which the Bible is a record is only the moral and religious education. But to this in later times, and in some sense it may be said in our own day, there has been added a new branch of education—the scientific—which in itself is perfectly distinct from the other, and not only no part of the religious and moral development, but apparently rather at variance with it ; for it has introduced man to the knowledge of a vast system of secondary causes, previously unknown and unsuspected, which seem to separate him from God, and to exclude the idea of the immediate divine presence and agency, which was the condition of his early piety. Whether it really does this, or only seems to do it, is the question of deepest interest to all religious minds. If that system of secondary causes is, as men of science are apt to regard it, an adamantine clockwork, without any provision for continual adaptation to varying circumstances, it is to my thinking of the smallest possible importance whether we admit or deny the being of God. For at the best He is now *functus officio*, and enjoying an everlasting holiday, only differing from the epicurean inasmuch as it has been earned by work now done. The great problem of our day seems to me to show that the childlike belief of man's early days is consistent with the fullest acceptance of all scientific truth,

and that there is no reason why this should quench faith
or stifle prayer.   I think that an important step is gained
when it is shown that science at least does not and cannot
disprove this, and that it is consistent with all our experience of human action.   It is only as a slight contribution towards this object that my Address* could have any
value ; but it has been a great satisfaction to me to know
that it has relieved the minds of some intelligent persons
from distressing perplexity.   The Duke of Argyll's ' Reign
of Law ' is a most valuable aid to thought on this subject.
The fact is that people have been stunned by the rapid
rush with which science has been advancing within our
generation, and are only now beginning to collect themselves and to take a stand from which they can survey
the phenomena soberly and calmly.   But if I am not mistaken they *are* beginning.   Allow me to say how much I
have been delighted by the truly liberal and generous
spirit that pervades your sermon, and by its sound, though
unhappily not generally recognised, teaching on the right
use of the Bible, which, even when it is admitted, as a
general principle is so rarely carried out into its legitimate
and most important consequences."

[The next letter contains amongst other matter the first
intimation of those physical infirmities, the gradual increase
of which led to the Bishop's resignation of his see.]

To the HON. and REV. W. H. LYTTELTON.

1, REGENT STREET, *February* 23rd, 1867.

" You are quite right in supposing that I have no objection to Church Congresses in the abstract ; and I am
willing to believe that much good may have resulted from

* " On the Relations between Science and Literature," " Remains,"
vol. iii .p. 284.

those which have been already held ; and if the proposed place of meeting had happened to be in my diocese, I should certainly have thought it my duty to preside ; but there is one objection which of itself would prevent me from attending at Wolverhampton, viz. that I have already declined an invitation which I received from a lady who lives in the neighbourhood to stay at her house during the Congress. It is true that I did so because at the time I received the invitation I had been long so deaf · that I could hardly have taken part in any discussions. Since I came up to London I have been relieved as to one ear, though I am afraid that the other will never again transmit any sound. But I must frankly say that if there had been no such objection I should not have liked to attend for the purpose of volunteering an address on a *question brûlante* such as that of the Bible and science, and I do not think I should have been quite justified in so doing. I do not consider a Bishop as the most suitable person to provoke a discussion of a subject on which opinions are so widely divided, and I, perhaps, the Bishop who is least fitted for the task, and this on two accounts : first, because I have reason to fear that the 'authority,' which you seem to ascribe to me, would be confined to a very small part of the assembly, and with the rest would be below zero ; and next, that I could not trust myself. I am conscious of being almost irresistibly disposed to put things too plainly and strongly. I find that my last Charge, though written with more than my ordinary caution, has given great offence to a number of persons whom I highly respect, and, considering what appears to be the prevailing character of the attendants at Church Congresses, I feel that my opinions could hardly be advocated by any one who was less able to recommend them by personal influence and popularity. I should like to see the subject treated by some one who had no claim to the questionable advantage of official authority, and I know of no one whom I should think more competent than yourself."

To the DEAN OF WESTMINSTER.

February 27th, 1867.

" I am much obliged to you for your Christmas sermon, which I have read with unmixed pleasure, as I could entirely agree with you in your broad view of the controversies about the Real Presence.

" My only doubt in the eucharistic question is, whether it is possible either logically—which I think it is not—or practically, for a permanence, that the same Church should celebrate the Anglican communion and the Tridentine mass, as equally legitimate and conformable to her doctrine.   This of course does not affect the question as to the policy of a temporary or exceptional connivance."

[The following series of letters to Mr. Dundas have reference to some contemporary conversions to the Church of Rome :—]

To W. DUNDAS, Esq.

ABERGWILI PALACE, *April* 23rd, 1867.

" I had not heard the report which you have communicated. If it should prove true, I shall lament it the more, because I am afraid that every such perversion is contagious among persons of the same rank, but in itself hardly any could be more deplorable than the one you mention.

" I am much obliged to you for the expression of your good opinion of me.   But as I am utterly a stranger to him, and without either a personal or official plea for interfering with his religious convictions, whatever way I might take of approaching him would be subject to great disadvantage, and much risk of doing harm rather than good, and for such a cause as you suggest his own Diocesan is both eminently qualified and the person whose station might most naturally and fitly suggest such an attempt.

"But I must own that I should not think any one qualified for it who was not acquainted with the convert's character and turn of mind, and with the methods which have been employed to make a proselyte of him. I should be very much surprised to hear that they have been such as would be in the least affected by any discussion of the peculiar doctrines of the Church of Rome. I doubt very much whether a proselyte was ever gained to the Church by such discussion. An expert Romish controversialist would never willingly permit the question to be brought to that issue ; he would anticipate such a result as that which you mention as related by Macaulay. It was not through any change of opinion as to particular dogmas that any of the Oxford Tractarians, Newman, or Manning, or Oakeley, or Ward, were won. Newman never believed in Transubstantiation before he became a Romanist. It was by wholly independent considerations of a general kind that they were led to adopt implicitly all Roman doctrine : such as the unity of the Church, our Lord's promise, the necessity of a visible infallible authority (the argument by which Le Maistre maintained the monarchy of the Pope). Such abstract considerations may have had a like effect in this case. Nothing appears to me less probable than that he has given way to any arguments which might be refuted by appeals to the evidence either of dogmatic theology or of ecclesiastical history. It is far more likely that he has been partly overawed by the dogmatic tone of his teachers, commanding him to submit to an infallible Church, and to seek safety and repose of conscience within her pale, and partly attracted, as most young persons and women, through the imagination and the sentiments, which are not merely incapable of being moved by the logical arguments, but absolutely deaf to them. If this is the case I see no remedy for the mischief."

[On the same.]

April 30*th*, 1867.

" It has been a very great relief to me to learn that the report of the perversion is unfounded. I should have answered your letter sooner, but was prevented by a very pressing special engagement. It is necessary to be cautious in speculating on the character of another man's mind; especially for those who know nothing of him from personal acquaintance, which is my case as to Newman. But although it may be true that there was a want of balance and harmony in his nature, I doubt very much whether his secession was owing to the predominance of the imaginative element or to his proneness to the sensuous in religion. I see no reason for thinking that this was the attraction by which he was carried to Rome. My view of his character and internal history is, that his mind was essentially sceptical and sophistical, endowed with various talents in an eminent degree, but not with the power of taking firm hold on either speculative or historical truth. Yet his craving for truth was strong in proportion to the purity of his life and conscience. He felt that he was entirely unable to satisfy this craving by any mental operations of his own, and that if he was to depend on his own ability to arrive at any settled conclusion he should be for ever floating in a sea of doubt;

therefore he was irresistibly impelled to take refuge under the wings of an infallible authority. No doubt this was an act of pure self-will. He bowed to an image which he had first himself set up. There was at once his strength and his weakness. He could deceive himself, and could not help letting himself be deceived.

"That is the impression which all I know of him has made on my mind. But it may very well be that your theory is better grounded than mine, and the real question is which is most in accordance with the facts of the case."

[On the same.] .

May 6th, 1867.

"I am much obliged to you for the Manchester paper. I own I should be very loth to believe Newman capable of any conscious untruthfulness, or of any that is not implied in the sceptical and sophistical character which I ascribe to his mind. But I believe him to be at bottom far more sceptical than his brother Francis; and the extravagant credulity with which he accepts the wildest Popish legends is, as it appears to me, only another side of his bottomless unbelief.

"Dr. Pusey is to me not, indeed, an object of horror, but a painful enigma. I cannot help thinking him less ingenuous than Newman. And when I consider the changes through which his views have passed, and his present dogmatical intolerance on the one side and his leaning to Rome on the other, I recoil from the thought of the mental process—I fear a moral self-maiming—which alone I can conceive capable of leading to such a result."

[On the same.]

January 8th, 1869.

"I believe that some time ago when you did me the honour of writing to me on the same subject I expressed the opinion that inquiry, discussion, and rational conviction seldom had anything to do with conversions to the Church of Rome. That opinion has been confirmed by subsequent observation. I do not believe that the case you mention is one of the rare exceptions to its truth, or that it affords a parallel in a single point to that of Chillingworth. But I have not the slightest personal acquaintance with him, and am therefore totally unable to say whether any, and what, 'social and religious influences could be brought to bear upon his mind.' But, judging from general principles of human nature, I should say that no time could be chosen for an attempt to reconvert him more unpromising than just after he has taken such a step. I do not know whether you mean to suggest a public controversy as an expedient for this purpose. I confess that I should very much deprecate such an attempt, as both useless and undignified. I was not aware that 'public discussions and challenges' had ever produced the effects you ascribe to them. Indeed I cannot say that I ever yet heard of their having changed the opinions of any who took part in them, as either speakers or listeners.

"I am very sorry that Rome should have made a convert, who, if he chose, could raise an army for the Pope, stud the whole island with cathedrals and convents, and carry on a vast system of propagandism among the lower classes. But it still remains to be seen whether he will do any of these things; and if he should, I am not sure that he might not have done more harm to the Church of England if he had remained within her pale, and had thrown all the weight of his wealth and influence into the scale of the Ritualists. I return the *Daily News*. The article on the subject in the *Times* appeared to me more sensible."

[On the same.]

January 15th, 1869.

"I am much obliged to you for the extracts you have sent. I had not supposed that you meant to credit the convert with the character of Chillingworth. But I meant to intimate my belief that it is only for men gifted with such a mind and character that there is any chance of escape when they have once been taken in the toils of Romanism. Since I wrote, I have received Mr. Ffoulkes' most instructive and valuable letter to Archbishop Manning, 'The Church's Creed or the Crown's Creed?' He observes : 'You, and very many more probably, seemed to have joined the Roman communion, not only pledged never to find fault with it, but to see with its eyes, hear with its ears, understand with its understanding, stand or fall by its judgment.' Mr. Ffoulkes himself was not required, and, as he says, would not have consented to give this pledge. And so probably it was with Chillingworth and Arnold. But I am afraid that their last convert was more than willing so to pledge himself; as his very object was to let his mind and conscience go to sleep, without fear of waking, in the lap of an infallible Church. How vain must it be to invite persons in such a state of mind to enter into or to listen to a controversial discussion ! Nor do I believe that theological duels, such as that which was fought some years ago between Messrs. Pope and Hennessy, ever produce any appreciable effect on the audience. It would be, I should think, about the last means to which an intelligent convert to Romanism, who remained open to conviction, would resort for enlightening his judgment. In general the result, as I believe, depends entirely on the state of the mind on which the argument falls. Otherwise, it is the Protestant cause that has most to hope from free discussion, in which I believe Romanists never engage willingly, as they find that in nine hundred and ninety-nine cases out of a thousand their sophism of an infallible Church, claiming passive obedience and implicit faith, answers much better. They work most successfully underground, and dread such a convert as Mr. Ffoulkes."

[In 1867 Bishop Thirlwall was elected an Honorary Fellow of his old College. He acknowledged this much-coveted distinction in the following letter to Dr. Thompson]:—

To the Master of Trinity College, Cambridge.

1, Regent Street, 12*th June*, 1867.

" I accept with very great pleasure and thankfulness the privilege of an ' Honorary Fellow ' of Trinity College. A Fellowship of my College was the highest object of my early ambition, and has been the groundwork of whatever success I subsequently obtained.

" But the renewal of my connection with the College, which I owe to the spontaneous judgment of its governing body, is an honour which I prize still more highly, as indeed the crown of a career which is now drawing near its close.

" I feel its value to be enhanced by the kind terms in which you have announced it, for which I beg you to accept my special thanks."

[This and the next three letters are on points connected with the interpretation of the Psalms.]

To THE REV. J. J. STEWART PEROWNE.

ABERGWILI PALACE, *May 20th*, 1867.

" The latest account I have met with of the proceedings against Galileo is in an article in the *Revue des Deux Mondes* (Nov. 1, 1864), by J. Bertrand, entitled ' Galilée, sa vie et sa mission scientifique d'après des recherches nouvelles,' and it probably contains every material fact of Galileo's history. There is also a ' Life of Galileo,' by Drinkwater-Bethune, published by the Useful Knowledge Society, which, however, if I possess it I am not able to find. But I doubt very much that you would be able anywhere to verify the statement of Father Sanchez.* It is, indeed, in itself highly probable, except that there is no reason for attributing to the argument drawn from Psalm civ. 5 any pre-eminence over the many others of the like kind which were opposed to Galileo's doctrine. But we must distinguish between three stages in the history of this opposition.

" First, after the appearance of the ' Dialoghi,' Galileo was assailed with a shower of objections derived from Scripture. Bertrand gives some samples of these, among which the two miracles of Joshua and the dial of Ahaz are the most conspicuous. Next came the proceedings of a congregation appointed by Urban VIII. to examine the ' Dialoghi,' by which they were condemned. And, finally, the interrogations to which he was subjected, according to some with the infliction, but most probably only with the formal threat, of torture, which extorted his recantation. Bertrand observes that no minute (*compte rendu*) was allowed to be taken of the examination, so that the truth as to this can never be ascertained ; but he thinks it most pro-

* [Quoted in my work on the " Psalms," in a note on Psalm civ. 5.—J.J.S.P.]

bable that the motive of this secrecy was more to conceal the indulgence (which it might be imprudent to reveal) than the excessive severity of the holy office. As little, I believe, have the proceedings of the Congregation—though they may be preserved in the archives of the Inquisition—ever been published. It was most likely in some of the controversial writings called forth by the 'Dialoghi' that Sanchez found the argument from the 104th Psalm. But I need not say that even in Italy these pieces must now be very rare. There might, however, be an allusion to the argument in the works of Galileo; only Bertrand observes that he made no reply to any of the arguments drawn from Scripture, only to the (so-called) philosophical, which he treated very roughly. In Ponsard's new play, *Galilée*, he defends himself against one objection only—

'Mais à la Bible enfin je ne suis pas contraire ;
Josué se ployait au langage vulgaire.'

To THE REV. J. J. STEWART PEROWNE.

ABERGWILI PALACE, *May 4th*, 1868.

"I have now received your kind present of the second volume of the Psalms ; and while I thank you for it, must also congratulate you most heartily on the completion of so important a work—the first, I believe, that has ever enabled the English student to read the Psalms intelligently as well as devoutly. I hope that it will operate powerfully in promoting both the cultivation of Hebrew and a critical study of the Old Testament. It is also a great satisfaction to reflect that the termination of a task, which must have occupied so much of your time, leaves you in possession of leisure which will, no doubt, be not less usefully employed."

[On Psalm civ. 4.]

To THE REV. J. J. STEWART PEROWNE.

ABERGWILI PALACE, *August* 10*th*, 1868.

" I always find it profitable to myself to give fresh consideration to any difficult question lying within my sphere.

" As to Psalm civ. 4, I do not feel the same difficulty which you have found in the plural 'ministers.' It seems to me an example of a common Hebrew taste, which preferred variety to symmetry. I think we have a nearly parallel case in Micah iv. 13 : 'I will make thine horn iron, and I will make thy hoofs brass." But there is another difficulty which I have always felt in the way of that which otherwise I should without hesitation believe to be the true rendering; that is, what strikes me as the harshness of the construction, if the verb is supposed to be followed immediately not by the object but by the predicate. It is possible that this difficulty arises only from my ignorance or forgetfulness, as none of the commentators notice it. Perhaps you know of parallel passages. I have never read the Old Testament for the purpose of looking for such ; but I think, if I had seen any, they would have struck me. *A priori* I should have thought it almost incredible that the language should have been left in such a state as to make it immaterial as to the sense whether you wrote, ' Who maketh the clouds his chariot,' or, ' Who maketh the chariot his clouds,' and that the reader should have to infer the author's meaning, not from the order of his words, but from extrinsic considerations such as those which you have discussed. I cannot help thinking that more attention should have been paid to this question, and that it should have taken precedence of every other ; because if in this respect the rule of Hebrew syntax was the same as our own, the only remaining doubt would be in what sense we are to understand the words, ' He maketh

His messengers winds, His ministers a flaming fire,' which would then be the only possible rendering. And in itself it would give a very good sense as meaning, ' He endows His messengers with the might of the wind, His ministers with the all-pervading subtilty of fire '—or as any one might paraphrase it better. But it would be only the irresistible compulsion of a grammatical necessity that would induce me to adopt this rendering ; because, however satisfactory in itself, it appears to me quite foreign to the context. The Psalmist is evidently speaking of God's doings in the visible creation, not of the secret agency by which He accomplishes his ends. It was therefore very much to the purpose to say that wind and fire are his servants and do his pleasure ; but not at all to say that He has unseen servants who act as wind and fire.

" It would also, I think, have been more important to inquire whether such an idea of the ministry of angels was familiar to the Hebrew mind, than to show that it had been accepted by a modern writer, and by such a writer ! You would not, I imagine, consider Psalm xviii. 10 as indicating such a view, as you have not there thought it necessary to notice the relation in which the ' cherub ' stands to the ' wings of the wind.' As to the modern authority, I cannot share your admiration of the passage you cite from Newman any farther than as regards the expression. In the thought it appears to me only to illustrate his great intellectual deficiency, the utter want of historical tact and judgment, which alone enables one to believe the sincerity of his professed all-absorbing credulity. He was in this respect a born Papist, and finds his natural element in the Golden Legend. The conception that all the work of the universe, all mechanical, physical, chemical, and physiological movements, from planetary and sidereal rotations to the dislocations of the molecules of an atom, are carried on by the agency of an order of personal beings, is one which my mind utterly rejects, and I believe that no mind could attempt to realise it without feeling itself in danger of losing its senses. Surely it is one thing to believe that all is regulated by a Supreme Will, and quite another thing to believe that this Will employs a machinery like that of the " Rape of the Lock." But to sum up, I am sorry that I have not sufficient materials for a definite conclusion. But you will have seen that I consider the first and main question to be one of syntax, and until that is settled by competent judges I can pronounce no decided opinion on the sense. Until I am satisfied that a Hebrew writer *could* have placed his words in an order which an English translator is forced to invert, if they are to be understood in a certain sense, I cannot believe *that* sense—however otherwise commending itself to my judgment, as alone consistent with the context—to be the true one."*.

[On the authorship of the 110th Psalm.]

To the REV. J. J. STEWART PEROWNE.

ABERGWILI PALACE, *August* 11*th*, 1868.

" I now proceed to the consideration of your second question, which is beset with difficulties, not only more and greater, but of a far higher order than those raised by the first. I feel them so strongly that I shall not venture to pronounce any dogmatical opinion on the subject. But I will draw your attention to some aspects of it which you seem either to have overlooked, or not to view in the same light as I do.

" I think it will be convenient first to consider the Psalm by itself, just as if no reference had been made to

* [In the last edition of my work on the Psalms, I have shown, by reference to other passages, that this inversion of order in the Hebrew, which to the Bishop seemed so unlikely, is actually employed.—J. J. S. P.]

it in the New Testament, and then to see how our conclusions about it must be modified by our Lords' language.

"1. I think there can be no doubt that whoever was the author, it must be considered as a Messianic Psalm— a picture of a state of things which had not been fully realised, either in the literal or the spiritual sense, before the coming of Christ. This character of the Psalm, as manifested by its contents, would not be more strongly marked if it is considered as the work of David, and the only question is whether, without some special revelation beyond what would have been required for any other author, he could have spoken of the person described in it as his 'Lord.' I will only say that it does not appear to me inconceivable, but quite natural, that he should so style one who answered to the description given of the future victorious king. Only I am not sure that there is anything in that description that might not be accounted for, without any peculiarly distinct *consciousness—some* consciousness the writer must have had, whoever he was— in David's mind, partly by the promises which he had received (2 Samuel vii.), and partly by traditional expectations of the coming Great One.

" 2. How, then, is the case altered by our Lord's reference to the Psalm?   Here we find ourselves in the presence of two opposite theories as to our Lord's intellectual state. According to that which invests Him with the fulness of divine as well as human knowledge, there is of course no room for doubt about the authorship of the Psalm.   You, however, seem willing to admit that of Neander, Meyer, and others (among the rest Pressensé, "Vie de Jésus"), that our Lord was not habitually conscious of facts such as 'matters of literary criticism,' which did not fall within the range of His human knowledge.   But then arises the question whether even on this theory we are not compelled to suppose that He would not have argued as He does with the

Pharisees on the Psalm if a certain knowledge of its real authorship had not been supernaturally infused into Him for the special occasion. This leads us to inquire what the argument was. And here it is to be observed that, strictly speaking, it was no *argument* at all. Still less was it an argument proving that the Christ was foreseen by David to be the Son of God. As far as our Lord's words go, they are simply questions which might have been put by one who wished to suggest to the Pharisees that they were mistaken in believing that David was the author of the Psalm. Nothing of course could be further than that from our Lord's intention, though I see from Alford that De Wette actually thought so. But if He did not take, but stand on, the same intellectual level in this respect with the Pharisees, can it be said that His questions, if David was not really the author of the Psalm, tended to mislead them, and, therefore, that this was a case in which, if He had needed a supernatural revelation of the truth, He must have received one? I must own that is not at all clear to me. But that which most perplexes me is the difficulty I find in understanding the precise drift of our Lord's questions, or why they should have had the effect of putting the Pharisees to silence. One would think that they could have been at no loss for an answer, according to the current Messianic notions of the day. They knew that Messiah was to be of the lineage of David. They also believed that He was to be a greater than David, though the precise degree of His superiority might be open to doubt. But this might suffice to remove the appearance of inconsistency between David's language and his relation to the expected Messiah. Nor does it appear elsewhere that the question between our Lord and His opponents was who and what the Messiah was to be, but whether He was the Messiah. If the Pharisees had not believed that the Psalm related to the Messiah, the question would have been futile.   The argument, whatever it may have been, turns upon that quite as much as it does upon David's authorship ; and though the title of *Lord* implied a dignity higher than David's, it can hardly be said to carry so much as the sitting on Jehovah's right hand, or even as the everlasting priesthood,   But if so, the alleged occasion for a supernatural infusion of superhuman knowledge seems to lose almost all its importance, as the only result would be the addition of a title, which could have no such meaning except in the mouth of David, but which is thrown into the shade by other attributes which do not depend on the supposition of his authorship.

"On the whole, the conclusion to which I am led, as far as the great obscurity and imperfection of the data permits me to draw any, is that we are left very much in the same position with regard to the Psalm as if our Lord had not asked the questions about it, and that though we may be at liberty we are not 'compelled' to attach any greater weight to it than it would have if it was not written by David.   All that 'falls to the ground' in our Lord's argument, is a particular which does not seem to have any bearing upon doctrine, and to be indeed immaterial.

"It may be that I have overlooked some essential point. If so I hope you will have the goodness to set me right."

[The next three letters form part of a correspondence which arose out of a Charge delivered by Bishop Ewing in 1866 on "Materialism in Christianity."   The Charge and the correspondence, which included letters from Mr. Erskine of Linlathen, and Dr. J. MacLeod Campbell, are printed at length under the title of "The Relation of Knowledge to Salvation" in "Present-Day Papers," Third Series.]

To THE BISHOP OF ARGYLE AND THE ISLES.

ABERGWILI PALACE, *July* 15*th*, 1867.

" I found your letter to the Primus on my return. . . . .

" As I am not acquainted with your Primus, I cannot form any opinion as to the impression your letter is likely to make on him ; but am rather inclined to doubt whether it will improve your position in his view. But at least it seems to me to contain nothing which you have not a perfect right to say. So, however, I thought as to your Charge, and it may be that he will be as little satisfied with your vindication or explanation as with that which was to be vindicated or explained. But I think I am bound to say a word or two on the P.S. which is intended in part to meet an objection raised by myself. I feel sure that on the subject of the knowledge of God in its bearing on Salvation we are at bottom quite agreed. But I cannot help wishing that you had expressed yourself a little more clearly and precisely. To say that 'Salvation consists in the knowledge of God' is evidently an unsatisfactory way of speaking, as it requires an explanation, but it is not more obscure than the phrase 'to be in the Spirit of God.' Your statement that 'Salvation' is the '*product* of knowledge,' or that knowledge is the *means* of Salvation, does not seem to me to be at all supported by the words of our Lord. Those words do not seem to me to say anything about the *means* of Salvation, but about Salvation itself, or 'life eternal,' which is described as a 'knowing.' But it is no more possible that this 'knowing' should be a merely intellectual process, than that the 'life eternal' should be a mere endless being. For if so, both would be something common to angels and devils. It must be something more than knowledge, viz. a loving adoring knowledge, of which only good spirits are capable, not one which creates fear and torment. Unfortunately our word to 'know' does not suggest the idea as do both the Hebrew 'yada' and the Greek γιγνώσκω (which makes the γνωτοί τε γνωταί τε of Homer * equivalent to 'nearest and dearest'). It is in this sense that God says of Israel (Amos iii. 2), 'You only have I *known* of all the families of the earth,' not meaning to limit his omniscience, but to express his tender care. And in a like sense, Nahum i. 7, 'The Lord *knoweth* them that trust in him.' This knowledge is the ἐπίγνωσις of St. Paul (Ephesians iv. 13, and 1 Corinthians xiii. 19). Not I apprehend a *means* or a stage, but the consummation, the beatific vision itself. I would therefore rather say that salvation or eternal life consists in the love of God, because this implies some degree of knowledge, whereas knowledge does not imply any degree of love (1 Corinthians xiii. 12).

"I do not think you are warranted in so contrasting the 'holding justification by Faith alone' with the tenet 'that we are saved by instrumentality acting apart from the intelligence.' I should myself be equally loth to adopt either tenet in its naked literality, because both are equally Antinomian. Properly explained, the first may be a very sound and wholesome doctrine. But is it certain that either any church or any school would admit your statement of the second to be a fair description of its views? If the sacraments are means of grace, it cannot be denied that they are in their measure and degree means of salvation, and this would be perfectly consistent with the doctrine of justification by faith rightly understood. The measure and degree may be exaggerated by one party; unduly lowered by another; but this is not sufficient to establish a contrast between the things themselves.

"Another point on which I am quite unable to agree with you is your view of Scripture as realising the

<hr>

* Iliad, xv. 350.

promise of the Holy Spirit. That in this promise our Lord had writings of any kind in his view appears to me utterly uncredible in itself, as well as destitute of all evidence, if not absolutely inconsistent with the language of St. Paul (1 Corinthians xii. 4 foll. and Ephesians iv. 4 ff.) The peculiar value of the New Testament, as the only trustworthy record of the original revelation, does not appear to me either to need or to be enhanced by such a hypothesis. Indeed I hardly understand how you reconcile it with the gift of the Spirit at a time when not a line of the New Testament was written.

"I am forced to break off, and will only beg you to excuse the haste with which I have been forced to write, and to inform me how to direct the proof."

July 29th, 1867.

"I am much obliged to you for the sight of the enclosed paper. I am not sure in what way it was meant to bear on my remarks in my letter to you. But it contains some propositions which, if I understand them, I could not adopt. I have not now leisure to discuss them, but will very briefly notice one or two. It is very true, as a matter of fact, that gratitude enters very largely as an ingredient in our love towards God : as it does in that of children to their parents. But this I consider as a mark of imperfection, of moral and intellectual childishness and selfishness. Mr. Erskine seems on the contrary to treat it as not merely the natural but the normal state of things: to identify love with gratitude, and to make the benefits, which we either have received or expect from God, the measure of His 'love worthiness,' as if His rightful claim to our love depended upon them ; which would appear to degrade Him into a property or an instrument to be valued in proportion to its usefulness. I am loth to attribute such an opinion to any one, but if the meaning is not this, I think it should have been differently expressed ; and, after a repeated perusal, I can find no other which seems to me in accordance with the general drift of the paper. The interpretation of our Lord's words in Matthew xi. 28 seems to me quite inadmissible, even in the application proposed by Olshausen to the Cross, much more in the sense that our Lord spoke of His own filial obedience as a yoke and a burden. He was speaking to those who were ' heavy laden,' and inviting them into a state in which, if they would ' learn of Him,' and in proportion as they did so, they would ' find rest to their souls.' It is, as I apprehend, not the exchange of one yoke or burden for another that is meant, but a training which leads to perfect rest and liberty—that which Christ himself already enjoyed.

" You seem to have added at the end some words of your own for the purpose of connecting the concluding proposition with your own statements as to the necessity of knowledge. And undoubtedly in every act of faith, in every religious act, there must always be two elements, a thought and a feeling. Without the one it would not be properly an *act ;* without the other it would not be *religious.* It seemed to me that, while insisting on one of these factors, you had neglected the other."

September 4th, 1867.

" Even without the privilege of a personal acquaintance with Mr. Erskine, I feel, in reading his remarks, that I cannot differ from him on such a subject without distrusting my own judgment, and must hope that there may be only the seeming of a difference, arising from a misunderstanding. I think I observed in my last letter that I did not clearly see the bearing of Mr. Erskine's first Paper on the subject of my criticism of your Charge, and I am now under the disadvantage of writing without the means of referring either to my own remarks or to his. It may be owing to this that I do not see why he lays so much stress on 'the necessity of having something to awaken an emotion.' Am I supposed to have denied that? What I might have said, though I am not aware that I did so, is, that there may be emotion (certainly not without a cause, but) either absolutely without or with a minimum of consciousness. Such, I would say, is the state of the infant on its mother's breast. Again, I had certainly not suspected that *fear* would have served Mr. Erskine's purpose of illustration as well as *gratitude*. No doubt, if you fear, it must be somebody or something; and if you are grateful, it must be to somebody for something. But have I directly or indirectly denied that? Otherwise the difference between *fear*, the most purely selfish, painful, and loveless of instincts, and *gratitude*, is so great, that the little they have in common would seem immaterial. But when Mr. E. adds, 'I conceive that gratitude must remain a permanent element in our normal spiritual condition,' we come to a point at which our views certainly diverge. All that I can do is to endeavour briefly to explain my own. The love of the infant for its mother is at first purely instinctive. That of the child may be continually strengthened by the experience of kindness before the awakening of reflection, still more before the actual forming of any judgment on the character of its object. But it may happen, and I suppose often happens, that, as the intelligence expands and knowledge is enlarged, the child makes the painful discovery that the person whom it most tenderly loves is not loveworthy.   The gratitude which it does not cease to feel is not accompanied by approbation or respect.   It remains only as a selfish, irrational instinct.   With regard to God, the case is exactly the reverse.   The more we discover of His nature, the more we must find Him worthy of our love ; and the perception of His loveworthiness must tend to swallow up our sense of benefits received from him.   The contemplation of this glorious object must, in its supreme degree, absorb all reflection on self, and just on this account it is ecstasy, rapture, the perfection of bliss.   It is a state of admiring love.   And I do not see how the sense of gratitude, which implies reflection on self, could add anything to its felicity.   It would, I think, be a descent to a lower stage of spiritual life.   And yet such a state of ecstasy does not imply any illusion.   The relation of the creature to the Creator, of course, must always remain the same, and may be implicitly acknowledged though it is not distinctly present to the mind.   So far as there is consciousness, there must be a consciousness of dependence and a sense of gratitude.   But I conceive that the supreme happiness is so far from depending on the distinctness of that consciousness, that ultimately—as mathematicians would say, at the *limit*—it excludes such distinctness.   This may seem to be at direct variance with the proposition that our normal (if by that is meant our highest spiritual) condition must be imperfect without gratitude.   But it may be that the nature of a creature is incapable of such contemplation beyond certain limits of time, and that its highest permanent condition is one which fluctuates between ecstasy and reflection.   Only I would still say that ecstasy is the crest of the wave.   Also, 1 am aware that this is a mystical speculation, relating solely to a heavenly state, and that as long as we continue upon earth the sense of creaturely dependence will be indispensable for our safety, and relatively to our earthly condition an essential element in our happiness. I cannot assent to Mr. Erskine's interpretations of Scripture in the passages he cites, but I am persuaded that his doctrine does not at all depend upon their correctness. On looking again at the Paper, I cannot help thinking that there has been some confusion in Mr. E.'s mind between the objective and the subjective, which is betrayed by his illustration of the branch. The creaturely relation is necessary and eternal : but the consciousness of it may be suspended or even cease altogether."

[The next four letters refer to the Pan-Anglican Conference of 1867, in which Bishop Thirlwall played an important part. He addressed a strong remonstrance to the Archbishop against the Assembly,* and his " weighty appeal " during the meeting went far to ward off mischievous action. The Conference was summoned by Archbishop Longley at the suggestion of the Canadian Church. Its " objects were undefined," but there was an understood feeling, which found vent before the proceedings were over, that the real business was to procure the formal condemnation of the Bishop of Natal. The practical outcome of the Conference was a Pastoral, signed by all the assembled prelates, and a series of thirteen resolutions. Two of these had reference to the vexed question of the Bishopric of Natal. An informal condemnation of Bishop Colenso was signed by fifty-six Bishops *after* the close of the Conference. A good account of the whole proceedings is to be found in Bishop Ewing's " Life," chap. xxviii.]

* Reprinted in the " Remains," vol. iii. p. 445.

ABERGWILI PALACE, *September 18th*, 1867.

" I expect to have the pleasure of meeting you at Fulham next week. I do not know how it is that it was so generally supposed that I had declined attending the meeting, whereas I had expressly declared my intention to attend it unless prevented by a contingency which has not occurred, and which is avowedly excluded by the programme of the proceedings ; which is so far from embodying Archdeacon Denison's views and wishes that, as you will have seen, he is getting up a protest against it. But though I think myself bound to comply with the Archbishop's summons, I go with the melancholy conviction that I shall be, in the French sense, assisting at a proceeding which can hardly fail to be either, from its nullity, ignominious or positively disastrous to the Anglican Church—as it would be if it should be found to be beyond the Archbishop's power to exclude that which Denison and many others consider as the proper business of the meeting. I read with pain the reflections of the *Times*, the *Spectator*, and the *Pall Mall Gazette* on the programme, because, as far as regards the policy of convoking such a meeting for such a purpose, they seem to me unanswerable. And one thing that strikes me as very remarkable is that, with regard to the calling of the meeting, the Archbishop appears to have relied entirely on the 'guidance of the Holy Ghost,' but referred the agenda to a committee, in which I see with surprise the names of the Bishops of London, Llandaff, Lincoln, Ely, and Chester. The responsibility incurred by those who recommended such a programme is, to my mind, awful and dreadful. My only consolation is that no one can charge me with any share of responsibility, either with regard to the holding of the meeting or the business to be transacted in it. As the time draws nearer it seems

more and more clear that it must go to wreck on one of
the alternatives which I pointed out in my letter to the
Archbishop—futility, or mischievous activity ; and I hardly
see a remark in the papers which appears to me a great
objection which I had not in substance forestalled.   How
truly should I rejoice if my forebodings should, in some
way to me utterly inconceivable, be belied by the result ?
Possibly some new light may break in upon me at Fulham
before the meeting.   It is very unfortunate that just now I
find myself suffering under one of my frequent attacks of
deafness, which, if it should last through next week, would
render the meeting to me little better than a dumb show."

To THE BISHOP OF ARGYLE AND THE ISLES.

ABERGWILI PALACE, *November 6th*, 1867.

" I enclose Mr. Erskine's letter.   The question is one
on which we must wait content with our several portions
of truth for the fuller light of a future state.

"Considering the nature of the document, I think we
were justified in signing the Lambeth Pastoral, though it
contained several expressions which were perversely ill-
chosen.   'The wrath of God' can only be understood
(consistently with our definition of his nature) as a figura-
tive expression signifying a state of relations, in which
consists all the misery of man, with whom alone the fault
rests.

" My letter to the Bishop of Cape Town was a reply to
one from him on the remarks which I made in my Charge
on his 'trial' of Bishop Colenso.*   As I find I have a
duplicate I send it by this post, though as it has nothing

* "Remains," vol. ii. p. 143.

to do with the Conference there is little to interest you
in it."

April 20th, 1868.

"I not only thank you but am very thankful for your
paper on the Encyclical—that is, not only for the present or loan, but for the contents. You have not said a
word too much in praise of the Bishop of London (Tait),
or at all exaggerated the importance of the part which he
took in the discussions at Lambeth. His position gave a
weight to his opinions which could not belong to those of
any other bishop present, and he availed himself of it
with a moral courage combined with good temper which
was truly admirable. When I consider the unspeakable
value of his services to the Church, especially at this
juncture, which is likely to become more and more
critical, I feel deep anxiety that so gracious a life may not
be endangered by excess of labour and self-sacrifice.

"Now a word on your paper. I agree with you entirely
as to the dogmatical grounds of your objection to the
phrase that 'Christ died for us to reconcile his Father to
us.' But I think you do the Encylical too much honour
when you treat it as if it was an exposition of doctrine
and not simply a pastoral exhortation, which allows and
even requires a much greater latitude of expression. The
form of the document was adapted to the purpose for
which it appears to have been framed, *i.e.* to seem to say
as much while saying as little as possible—maximum of
sound and show, with minimum of tangible substance. In
the obnoxious phrase which, no doubt, inverts the true
idea of reconciliation, I believe that the author merely
adopted the common way of speaking without reflection.

I recollect that some years ago, having in a Christmas sermon preached at Carmarthen dwelt on the love of the Father, manifested in the sending of the Son, I soon after received an anonymous letter expostulating with me on the new and shocking doctrine that I had broached. But I think it would be hard to convict the Encyclical of heresy on this ground. And that not only because the identical expression occurs in our second article, but because it seems to be fully borne out by the language of Scripture. If you do not scruple to say with St. Paul (and the Catechism) that all are by nature 'children of wrath,' that 'wrath of God' which 'cometh on the children of disobedience,' why should you hesitate to say that the work of Christ whereby we become 'children of grace' may with equal propriety be described as reconciling us to God, or to be reconciling God to us? Such language may seem to be open to the objection that it implies 'a change upon the nature of God' wrought by the work of Christ. But this is an unavoidable effect of human infirmity. We cannot conceive a transition from a state of 'wrath' to a state of 'grace' in ourselves, without a corresponding change—not, indeed, 'upon the nature,' but upon the mind of God. We are, or ought to be, aware when we use such phrases that we are speaking of God's *humanity*, and not, in logical accordance with the description of the first article, as of a Being without 'passions.' Tried by that test the Bible would be full of heresy from one end to the other. The Encyclical attributes no changeableness to God which is not implied in the words of the Baptist (John iii. 36.) It is true that St. Paul, in the same context in which he speaks of men as 'children of wrath' (Ephesians ii. 3), speaks of God as 'rich in mercy,' and as 'loving us even when we were dead in sins.' To show that not only there is no inconsistency between those seemingly contradictory statements, but that the one involves the other—love of good being inconceivable to us without hatred of evil—belongs to a sermon or a treatise not to a Pastoral, which may assume the conciliation, and use either of the scriptural phrases at pleasure. I am particularly thankful for your concluding pages on the authority of the Conference and the relative positions of the two African Bishops. I am very sorry that this was not made public.

"Nothing, I believe, can save the Irish Church as an establishment. The question *whether* it is to be 'disestablished' may be considered irrevocably decided. But the question *how* it is to be disestablished remains, and Blakesley (the Hertfordshire incumbent), in a letter to the *Times* of Wednesday, the 15th inst., has shown, I think conclusively, that it is one of enormous difficulty, unless the Irish Anglican communion is to be left in a state of hopeless anarchy, which Gladstone at least does not intend. But the knot is one which it will task his statesmanship to the utmost to untie. The excitement which prevailed in London when I left was such as I had never seen since the first Reform Act. I hope when you go to London, if not sooner, you will fall in with the 'Memoirs of Baron Bunsen,' which have just come out. I do not know whether you were at all acquainted with that admirable man. If not you cannot imagine the interest which the book has for those whose privilege it was to know him intimately, as I did, for half a century. But in much of his correspondence, especially his letters to Arnold, there is a great deal that bears on the present state of the Church and on questions of the day. We want some one like him, standing aloof from all party strife, yet with the deepest interest in the subject, and taking a comprehensive survey of the whole field and of all the movements that are taking place in it, to give us a word of timely warning and guidance."

To THE BISHOP OF ARGYLE AND THE ISLES.

April 27th, 1868.

" I am much obliged to you for the sight of Mr. Campbell's letter,* which I return. You have certainly nothing to reproach yourself with as to the signing of the Encyclical, as you were, I believe, the only Bishop who made any objection to it. On the other hand, I was one who contributed to silence your scruples, which I remember you communicated to me. I thought the phrase which offended allowable, though ill-chosen, and I am glad to find that Mr. Campbell's letter appears to confirm my opinion.

" I believe with you that the 'stream of tendency' is against the Established Churches, and will, sooner or later, sweep them all away. Whether the Church of England will gain or lose by that event must depend mainly on the constitution of the disestablished Church. But the more immediately pressing question seems to me to be whether, before it is touched from without, the Church must not fall to pieces, rent by internal divisions. This would he the worst catastrophe of all, and our 'unions' and 'associations' seem to be doing all they can to bring it about."

[On the Talmud, &c.]

To THE REV. H. D. M. SPENCE.

1, REGENT STREET, *November 25th*, 1867.

" When I received your letter I was on the point of writing to you, and on the very same topics. . . . .

" On Wednesday, the 11th of December, I have to set out for the opening of a church between Brecon and Crickhowell the following day. . . . . .

* " Present-day Papers," Third Series, " Reconciliation."

"I was going to speak about that article on the Talmud in the *Quarterly*. I brought up the fourth edition with me, and also that of Albert Réville, and yesterday read both. Do you know I was a little disappointed with the *Quarterly* Talmud? It seemed to me to be disagreeably pretentious in tone and deficient in lucidity of exposition. But the great question is, whether it does or does not convey an untrue or highly exaggerated notion of the value and character of the Talmud. I must own that I strongly suspect it does, and that, so far as it contradicts the commonly prevailing opinion of Rabbinical lore, it misleads. I suspect that the really good things in the Talmud are scattered over a mass of worthless trifling, curious, it may be, but serving no better purpose than amusement. One can easily imagine that, if this is the case, the gems would sparkle the more brightly for the rubbish in which they are embedded. It is true that in so vast a compilation you cannot safely draw any conclusion from particular examples as to the spirit and character of the whole. But it is at least an evil sign that it should be possible for any of the writers to represent the Lord as devoting a portion of each day to the study of the Law, and as refreshing himself by playing with Leviathan. This impression of mine was confirmed by the article of Albert Réville, and also by a letter of 'H. J. R.' (Rose) in the last *Guardian*. Rose has, I know, been a student of Rabbinical literature for forty or fifty years, and I believe his estimate to be the more correct. I should think it very likely that a whole encyclopedia of science might be called into play to illustrate the allusions to various branches of knowledge contained in the Talmud. But it would not follow—as the writer in the *Quarterly* seems to suppose—that those allusions add a single particle to our stock of real knowledge, oftener perhaps they may only illustrate the weakness or obliquity of the author's intellect.

"The New Testament shows how far those who in our Lord's day sat in Moses' seat had corrupted the interpretations of the Old Testament, much as the Popish doctors have that of the New. And the course of historical events after the fall of Jerusalem tended constantly to intensify all the causes of that corruption.

"Still I quite understand how desirable it must be for every Hebraist to make himself master of the key which will open the Talmud to his researches. But I do not think that any one would do wisely or rightly to devote a large portion of his time—and I suppose a whole life would hardly suffice for more than a partial acquaintance with it —to the study of the Talmud without some clearly defined practical object. I apprehend that if the Talmud is ever to be thrown open to readers who cannot consult the original text, it must be by the conjoint labours of an association formed for the purpose. But a private, desultory, rambling through the immense labyrinth, without mark or limit, would seem to me an unjustifiable waste of time and strength.

"I am not surprised that you should chafe under the necessity which confines you to what most men would consider as very ample occupation. But, my dear Spence, ought you not rather to be thankful if your power of continuous application has not been permanently impaired by immoderate exertion, and to begin to reckon and see whether the whole amount of your work is the greater or the less for your having done so much at once, instead of distributing it over a longer period? I take in no French Review but the *Deux Mondes*, and can hardly accommodate that, consequently I have no chance of seeing any other except at the Athenæum. Last night I looked there for the *Revue Nationale*, but in vain. I think you must have meant *Revue Moderne*. If not, it is curious that this seems exactly to answer to your description. There is very free speaking in the last number, particularly in an article on the 'Politique du Grand Livre.' I also observed that it seems to be an organ of Orleanist opinions. For the author of the first article is Auguste Laugel, who is somehow strangely identified with the Duc d'Aumale. The Duc (you perhaps remember) published an article on the 'Constitution of the French Army' (first in the *Revue des Deux Mondes*, then separately), under the signature of Auguste Laugel. And yet Auguste Laugel has an independent and very conspicuous existence as a scientific writer; and, moreover, was enumerated among the guests of the Duc d'Aumale who met the Prince of Wales the other day at the Duc's country seat. I have only reached the end of Vol. I. of 'Auf der Höhe,' and consequently am not yet able to judge of its merit as a whole, which will mainly depend on the third volume, in which so many German (and Danish) novelists fail after the most promising beginnings. I liked almost all very much, only toward the end of the volume I found a few chapters rather too German or subjective for my taste. But the delicate haze suffused over the whole forms a most amusing contrast to the hard, realistic Dutch painting of my other novel, in which I am still only at the third volume.

"I do not wish you to give up the study of the Law; but pray take care to have at the same time a good game of play with Leviathan."

[On the Ritual Commission.]

To THE REV. H. D. M. SPENCE.

1, REGENT STREET, *February 8th,* 1868.

". . . . My Horæ Subsecivæ here are very few and short. You do not know what a mass of reading is imposed on me as a member of the Ritual Commission. As such I receive a shorthand writer's report of every syllable that has been said in the Mackonochie case. At present, indeed, it extends to only twelve days, but perhaps you can conceive that the stream of words which may flow in that time from a set of voluble lawyers must cover a considerable volume of paper. And the privilege of receiving of course involves the duty of reading, as the subject is intimately connected with the business of the commission. The verbiage is of course oceanic, as the nonsense of the Talmud, but must be waded through, which the other happily need not. I do not, however, say that I am not a good deal amused by the forensic digladiation, and shall certainly read the judgment, which is to disentangle the truth (if there be any on either side) from the mass of sophistry, with some interest. But this, coming among so many other things, will prevent me from forming an acquaintance with Spielhagen for some time to come; and I imagine from what you said that even if ever I had an afternoon to spare—which I never have—that would not carry me a great way through him. In the short intervals which I can catch I am now reading a book which I can recommend to every lover of history, 'Lanfrey's Histoire de Napoléon I.' It is, I believe, the first trustworthy history of the man that has yet been written; and, indeed, it has only been since the publication of materials which have been brought to light within a few years that such a history could have been written, even by one whose aim was truth, and not, like Thiers, falsehood. His romance will henceforth be properly appreciated. There are at present only two 12mo vols. of Lanfrey's, going down to the Peace of Amiens. As it shivers the idol of the Invalides to pieces, it will not be without its effect on the fortunes of the dynasty. I have no doubt that the nephew would gladly have bought it up for many times as much as Thiers got for his apocryphal legend."

U

To Mrs. Thirlwall.

1, Regent Street, *February* 14*th*, 1868.

" I was very glad to receive your kind letter, which was forwarded to me from Abergwili. I left the country on the 21st of January, for the purpose of attending the meetings of the Royal Commission on Ritual, of which I am a member. It has been sitting only twice a week, on two successive days, but I could not afford to spend two of the remaining days on the road for the sake of three at home, and have therefore remained here without interruption. . . . .

" I think I did see that letter of Mr. Macrorie you speak of. He must be a man of great resolution to undertake such a charge, which I should imagine nothing but a strong sense of duty could render tolerable. Still I cannot help sharing the doubt which is felt by many as to the expediency of sending him out in such a character. The Church of Natal is certainly in a very unhappy state, but the proposed remedy may be worse than the disease. The object assigned is the removal of scandal. But I must own I see much more clearly how the scandal is likely to be increased by the spectacle of two rival Bishops, professing to belong to the same communion, than how it can be lessened by such means. That this measure will tend to heal the present breach and restore peace I have never seen pretended by any even of its warmest advocates. My fear is that it will not only inflame but perpetuate discord, and that the members of our Church in the colony may never again be united under one Bishop. This is, indeed, as you say, a very stirring time—in fact, a crisis big with change, the nature and extent of which no human mind can foresee, and in which there is certainly ground for much uneasiness. The radical measure brought in by the Conservative party, in a way which has shaken the confidence of the country in the principles of its leading public men, cannot but excite very grave apprehensions when it is considered as virtually placing the Government in the hands of the class to which the Trade Unionists belong, though it may be hoped that their detestable principles do not pervade the whole. The prospect is further clouded by Fenian conspiracy, the American grudge, the Abyssinian adventure in which we are setting elephants to hunt down a wild cat, and, closer at hand, what the *wicked* but often truth-telling *Times* calls, only too appropriately, the ' Outrage Epidemic,' in which, when Mr. Speke mysteriously disappears,* not only numbers of similar stories come to light, but it seems as if you could hardly walk about any of the less frequented parts of London without like danger. But though we cannot and ought not to shut our eyes to our real position, we must leave the event to the counsels of Providence. . . . .

" Within the last few months some of my oldest friends and schoolfellows,† but younger and seemingly stronger men than myself, have been taken away. I only wish to remain as long as I am of any use to any, and do not at all know how long that may be. . . . ."

To Mrs. Bayne.

Abergwili Palace, *June 17th*, 1868.

" . . . . You, being a thoroughbred city mouse, will smile when I talk of the gaieties of the season in the country ; but I must tell you that this week I have had, and am having, a succession of large parties of haymakers. There is only one gentleman among them, ánd he is a horse, who, when

---

* The Rev. B. Spoke's disappearance, just recently brought to mind again in consequence of his distressing death, turned out to be the result of mental aberration.

† Lord Justice Turner, &c.

they have laid all flat, goes about with a system of hay rakes behind him to toss it about and accelerate its maturity. This is the most critical and anxious time of the year for owners of meadows, but to me, when the weather is propitious, the most delightful. The present haymaking is in both respects very remarkable. We began to cut last Monday under a very gloomy sky; and as we had had some three weeks of uninterrupted fine weather, I resigned myself to what seemed the certainty that a change was at hand which would ruin my crop. Yet not a drop of rain has yet fallen, and yesterday afternoon the clouds broke again, and the evening was one of perfect beauty. The scene was one which I am sure was never surpassed at any opera : in the foreground the roses, rhododendrons, and the like, over which you look to the field spread with little haycocks (how you will laugh !), and behind the masses of foliage a verdure which I never saw richer, softer, lovelier, than this year. And this near sunset was lighted up by a parting gleam of quite magical radiance. I am serious when I assure you that I do not believe it was ever surpassed by the Bengal lights of the most splendid transformation scene, or by the stage effects in the *Huguenots* or *Faust*, or wherever else it is that Londoners see the beauties of nature in the highest perfection.

" You will no doubt have the advantage over me in hearing the *Spanish Gipsy* read by Mrs. Stirling. I have the book, and should have been in it now, if I had not postponed it to Morris's ' Earthly Paradise.' He is the author of the ' Life and Death of Jason.' That was exquisite poetry, and yet I think this is even more delicious. It comes out quite as a godsend when I can take it out on the grass and read it, while the haymakers are at work, and the dear horse pacing up and down, quite unconscious of the help he is giving. The ' Season ' is not complete without such a reading in harmony with it. I leave off while all is fair and promising. If the hay should really be got in without rain it will deserve to be kept in bottles, labelled ' Hay of 1868.' "

[On the Irish Church.]

To LORD ARTHUR HERVEY.

ABERGWILI PALACE, *June* 18*th*, 1868.

" I have to thank you for your kind present of your Charge, and I know you will not take it amiss if I make one remark on it which may not be quite in harmony with your view of the subject. I do not think you have exaggerated, or indeed easily could exaggerate, the gloomy and threatening aspect of Church matters. And I quite admit that the Church of England cannot, in her own interest, be indifferent to any danger that threatens her Irish sister. Nor can any one desire more heartily than I do to see the Irish branch of the Church able to cope successfully with the Roman adversary, and to assume an attitude of peaceful spiritual aggression. But that her present position is the most favourable to this object seems hardly to be maintained by her warmest advocates. This leads me to the remark I wish to make on the view you take of the present controversy. Whether the fact that the Irish Church has become ' the rallying cry of a party,' is due exclusively to the cause to which you ascribe it, and not in any degree to the march of events, raising all Irish questions into extraordinary prominence in the public mind on the one hand, and on the other to the incapacity of the Government to deal with them ; this is a point on which, of course, people will hold different opinions, generally according to their political bias. But it seems to me that, if the case is as you represent it, it suggests the question, how it has happened that the Irish Church *could* be used as a party rallying cry when no other institution or interest in Church or State was found available for such a purpose? Does any one believe that if the Irish Church had not existed the anomalies of the Church of England in Wales—considerable, and in one respect similar to the Irish, as they are—would have served the same purpose? Bright's speech at Liverpool shows, I think, that they neither would nor could. But if so, can it be rightly considered as merely an unlucky accident, arising out of party strife, that the Church of Ireland is now threatened? Does it not rather appear that this was the inevitable result of a precarious, because radically false, position, and that the only effect of the extraordinary conjunction of foreign and domestic politics, to which on a superficial view it might seem to be owing, has been to hasten the events by a few years? If so, is it not best to look the past in the face?"

[On the same.]

To Lord Arthur Hervey.

Abergwili Palace, *June 26th*, 1868.

" Your argument would appear to me irresistible if I could admit your premisses ; but the proof that these are in the last degree precarious and questionable, lies in the fact that they have been actually debated over and over again both in and out of Parliament. No doubt the opposition to the Irish Church includes all those who are adverse to the principle of establishment, but it does not in the least follow from that that the principle of establishment is involved in that opposition. To assert this would be to assume, in the teeth of patent facts and of your own more or less express admissions, that there is nothing peculiar in the character of the Irish Church to distinguish it from other establishments. In the presence of those admissions, the statement that 'no wrong or injustice is done to any one by the continuance of the Irish Establishment,' implies the proposition that a 'sentimental grievance' is not a real grievance, still less the worst of all grievances, but one which may be rightly and safely ignored.

" When you take the ground that 'wisdom' requires that the Irish Church should be maintained, notwithstanding its anomalous position, for the security of the English Church, you tacitly assume two things—1st. That the Irish Church is actually a bulwark and a source of strength, not a burden and a weakness, to the Church of England, and more particularly that its continuance places the Liberation Society under a disadvantage in their appeals to public feelings, a proposition which seems to me paradoxical; and 2nd. That Ireland may be 'wisely' treated, like the Papal territory, as existing only for the sake of England, and its ecclesiastical Establishment for the sake of a kindred English institution. What is this but to say that Ireland shall to the end of time be governed by the bayonet? I do not say it is impossible that such may be the case whatever we do; but no statesman capable of grasping the importance of the subject as an Imperial question would feel himself at liberty to act on such a supposition. Among all the topics which have been urged on the Conservative side none surprise me more than that of the alleged 'suddenness of conviction' as to the disestablishment of the Irish Church in the leader of the Opposition and his followers. It is so directly opposed to all my recollections, and to what I had imagined to be the most patent and notorious facts in recent history. I cannot recollect the time when there were two opinions among Liberal politicians as to the Irish Church. I do not know of any conviction that more generally pervaded the public mind, before the opening of the present session, than that the state of Ireland would and must occupy the attention of Parliament above, if not to the exclusion of, every other question. The disclosure of the policy which the Government meant to adopt was looked for with the most anxious expectation. It turned out—as no doubt might have been foreseen—to be that of the man of phrases, utterly null. The Opposition took the place which the Government had abandoned, in the consciousness of its incapacity, intellectual as well as political, to deal with the Irish difficulty. That it should be taunted with the 'suddenness of its convictions' appears to me astonishing. But if the taunt was as just as it appears to me unfounded, it would be totally irrelevant—an *argumentum ad hominem*, not *ad rem*. That party feeling should have had no influence in this case would indeed be a marvellous exception to universal experience; but the fact cannot in the least affect the merits of this question, any more than of the others in which this element entered as largely, without being ever supposed to exclude the operation of great principles. This is an *argumentum ad hominem* with two edges. No doubt the fate of the Established Church of England depends on the prevailing disposition of Parliament, and they again on the prevailing disposition of the public mind. But whenever it falls, its fall will not be owing to a mere party combination in Parliament, but to the prevalence of hostile views out of doors. That the hostility will be stronger and more dangerous if the Irish Church should be (in some sense or other, for in what I do not pretend to know) disestablished, seems to me, as I have said, a simple paradox. But if the fact were so, it would be beside the question."

[On the same.]

To MRS. THIRLWALL.

ABERGWILI PALACE, *February 15th*, 1869.

"I am much obliged to you for your kind remembrances of my birthday, not at all the less because the completion of another long step down the vale of years does not appear to me exactly a subject of congratulation, though I feel how much reason I have to be deeply thankful for having been preserved in tolerable health and strength to such an age. The affairs of the Irish Church and of our own occupy much of my thoughts, but have not yet begun to break my rest or injure my health. You are undoubtedly right in your opinion that the greatest danger of our Church lies in her internal divisions. The case of Ireland is so entirely different from that of England that the disestablishment of the Irish Church would not of itself any way alter our position. It has never been to us a source of strength, but much rather a burden and a weakness, and I think it quite possible that both may thrive the better for the political severance. Nevertheless, it is not without reason that so many of our bishops and clergy anticipate alarming consequences to the English Establishment from the fall of the Irish. When the disestablishment is advocated on the broad ground of 'religious equality,' those who take that ground can hardly refuse to apply it to both Churches alike, and whatever is done in Ireland may serve as guidance in dealing with the same question in England. But yet if the Church was only compact and firmly united in itself, I believe that it would be long able to resist any assault from without. As it is, we have the hitherto unheard-of fact, that a considerable party among our own clergy are more or less openly desirous of a separation between Church and State. . . . ."

[The following six letters deal with questions of criticism connected with the view of a Future Life in the Old Testament * :—]

To THE REV. J. J. STEWART PEROWNE.

ABERGWILI PALACE, *September 24th*, 1868.

" The consensus of critics ancient and modern against the genuineness of Od. Λ 567—626 (for which see Porson's note on the Orestes, ver. 5), seems to me (who am decidedly on the same side) irresistible. Otherwise I should attach little weight to the arguments you cite from B. Thiersch—I suppose from his work, 'Die Urgestalt der Odysee,' which I am afraid I do not possess, as I can only find one entitled, 'Ueber das Zeitalter und Vaterland des Homer,' in which he refers to his earlier work. But even if the question was quite open to doubt, it seems clear that no otherwise disputable conclusion could be safely drawn from the passage. It is not surprising that you should not have gained a clear view of the Homeric Νεκυία if the poet himself had none, and this is the opinion of many eminent critics. Nägelsbach ('Die Homerische Theologie') believes that Völcker has made it certain that the poet places Hades now above ground, now under ground. I think you would find this work of Nägelsbach interesting, especially the last section, 'Das Leben und der Tod.'

" But I do not see that the question of retribution after death depends on the passage of the Odyssey. In the Iliad there are two passages incidentally referred to by Nägelsbach which seem to contain a most unequivocal statement of the doctrine. In the one (Γ 7, 8) there is an invocation of some unnamed Powers who—

ὑπένερθε καμόντας
ἀνθρώπους τίνυσθον, ὅτις κ' ἐπιώρκον ὀμόσσῃ

<hr>

* [These letters have reference to my Hulsean Lectures on "Immortality," which I was at this time preparing for the press, and which were afterwards published with a dedication to the Bishop.—J. J. S. P.]

and at T 259 this office is specially assigned to the

’Ερινύες, αἴθ’ ὑπὸ γαῖαν
ἀνθρώπους τίνυνται   (and O 204)

With regard to the passage in Job, I have long been convinced that it does not relate to a resurrection or a future state, and that every expression may be satisfactorily explained from the close of the story."

To THE REV. J. J. STEWART PEROWNE.
ABERGWILI PALACE, *October 26th*, 1868.

" It is so long since I have read any of Nitzsch's sermons that I cannot say with any confidence whether they do or do not contain anything on the subject of a future state. I recollect nothing whatever relating to it. But the last portion of his ' System der Christlichen Lehre,' ' Von der Vollendung des Heils,' treats of it *ex professo*. From your inquiry about the sermons, I gather that you have not this work. If you would like to see it I could send it you. . . . . You recollect, no doubt, how remarkably J. H. Fichte's theory about the ' Naturvölker' is confirmed by Sir S. Baker's report of his conversation with that African king, whose name I cannot remember.

" I quite agree with you that *dédain* is a completely ill-chosen term for the feeling with which Socrates appears to have regarded the mythical envelopes of truths which he heartily embraced in their substance."

To THE REV. J. J. STEWART PEROWNE.
1, REGENT STREET, *February 9th*, 1869.

" I return the proofs of your Lectures by book-post, with many thanks for the pleasure which I have enjoyed in the perusal. The interest is not only sustained, but grows as they proceed. I was particularly struck by the new ground which you lay for the belief in a resurrection among the Jews which seems to me beautifully worked out. But does it apply to the mass, or only to the *élite* of the nation ?

"There still remains in my mind a difficulty as to the reticence of the revelation given to Moses. Your two remarks on the possible purpose of such a Divine reticence are very just and true. But in what sense can it be said that there *was* such a reticence, if, as you show to have been the fact, the doctrine was known to Moses ? Had he not the strongest motives for communicating it to the people, whom he found it so difficult to restrain by the fear of temporal judgments ? And can we conceive that while he was permitted and enjoined to hold out this motive, he was commanded to abstain from enforcing it by the great truth of future retribution ? "

To THE REV. J. J. STEWART PEROWNE.

1, REGENT STREET, *March* 15*th*, 1869.

" Having heard that some of your Cambridge hearers took offence at your treatment of the passage in Job (xix. 25), I think you will be glad to hear what I am going to say. Yesterday afternoon I had the pleasure of hearing the Bishop of Peterborough preach a magnificent sermon to an immense congregation at Whitehall Chapel on Job xix. 25, foll. He began with a lucid exposition of the opposite principles of interpretation of prophecy adopted by what I will call the narrow and the broad school, and then proceeded to show how these principles are applied by each to his text. He then dwelt for some time and with much pathos on the apparent sanction given to the literal interpretation by the use which the Church makes of the passage in the Burial Service. But he laid it down, not as a doubtful opinion, but as something quite clear and certain, that the letter of the words *could not* refer to Job's *resurrection*, but only to his *recovery*. He then entered on an analysis of the *drama*, for the purpose of showing that, as a whole, it contained the germ of the doctrine which was erroneously supposed to lie in the letter, that the righteous sufferer of the Old Testament was a type of the still holier and more deeply afflicted Son of Man in the New; and that all truly Christian sorrow might take to itself the like consolation in the assurrance—' I know that my Redeemer liveth.' All this was brought out in a strain of the highest eloquence. Unhappily the Bishop never writes his sermons, so that unless there was a shorthand writer in the crowd this splendid discourse will have been lost like so many scores of others."

To THE REV. J. J. STEWART PEROWNE.

1, REGENT STREET, *March* 18*th*, 1869.

" I found the Bishop of Peterborough in the House of Lords on Monday, and pressed him so strongly to publish his sermon that I have great hope of seeing it in print.* He would have to write it out from memory, but sometimes does so. He expressed surprise at hearing that the view he took could give offence to any one, and seemed to think that it was the common one, at least among educated men."

---

* The sermon was never printed.

To THE REV. CANON PEROWNE.

ABERGWILI PALACE, *August 1st*, 1870.

"I can but count it an honour, of which I am scarcely worthy, that my name should appear in your pages.*

"I had thought of asking you a question connected with the same subject, and though it may be too late for any practical purpose, I will avail myself of this occasion to do so. I have been a little surprised that so many critics, whose opinion you have adopted, should have found no difficulty in making כָּבוֹד = soul, in Psalm lvii. 7, and elsewhere; and should not have thought it worth while to enter into any explanation of what seems to me so singular an expression. To me this interpretation seems open to two objections: 1. That the Psalmist is made to claim as *his* peculiar *glory* that which he has in common with all mankind; and 2. That the name of *glory* is applied, not, as I believe in all other cases, to an outward manifestation, but to that which is innermost in man. I should myself prefer the interpretation *tongue*, provided this is taken in the largest sense, as including the gift of music and poetry, which was indeed the glory of the sweet singer of Israel. But it may be that I have overlooked some simple solution of the apparent difficulty.†

"I am really glad that the Company adopted 'waste and void.' It gives me some hope about a similar change which I shall venture to propose in [Genesis] iv. 12—14."

---

* In reference to the Dedication.

[† In reply to this, I pointed out that in other passages, *e.g.* Gen. xlix. 6, Ps. vii. 5, "glory" (E. V. "honour") was used in parallelism with "soul" or "life;" and the Bishop expressed himself as satisfied with the explanation. —J. J. S. P.]

CHAPTER IX.

ST. DAVID'S, 1869—1874.

Æschylus—Reminiscences of Rome—Rev. C. Voysey—Bishop Ewing's
"Present-Day Papers"—Revelation—Atonement—The Rule of Faith—
Bishop Thirlwall and "Favourite Texts"—The Elementary Educa-
tion Act—St. David's Cathedral—Abraham's Sacrifice—The Franco-
German War—Bishop Thirlwall and the Old Testament Revision Com-
pany—Bishop Thirlwall and Bishop Wilberforce on the Athanasian
Creed—Lampeter—The Welsh Church—Day of Intercession for Mis-
sions—Adult Baptism—Bishop Thirlwall and the Rev. Malcolm MacColl
—Early Liturgies—The Laying on of Hands—Revision Work—Death
of Bishop Wilberforce—Feast of Epiphany—Confession and Absolution
—Thirlwall's Generosity.

To THE REV. E. H. PLUMPTRE.

[On his translation of Æschylus.]

ABERGWILI PALACE, *January 6th*, 1869.

"Your kind present reached me two or three days ago,
but I deferred thanking you for it till I had looked into it
a little. I have now done so sufficiently to appreciate in
some degree the skill and success with which you have
encountered the enormous difficulties of the undertaking,
conceived as you have conceived it, and the ease and freedom with which your translation moves under the conditions which you have imposed upon it. I may congratulate you on having rendered a great service both to
English and to Greek literature. I do not indeed
imagine that the number of English readers to whom the
original is a sealed book, but who are capable of enjoying
the translation, is or ever will be very great—what proportion of the 'reading public' reads Shakespere, or any

of our old dramatists ?—but they are the minds which best deserve to be cultivated and enlarged by the highest kind of intellectual enjoyment.

"I also believe that your translation will do much to foster and refine a taste for Greek literature in students who have access to the original texts. And this is now a thing of very great importance. While I agree with Mr. Farrar as to the desirableness of saving that vast amount of time which is now wasted in so many schools on a rudimental study of Greek which is never turned to any profitable account, I am the more anxious that the taste for the great masterpieces of Greek literature, which has hitherto distinguished our educated classes, should not be suffered to die, but be more and more carefully matured, and I am persuaded that one who is already familiar with Æschylus will find his enjoyment of the original very much heightened by a comparison with your translation. The best, indeed, can be no more than an approximation ; but the distance which separates it from the original is just that which makes it most instructive."

To ARCHDEACON CLARK.[*]

1, REGENT STREET, *February* 10*th*, 1869.

"If it had so happened that, instead of being a venerable Archdeacon, you had been a Thessalian witch, you might have been suspected of some magical incantation by which you had charmed away our English winter climate, and sent us that of Rome in its place. While you have been shivering under all your wrappings, indoors and out of doors, I have been sitting for hours with window open, and letting the fire go out without missing it. If I was a botanist I would fill a page with a list of the spring

* Late Archdeacon of St. David's, and Examining Chaplain to the Bishop.

flowers that have been seen in fields and gardens during the last two months. But I will content myself with one solid fact of my own experience. I was staying lately at the Deanery, Canterbury, on the occasion of the Archbishop's enthronement. As I came down-stairs in the morning, I observed a fig-tree growing on the wall in a pretty advanced state of fruitage. When I made the remark to Mrs. Alford, she told me that they had already (in January) eaten of the fruit of their fig-tree. Can Sorrento beat that? But then you must know that in the first week of this month the thermometer stood at 71 out of doors—a thing, it is believed, absolutely without any recorded parallel. And this has continued ever since you went away. On the other hand, we have had extraordinary torrents of rain and floods, and the frequency and violence of the gales (once, I think, generally attributed to witchcraft) has been such as no one remembers.

" Yet I would willingly have braved the rigour of a Roman winter, if I could have exchanged the sight as well as the climate of London for that of Rome. What would I not give for even a three days' ramble over my old haunts! I am very much obliged to you for your kind offer, especially of photographs. I have seen those fine views of the Forum. But they would be more of a luxury than I can afford, because, though foremost in beauty, they are more deeply impressed on my memory than any scenes in Rome. But there are others which, if they are to be had at a not extravagant cost, I should be very glad to possess—views of spots which have begun to fade in my recollection, and of which I should like to recover the details. Such are the Termini, the Aventine, Monte Cavallo, the Baths of Caracalla, the crypt of S. Clemente, the road at the western foot of the Palatine, between the Baths and the Forum Boarium. If there are photographs on a small scale of these or any other scenes of like interest

x

—which I would leave to your judgment—I do not know anything that I should value more as a memento of Rome. I believe the Piazza del Popolo has been entirely altered since I saw it, by a scala leading up to the Pincio—that would interest me much, also the Villa Borghese. I am more curious about the business of the expected Council than about the prospects of the temporal power, as its fall seems to me more likely to strengthen than to weaken the Papacy, and to deteriorate than to improve its spirit. I cannot make out whether its objects are yet definitively fixed. If so, one would have thought they must have transpired. We hear talk in several quarters about the Council effecting the reunion of Christendom. Could any one have ventured to talk about that if he was aware that the subjects of deliberation were to be such as the Assumption of the Virgin !

" Our own ecclesiastical affairs are in a very perplexed state. Still, I believe that the decision of the Privy Council in the Mackonochie case has given very general satisfaction to all but the Ritualists. They are endeavouring to console themselves, partly by abuse of the court, and especially of Lord Cairns, and partly by putting constructions on the judgment, as to points which were not in question, by which they hope to embitter it to their opponents. On the other hand, the prosecuting Association is going, as it is said, to beg the question of vestments, and a passage in the judgment leads me to believe that they will be successful. The doctrinal question itself is to be tried with Mr. Bennett, who has been, I think, the most audacious in his utterances, which would nearly satisfy Manning. Mackonochie has lost himself, even with many of his own party, by the extreme silliness and intemperance of his language. He has become an uncompromising Liberationist, and urges his injured and oppressed brethren to agitate for separation between Church and State. But none seem prepared to respond to his appeal. Denison himself counsels moderation and obedience ; and nobody seems to understand why Mackonochie does not set the example of liberating himself from State bondage. . . . ."

To the Rev. C. Voysey.

Abergwili Palace, *March 22nd*, 1869.

" Your letter was brought to me from the House of Lords just as I was on the point of leaving town.   I have always been decidedly opposed to any attempt to narrow the freedom which the law allows to every clergy-man of the Church of England in the expression of his opinion on theological subjects.*   And it may be that, if I permitted my name to be placed on your Defence Committee, I should in fact and in the way of logical inference be only making a practical avowal of that opposition.   But the inevitable effect would be to ' compromise ' me most deeply, and to impress ninety-nine out of every hundred of my clergy with the conviction that I shared your opinions.   What they are at present I do not know, and am unable to form a judgment whether, in the writings which have given occasion to proceedings being instituted against you, you have confined yourself to a ' reverent discussion of religious topics.'   The clergy who urged the Archbishop of York to institute those proceedings do not seem to have been of that opinion.

" My position is entirely different from that of Bishop Hinds, much more from that of the laymen you mention ; and it seems to me to render it my duty to avoid giving a needless and violent shock to the feelings of those who are placed under me."

* See p. 234.

x 2

[The next three letters are on the subject of the "Present-Day Papers." They were a series of essays "on Prominent Questions in Theology" by various writers, edited by Bishop Ewing.]

To the Bishop of Argyle and the Isles.

ABERGWILI PALACE, *December 3rd*, 1869.

" Until I received your letter I had neither seen nor heard anything of your 'Present-Day Papers,' which I have read with much interest. I cannot say that the prospectus enables me to form a very clear idea of their prime object, and I am afraid you will think me captious ; but I am not quite satisfied with your remarks on Revelation.* They appear to me to be only partially just, and that not exactly in the sense required by your argument. It seems to me an arbitrary assumption to describe revelation as a 'giving of light,' for the purpose of showing that it is erroneously regarded as 'a mystery,' and equally so to say, as you do farther on, that it is '*the making manifest* by the admission of light.' I cannot help thinking that the proper sense of the word suggests the possibility of the thing being quite consistent with mystery—of a revelation which is the revelation without being the elucidation of a mystery. Fancy a theatre in which a curtain intercepts the view of the stage. When the curtain rises the spectators may see something which they could not see before ; but whether they will see it clearly or dimly must depend on the design of the dramatist, which may require that the background be kept dark or seen as through a haze. The revealing only amounts to the withdrawing of one obstacle to sight, it does not imply the opening of a

* See the Preface to the First Series of " Present-Day Papers."

perfect vision. It seems to me that this is not an inapt illustration of the actual state of the case. If there had been no revelation we should have seen nothing of that which is behind the veil. As it is, we see but ' through a glass darkly.'

" It is true that by a process of abstraction we may confine our view to a few objects in the foreground which we see most clearly, and may say that as to them, and when they are taken as the whole, the revelation is complete. But I am not at all sure that this is your meaning, nor that I understand in what sense the Christian revelation is, or was ever meant to be, 'a key to the difficulties of Nature.' I gather from some allusions in your ' Paper ' that the periodical is directed mainly against Romanism, or, more generally, the sacramental system on the one hand and against Calvinism on the other, and I am confirmed in the supposition by your letter of last week to the *Guardian*. But I doubt whether this will be clear to all readers. Is not this letter itself an illustration of my position, that there may be a revelation which does not manifest the thing revealed ? Before the revelation brought by your letter I was entirely ignorant of your undertaking. But how far is it from being manifest to me now ! No doubt, when I see the numbers which have been published, I shall understand it better ; but I do not venture to pledge myself to take any part in such undertaking. There seem to be now hopes that the excellent Archbishop's life may be spared for some years to come ;* but whether he will ever be able safely to resume episcopal work seems to be much more doubtful. It is grievous to think of such a man being laid aside as 'a broken vessel ' in the prime of his intellectual vigour."

* Alluding to the serious illness of Archbishop Tait in 1869.

To THE BISHOP OF ARGYLE AND THE ISLES.

January 27th, 1870.

"I have to thank you for another number of the 'Present-Day Papers,' which I have read with great interest, as well as that on the Atonement. The second on the Eucharist, which I understood you also intended for me, has not yet reached me. All that you write has a stamp of freshness and spontaneity, which makes it interesting and profitable to me, even when I am not quite sure that I clearly understand your meaning, or am unable to adopt your conclusions; and this is the case with both of these papers. The subject of each is, as Mr. Campbell observes, 'high and difficult,' one on which none of us probably sees more than a part of the truth, at least, at the same time. I think that Law saw a part, and a fundamental part, of the truth. But I find in his essay things very hard of digestion, and which I cannot reconcile either with the language of our Church or with that of Scripture in its plainest sense. It seems to me that he attaches an arbitrary meaning to the words *atone* and *atonement*, and reasons upon that which is arbitrary in that meaning. His statement as to 'the very nature of atonement' as 'implying the alteration or removal of something that is not as it ought to be,' does not appear to me to be justified either by etymology or usage. I believe the derivation from *at one*—which delighted Coleridge—to be quite erroneous. It is the German *sühnen*, to *appease* or *propitiate*. But at all events it is our translation of the Hebrew *caphar*, *cophar*, *hide*, *hiding*, and so when applied to sin, *forgive*, *forgiveness*, as when God 'casts sins behind his back,' or 'into the depths of the sea.' This, however, may be no more than a verbal objection. Every one has a right to use words as he will, so longs as he explains the sense he adopts. But the peculiarity which seems to me to pervade Law's essay is, that his scheme effaces all distinction between justification and sanctification. It represents Christ's sufferings as merely exemplary. It virtually denies that He was 'given to be unto us *both* a sacrifice for sin and *also* an ensample of godly life,' inasmuch as it was only by the ensample of godly life that He could properly be said to be a sacrifice for sin. If all that was meant was, that our sanctification is the supreme object of the whole process of redemption, and thus pre-eminently 'the will of God,' I believe that this is a point as to which all theological systems, however widely diverging from one another as to the means, will be found in substance to agree.

"I am very thankful for the extract from Mr. Erskine's work, which seems to me beautifully clear and perfectly true. Only one can hardly help asking how many Christians have so much as an idea of this truth, and of those who have it, how many are thereby brought the nearer to realising it in their inward experience. But the general impression left on my mind by your remarks on the Rule of Faith is, that they do not discriminate between the case of churches and that of individuals. In a mystical sense, which each Christian must find for himself, it may be said that Christ is the Rule of Faith. But I do not see how He can be said to be such a rule in the sense of a common intellectual basis for a society or church, unless something be predicated of Him which would be a Confession of Faith. Confessions of Faith may often be evils, but they are necessary evils, wherever two or three come together as a church and have to answer the question, 'What are you? What do you hold in common?' It could hardly be sufficient in answer to say, 'We hold Christ as our Rule of Faith,' when all those from whom they are separated say the same, though for each of the two or three, individually, and in their closets, that might be quite enough.

"Many will be startled by your remarks on the hopefulness of our present prospects. I was glad to see them, having long been of opinion that there is a much greater amount of what may be called 'latent Christianity' among persons who pass for irreligious than the dogmatical theologians can conceive.

"I am not aware that the object for which the Roman Council was assembled has ever yet been authoritatively declared. Dupanloup, before he went to Rome, believed that it was to be a cure for Atheism. A friend of mine who was there wrote to me that he did not think the Pope had any special purpose, but expected that it would be the occasion of some miraculous intervention. It seems to me simply an attempt to galvanize the Papacy into a ghastly semblance of life. And yet I see Dr. Pusey is bringing out a new book on *healthy* union with Rome! A Mezentian operation I think."

1, REGENT STREET, *February* 18*th*, 1870.

"I have again to thank you for a Present-Day Paper on a very present and interesting subject.

"I believe that there is a very respectable amount of Biblical scholarship in the Church, but it is not equally diffused, and the Bishops have not always the lion's share. By this time you will have seen that your grief or alarm about the Bishop of Exeter's 'defection' was premature, and that he stands in his original position toward Dr. Pusey and Bishop Trower, which will probably reconcile you to him. If he made any concession in fact, he certainly neutralised its conciliatory effect by his speech in

Convocation.   All that is not quite satisfactory is, that it seems as if the speech would never have been made if the fact had not been prematurely announced.   But after all this is not absolutely certain.   And it may be that he always intended to make some declaration to the same effect."

[The next series of nine letters refer to the discussion raised by the reference of the Bishop to Haggai ii. 7 and Jeremiah xxiii. 6 in his Convocation Speech on the Revision of the Bible.   His speech and letters to the *Rock* are reprinted in the " Remains," vol. iii. Appendix.]

To THE REV. E. H. PLUMPTRE.

ABERGWILI PALACE, *March 8th*, 1870.

" On my return home a few days ago I found your ' Biblical Studies,' which I am very glad indeed to possess, and for which I beg you to accept my best thanks.

" They remind me that there is a little thing which you could do for me, probably both better and with less trouble to yourself than anybody else.   You have no doubt observed the outcry I have raised by the words I dropped in Convocation about ' favourite texts,' and still more by the two examples I gave in illustration of my meaning.   While I was in London I received a letter on the subject from a Yorkshire clergyman, named Fausset, who it appears is, in conjunction with two Scotch divines, the author of a ' Critical and Experimental Commentary on the Bible,' in defence of the received version of Haggai ii. 7 and Jeremiah xxiii. 6.   I intended to answer it on return to my books, but shortly after my return received a copy of a newspaper called the *Rock*, of Tuesday, March 1, in which I found his letter published.   It then seemed to me necessary

that I should reply to it in the same paper, though one of
the last I should otherwise have chosen for such a discussion.   I have, however, written on the subject of Haggai,
and expect that my letter will appear on Friday next (the
Rock is only published on Tuesdays and Fridays).   I shall
follow it up when I can find time—this being my ordination week—with one on the passage of Jeremiah.   But I
should be glad to have an audience outside the circle of
the *Rock*, and it occurred to me that you might find room
in some corner of the *Contemporary* for drawing attention
to the subject. . . . . ."

To Rev. A. R. Fausset.

March 5th, 1870.

". . . . I hope you will not think me uncourteous if I
say that in my opinion your argument on the passage of
Haggai sufficiently answers itself.   I do not understand
you to attempt anything more than to show that the interpretation for which you contend is grammatically possible.
That would not be much, even if you had been successful,
because, though grammatically possible, it might be utterly
untenable.   But I believe that you have failed in that
attempt, and that if the grounds on which you maintain
the grammatical paradox were submitted to a jury of competent Biblical scholars, though they are probably the best
that can be produced, they would be pronounced quite
inadequate to the purpose.   And I more than suspect that
such an interpretation would never have commended itself
to your judgment if you had not believed that what seems
to you revealed truth is at stake, and that the interpretation which you reject is 'anti-messianic.'   The point as to
which I should have felt most sanguine would have been
differently interpreted by eminent scholars, and this I think

would with judicious men be a reason for preferring some other for the pulpit."

To Rev. A. R. Fausset.

March 25th, 1870.

" I am much obliged to you for the information you have kindly given me, and shall be very glad to see what you and Dr. Pusey have written on the subject of my letter to the *Rock.* But as I do not take in either that or the *Record,* I should esteem it a favour if you would let me know the date of the impression of each at which your letter has appeared. Of course, if my letter has only had the effect of strengthening your conviction of the correctness of the opposite view, though I should still be curious to see how it produced this effect, there can be little prospect of any benefit resulting from any further discussion between us. But your reference to 'grammar,' 'the general analogy of Scripture,' and 'the voice of the Hebrew Church,' leads me to suspect that I may find the discussion transferred to a different ground—one of subjective feeling and self-constituted authority, on which every opinion is impregnable. When I consider of what absurdity the Rabbis have shown themselves capable, I am surprised at the weight attributed to their authority. That of Dr. Pusey I quite admit, but with a distinction. I have a high opinion of his learning as a Hebrew scholar, and am fully conscious of my own inferiority in that respect ; but I do not believe him to be open to conviction on any point in the remotest degree connected with dogma on which he has once made up his mind.

" When I wrote my letter I was not aware that Professor Plumptre had expressed the same opinion in a Paper which first appeared in a Scotch magazine, and which he has now republished in his 'Biblical Studies.' I consider his authority on this point as far higher than Dr. Pusey's, because he abandons the Authorised Version with a reluctance which would incline him to do the fullest justice to every argument that can be urged in its favour."

To Rev. A. R. Fausset.

March 31st, 1870.

" I have written to the *Rock* in answer to your letter containing Dr. Pusey's opinion, and I expect that my letter will appear there to-morrow. I am sorry that I did not before understand that Dr. Pusey's 'full letter' included other passages. I hope I may now infer that your extracts contain all that related to that of Haggai. With regard to that, Dr. Pusey's remarks have a little. lowered my estimate of his Hebrew scholarship, which was high, and has not raised my estimate of his judgment, which was low.

" I can only give a qualified assent to your general remarks. It seems to me that the first duty of a pious searcher of the Scriptures is to seek the truth. He will no doubt be glad to find as much as he can. That condition would prevent him from adopting an interpretation which would violate the laws of grammar, as Bellarmine, for the sake of the dogma, would have translated ' a smitten God,' instead of ' smitten of God,' in Isaiah liii. v. 4. But grammatical possibility, though an absolute *sine quâ non*, is not the only condition of a sound interpretation. In a question between two renderings there are various other considerations which *ought* to decide, if the object in view is truth, and not merely the gratification of a pious wish, however natural and praiseworthy in itself."

To Rev. A. R. Fausset.

April 13*th*, 1870.

" . . . . The ' note ' which you have transcribed appears to me a very striking example of that mode of dealing with Scripture on which I animadverted in my last letter, a mode unsound in principle, most dangerous in its consequences, one which opens the door to every kind of fanatical delusion, and tends to justify the language of Romish controversialists when they liken Scripture, in Protestant hands, to a nose of wax.

" ' The objects of desire of all nations cannot mean their gold and silver.'

" Why so ?   Not because the prophet's words suggest any other meaning, but simply because Henderson cannot make this fit into his scheme of expounding the fulfilment of the prophecy.

" And when I come to inquire into the nature of the difficulty which has led him to take this most unwarrantable liberty with the language of the Bible, I find that it depends on two assumptions, one clearly false, the other, to say the least, merely arbitrary.   His objection to taking the silver and gold for silver and gold rests upon the tacit assumption that a spiritual glory and a material glory are things which exclude one another and can only exist apart. For otherwise his remark (which I am afraid I saw reproduced in one of your letters) about ' parturient mountains ' would be both silly and profane, as if the *conversion of the nations*, manifested by their willingness to dedicate their treasures to the service of God, was, instead of being the great end of the whole dispensation, a ' ridiculously ' paltry object !

" How it is that you can ' heartily agree ' with this view, after having described the ultimate fulfilment of the prophecy to be, ' Then shall the nations bring those precious offerings which now ye so much miss,' I do not understand.

"The other assumption is, that the received version of Haggai ii. 9 is unquestionably correct. It would be nearer the truth to say that it is demonstrably incorrect, and that the LXX. gives the true sense. There is no question about a first and second *house*, but about a former and a latter *glory*. If the prophet is allowed to be his own interpreter, which seems not more than reasonable, he has decided the question at verse 3, 'Who is left among you that saw this house in her first glory?' . . . .

"I had always considered the current explanation of ' the desire of all nations '—in the sense of the *undesired need*, or the object of *an inarticulate, unconscious craving* —as, irrespectively of grammatical considerations, so improbable, that it could be hardly allowable to propose or accept it without a specific Divine revelation ; but your notion of manifold, rational cravings of the soul carries the license of fancy many degrees farther into a region of subjective feeling and speculation, beyond the sphere of rational discussion, into which I shall not attempt to follow you."

To REV. A. R. FAUSSET.

April 19*th*, 1870.

"I certainly am responsible for the opinion that the willingness of the nations to dedicate their treasures to God must be the result of their conversion ; but how that opinion pledges me to any *system* I am at a loss to understand, and you have not attempted to point out. I had supposed that it was a self-evident truth, universally admitted, perfectly independent of any question about the fulfilment of prophecy, and one that can only be disputed on

the assumption that men may act without motives, and
that a great change in their conduct, one involving
the sacrifice of their most valued possessions, may take
place without any previous change in their views and
feelings. I did not believe that Mr. Henderson, and still
less that you, meant to maintain such a paradox; but I
thought he must have overlooked that necessary implication, as I could discover no other explanation of the contempt with which he spoke of the Gentile offerings, the
result and manifestation of that conversion. But I did not
mean to charge him, and still less you, with intentional
profaneness or designed depreciation of the blessing. I
cannot, however, honestly give you the credit which you
seem to claim for the comprehensiveness of your views.
It seems to me, on the contrary, as I remarked in my
answer to your first letter, that you have throughout limited
your view to one side of the question. You have contented
yourself with an attempt—as it appears to me an unsuc-
cessful one—to extenuate the difficulty of the interpretation
you adopt, but you have ignored the fact that in that
which you reject there is no difficulty at all. You have
hitherto been unable to lay your finger on any weak place.
It seems, indeed, that you think that it is inconsistent
with your interpretation of a passage in the New Testament. But it will be time enough to consider that argument when your interpretation is universally admitted. I
am sorry that you have not thought it worth while to
explain it. I have read Hebrews xii. 24—28 several
times over, and am obliged to own that I cannot guess in
what way it is that you suppose it to bear on the question
between us. The attempts which you make in your last
letter to strengthen your position seem to me singularly
unfortunate. . . . . .

"In what sense you consider '*chochmah*' as a '*col-
lective* embodiment of wisdom' you leave me to guess.

The alleged analogy would seem to require that the heavenly wisdom should be conceived as made up of wise sayings. But that is an idea which I would not attribute to you on any authority but your own. I observed some time back that you appeared to me enormously to underrate the grammatical difficulty which others had felt to be insuperable. . . . .

"These laborious endeavours to get rid of the difficulty do but attest its continued presence; and the preference of an interpretation which labours under so many objections—obscurity, ambiguity, incoherency with the plain drift of the context, and grammatical (let us only say) anomaly, to one which is perfectly clear, simple, and consistent, as well as free from all grammatical objection—appears to me at variance with the principles of sober criticism. But it is a great comfort to me to find that after all there is no practical difference between us. I only plead for the interpretation, ' the desirable things of all nations,' which I am glad to see you adopt. I do not wish to prevent any one who feels himself edified by the thought, from considering this as a description of the Messiah, though I cannot do so myself. Least of all could I permit myself to doubt the sincerity of your conviction, and that you ' think it rests on solid objective' ground. That of course does not make it the less a mere private subjective opinion."

To REV. A. R. FAUSSET.

April 28*th*, 1870.

"I have received the three additional copies of your excellent work on the Prayer Book.

"As you may not see the *Rock* regularly, I take the liberty of mentioning that the number of Tuesday, the 19th, contains an interesting letter from Mr Wilkinson, of Derby, on the text of Haggai, on which I made some remarks which appeared the Friday following, the 22nd inst.

" I cannot help thinking that you have not made good your right to assume that 'the question in Haggai was as to the glory of the second Temple.' That assumption rests not on the Hebrew text, but on what appears to me an evident mistranslation.

"You have, as far as I know, nowhere explained your view of the fulfilment of the prophecy in the ' shaking of the nations' during the period of the Second Temple. I am not aware that history records any ' shaking ' so great and general as that which preceded and caused the fall of the Roman Empire, and which was attended by consequences so beneficial to the Church.

" It seems to me that there is a confusion of ideas at the bottom of the opinion which regards the prediction as to the future glory of Zerubbabel's Temple as fulfilled by our Lord's coming. No doubt, as a glorious person, He may be said to have diffused a glory around Him wherever He was, and therefore while He taught in the Temple, no less than in the cottage at Nazareth. But when I consider that the object of His coming was so far from being that of adding anything to the glory of the Temple, that it was rather to abolish its spiritual privileges, and to proclaim and (indirectly) to effect its destruction, I cannot conceive any interpretation of the prophecy more at variance with the facts of history."

To REV. A. R. FAUSSET.

May 7th, 1870.

" I only hope that you will not forget that there is a sense in which I have not denied that the Temple was glorified by our Lord's presence as that of a supremely glorious person, who, wherever He was, spread a glory around Him of power, wisdom, or love, of a different kind from those which He wrought in many synagogues and other places.   What was peculiar in his dealings with the Temple was that He declared it to have been made ' a den of thieves,' and announced (John iv. 21) the abolition of its privileges and its impending destruction."

To THE REV. CANON PEROWNE.

ABERGWILI PALACE, *April 6th*, 1870.

" I have to return my best thanks for your kind and most welcome present of the first volume of the new edition of your Psalms.   Let me congratulate you on the great improvement which has taken place in the general appearance of the book, but especially in the Hebrew type, which to me adds immensely to its value.

" It has been a great pleasure and comfort to me to read your Preface to the new edition.   After what has been said lately on the proposed Revision, particularly by persons who ought to have known better, a little good sense is really refreshing.

" Though you have noticed my remarks on ' favourite texts,' I do not know whether you are aware of the consequences it entailed upon me. . . . . . I therefore enclose some slips from a paper called the *Rock*, containing the correspondence, which will speak for itself.   As it is the only set I have, I should be obliged to you if you will let me have it again.

" I had meant to ask you whether you had seen a commentary on the Psalter (first half), by Dr. Moll, in Lange's ' Bibelwerk.' It seems very careful and elaborate."

[In reference to an article on " The Irony of Christ " in *Good Words*, October, 1870. The article is to be found reproduced in substance in Professor Plumptre's notes on the first three Gospels in Professor Ellicott's " New Testament Commentary for English Readers."]

To Rev. E. H. Plumptre.

October 8th, 1870.

" I am very much obliged to you for the sight of your article, which I have read with great pleasure, and I have no doubt that to most readers it will open an entirely new and highly interesting and instructive view of our Lord's method of teaching, besides guarding against sundry erroneous conclusions ; and I hope that the unquestionable truth of the concluding reflection will overcome any prejudice to which it might be exposed by its novelty. I think that all the cases are legitimate applications of the idea, though in some the application may be less obvious than in others, as the shade of irony is more or less delicate.

" Your calculation of the time which will be needed at our present rate of progress to bring us to the end of the O. T. must, I think, make most of us uneasy, and especially those who, like myself, would be most likely to have their labours cut short about the middle of Leviticus after an expenditure of time which might have brought them individually much nearer to the close of the whole. On the other hand, last July I received a letter from Dr. Jebb, in which he pathetically deprecated the wild precipitation with which the Company was setting to work, and reminded me that at the last revision an interval of two years was allowed for preliminary preparation, which he thought would not be too much now. Perhaps if he had been pre-

Y 2

sent at our meetings he would have been a little reassured. You suggest a subdivision of labour, which would no doubt save time in more ways than one, as I suppose in all deliberative bodies the rate of progress is inversely as the number of counsellors. But would it not be necessary that the work of each section should be subject to the revision of the whole company? And might not this consume all the time that had been saved? Should we not still be obliged to listen to a demonstration of such facts as that the termination in *th* has become obsolete, and superseded by *s* in our best writers?

" I hope that when we meet again you may be able to suggest some plan for economising our time."

[On the Elementary Education Act.]

To W. DE G. WARREN, Esq.

November 28*th*, 1870.

" I am very much obliged to you for your statement of the reasons which induced you to decline my invitation to attend the Conference which I propose to hold on Friday next. But I think it right to inform you that it was just because I knew you take a different view of the working of the Elementary Education Act from that which is commonly taken by friends of the Church, and because it is believed that you fell into some mistakes in a recent speech which you made on the subject at Carmarthen, that I was particularly anxious to have the benefit of your presence on the occasion, that you might have an opportunity of discussing any statements on the interpretation of the Act which might appear to you erroneous. I made the proposal simply in the interests of truth.

" No one can be more fully convinced than myself that

the Act was 'an honest effort on the part of the Government to meet the difficulty,' and I can add that I believe it will prove a great blessing to the country ; but it seems that persons who are so far agreed may yet differ widely from one another in very important practical conclusions."

[The restoration of St. David's Cathedral, to which allusion is made in the following letter, was an undertaking which the Bishop had greatly at heart. (See his Charges of 1866 and 1869 in vol. ii. of the " Remains.") The largest and most essential portion was restored during his episcopate,* and after his death the " Thirlwall Memorial Fund" was devoted to the continuation of the work.]

To WILLIAM THIRLWALL BAYNE, Esq.

ABERGWILI PALACE, ST. JOHN E., 1870.

" .... I continue to hear the best accounts of what has been done at the cathedral ; the work is making steady, though not rapid progress. I am afraid that hostility to the Church has quenched the interest which Celtic patriotism would otherwise have felt in the noblest monument of its architecture. I am not at all enjoying this cold weather ; but when I see what a source of healthy pleasure it is to the skaters on my pond, I bear my own misery more patiently, though I can hardly bear to think of those who are passing their nights wounded and untended in the open air. This house contains such a volume of cold air as no fire or stove can heat, and everything one touches pricks like a needle. I think on the whole the moment in the day in which I suffer least from cold is that in which I emerge from my bath, which happily has not yet been frozen over. . . . . ''

* Letter from the present Bishop of St. David's.

326 ABRAHAM'S SACRIFICE.

[On an Essay published first in *Good Words*, and afterwards in a volume of Sermons.]

To THE REV. CANON PEROWNE.

ABERGWILI PALACE, *January 6th*, 1871.

" I have given my best attention to your very interesting Paper on Abraham's Sacrifice, and probably should not be able to arrive at any more satisfactory conclusion if I were to keep it longer and read it oftener.

"I quite agree with you in your opinion of the interpretations which you reject. But that which you adopt seems to turn upon the question whether the killing of Isaac was an ἀδιάφορον, which might be converted into a virtuous act by a Divine command ; so that, as you put it, ' the only question is as to the authority,' and ' when this is made known unquestioning obedience is a duty.' Are we not thus led to the conclusion that the merit of Abraham's conduct consisted in this, that his conviction of the physical fact, of a Divine communication, was stronger than his conviction of the truth, that in slaying his son he would be breaking the law. of God ? If this is so, I do not see how the character of Abraham's act is to be distinguished from that of any assassination which has ever been committed under the impulse of religious fanaticism, in which the conviction might be quite as strong, though it was not wrought in the same way. I have never been able to reconcile myself to the principle that an act is right because God wills it, and that God does not will it because it is right. I could admit any explanation of the history of Abraham's sacrifice, sooner than that it was supposed to inculcate this principle.

"But I also find great difficulty in your Théodicée. The state of Abraham's heart was well known to God, without any ' trial ;' and it might have been made known

to Abraham in divers other ways. It was no more necessary for him to kill Isaac, in order to devote him to the
Lord, to whom he belonged alike, whether dead or living,
than it was for Hannah to kill Samuel. You assume with
Ewald that Abraham had indulged an excessive fondness
for Isaac, and ' had almost forgotten the promise in the
child of promise.' But where does this appear in the
history? Is it not rather disproved by his readiness to
obey the Divine command? But I know how much easier
it is to raise doubts than to solve them. I wish I could
propose any view of the narrative which would bring it
more into harmony with the genuine principles of Christian
ethics."

[On the same.]

To THE REV. CANON PEROWNE.

ABERGWILI PALACE, *January 10th*, 1871.

" It appeared to me that in your treatment of Abraham's
sacrifice you had confined yourself to one aspect of the
case, which is indeed the only one presented by the Scripture history, and had overlooked another not less real or
less important for a right estimate of Abraham's conduct. You considered Isaac as his dearly beloved son,
and the sole heir of the promise. So by the Divine command Abraham was called upon to sacrifice at once his
tenderest affections and his most cherished hopes, in obedience to the will of God. So considered, his conduct was
not only meritorious, but sublimely exemplary. And this
is the great lesson which the story conveys. But there
is another aspect in which it may and must be viewed.
Isaac did not belong to Abraham in the same way as one
of the lambs of his flock. Isaac was not a thing or chattel,
but a person invested with rights which were not subject

to Abraham's will, and secured to him, as one made in the image of God, by a divine ordinance. It may be that these rights—foremost among which was the right to life—were not indefeasible. All man-killing, though intentional, may not be murder. And the killing of a murderer was expressly enjoined. But Isaac had done nothing to forfeit any of his rights. The killing of him was a plain breach of a universal law, grounded on an unalterable fact. I do not see that God's secret purpose of preventing the consummation of the material sacrifice makes any difference in this view. The event showed that in this case God did not require a human sacrifice. But the impression left on Abraham's mind—at least on the reader's—is that it would not have been inconsistent with the Divine character to require it, and that, if required, it would be man's duty to make it. This is to me the perplexing and painful side of the transaction, from which I am glad to abstract, in order to dwell on that which is clearly noble and edifying. And I do not forget that we have no means of knowing whether this episode in Abraham's fragmentary history has come down to us in its original shape. We have no record of that which passed in Abraham's mind, which might possibly have thrown light on that which is questionable in his conduct. The sad misfortune is that, for one who has followed the example of his faith, there may have been thousands who have imitated him in that which seemed to sanction their own wilfulness.

[In answer to a request that he would preach at the re-opening of Kirby Underdale Church.]

To THE REV. T. J. MONSON.

ABERGWILI PALACE, *January 11th,* 1871.

"I am sorry to say that it is quite impossible. My

locomotive energies are not what they were ; and I have not enough courage to face such a journey.   Also, ever since I have been a member of the O. T. Revision Company, I find myself more and more distressed for the time required for my proper and ordinary work, and less and less able to spare any for that which is of supererogation. I can only be with you in spirit."

[The next three letters refer to the proceedings in Convocation in February, 1871, on the subject of the Revision Company.   A clear account of the incident is to be found in "Bishop Thirlwall's Letters to a Friend," p. 240, and the Bishop's speeches are reprinted in the "Remains," vol. iii. Appendix.]

To THE DEAN OF WESTMINSTER.

1, REGENT STREET, S. W., February 19th, 1871.

" It seems to be generally thought that the final resolution of the Upper House practically cancelled and rescinded that which they had previously adopted on the subject, and has thus as far as possible replaced things and persons in the *statu quo*, and I have in consequence been strongly pressed to retain my seat at the Board of the Old Testament Revision Company.   My own opinion is that, as far as regards myself, I could not desire more complete satisfaction than I have received.   But I should not feel myself at liberty to act on that opinion, and comply with the wish which has been expressed, until I hear from you that this is your view of the matter.   When I announced my intention of withdrawing from the Company by way of protest against the resolution which had been carried, I did so expressly on the ground that such a step seemed to me to be due, not only to myself, but to 'others,' (meaning *you*) 'who felt themselves aggrieved by the previous resolution.'   I am therefore anxious to hear in what light the case now appears to you, and whether you are perfectly satisfied that I am quite free in point of honour, and so in duty bound to continue to render whatever service may be in my power to the work of revision.   I must add that I have not the slightest personal feeling, inclining the one way or another, and only desire to do that which is strictly right.   As the Company is to meet on Tuesday I should be thankful for a few lines at your earliest convenience.

"Let me take this opportunity of thanking you for the letter of Père Hyacinthe.

"I do not even know whether you still allow the companies the use of the Jerusalem Chamber.   If you withhold it, that would be decisive."

To THE REV. CANON PEROWNE.

REGENT STREET, *February 20th*, 1871.

"I find that all parties concerned agree in thinking that after what passed in Convocation, which is universally considered as virtually and practically cancelling the obnoxious resolution which called forth my protest, I have no longer any ground which would justify me in absenting myself from the meetings of our Company, and I shall therefore have the pleasure of seeing you to-morrow. Though, so far as I am concerned, I can look back to that which has occurred with unmixed satisfaction, I quite understand that it may seem to call for some farther security against mischievous interference.   This has also been suggested to me by our secretary.   I am only anxious to avoid a split, which would probably have the effect of breaking up the whole scheme, and giving a triumph to the adversaries of revision.

" We meet in the Jerusalem Chamber."

To THE REV. EDWARD Z. LYTTEL.

1, REGENT STREET, *February 24th*, 1871.

" I am much obliged to you for your kind letter. But I think it ought not to be forgotten that, although the bishops adopted a resolution which is very much to be lamented, it was when they were taken by surprise, and did not clearly understand the point of the question before them, and they appear to me entitled to great credit for the very rare candour with which, on mature deliberation, they unanimously adopted the opposite view of the subject when it was fairly and clearly put before them. They showed that after all they meant what was right, and that it was only their discernment that was at fault."

[On the Franco-German War.]

To THE BISHOP OF ARGYLE AND THE ISLES.

ABERGWILI PALACE, *March*, 1871.

" I received your two letters of 19th January and 1st February, and those which you sent of my own through Mr. Ewing. The latter are perhaps the more likely to interest a reader, for having been written so entirely without a thought of publication, but it is not without some reluctance that I yield to your judgment about them. All that was clear to me was, that, if they were to appear in print, it should be exactly as you received them.* We are thanking God that an end

* See page 272.

has come of the bitter winter and the cruel war. The severity of the season was depressing in itself, but immensely aggravated by the thought of the horrible suffering which it superadded to the ordinary miseries of war.

"One cannot therefore but be thankful for the present relief. But otherwise a less satisfactory peace, one more heavily laden with all the elements of interminable warfare, envenomed by implacable hatred, was never concluded. The French may have deserved their humiliation. But there seems to be such strong reason for suspecting that the war was concerted by Bismarck, while he contrived to throw the appearance of aggression on the other side, that any sympathy, which one otherwise feels in the triumph of a righteous cause, is sadly alloyed by the reflection that it is at the same time the success of an unscrupulous diplomatist in ·a wicked manœuvre. The result, as far as we are concerned, is a state of things which ought to make our Government very uneasy. Europe at the mercy of two despotic Powers in the closest alliance with each other, and both hostile to us; while we have been left as scantily provided with the means of self-defence as if every neighbour was a bosom friend.

"I have just received a parcel containing eleven numbers of the *Revue des Deux Mondes* from 15th September, 1870, to 1st March, which has been kept in Paris during the siege. The *Chronique de la Quinzaine*, which exhibits the impression made on the most cultivated Parisian minds by the successive phases of the siege, forms an interesting historical document, independently of the great number of articles devolved to the subject of the war. That all should witness to the thirst for vengeance, which rages in every French bosom, was to be expected. But I am struck by the unabated intensity of the national egotism which finds in everything that takes place an occasion of self-glorification. France, the chosen people, Paris, the Holy City. The invader guilty, not only of brutal violence, but of sacrilege. Utter forgetfulness of the notorious fact that the Germans are doing what the French, when they declared war, hoped and meant to do. Or, perhaps, rather the great assumption that what would have been quite right in a Frenchman is an atrocious wrong when done by a German. And then there is Thiers, of all living men the most guilty in the matter of this war, wiping his lips and rubbing his brow and calling down general indignation on the Bonapartists as the authors of the calamity! As if he had not received 20,000 francs for the wicked romance in which he did his utmost to influence that passion for military glory, and had not made it the business of his life to inculcate the necessity of recovering the Rhenish provinces.

"I do not know how you are off for Church news. I do not think you would be less happy if you never saw any. But if you do, you will have noticed some proceedings of our Convocation, which are rather wonderful than admirable. Some people believe that the Church of England is on the eve of a ruinous disruption. The special cause of alarm is that, by the recent judgment in which the Ritualists have been defeated along the whole line, clergymen who have hitherto been used to turn their backs to the congregation while they say the Prayer of Consecration will be compelled to let their profile be visible during that act. *There* is a rock of offence for a Church to go to pieces upon."

[The following short letter is important from the fact that it is the only recorded instance of the expression of the Bishop's views on Eternal Punishment. It is in reference to the sermon of Professor Plumptre on the "larger hope" entitled the "Spirits in Prison." In the *Edinburgh Review* for April, 1876, Dr. Plumptre justly claims from the Bishop's words a full and unreserved acceptance of his views :—]

To REV. E. H. PLUMPTRE.

ABERGWILI PALACE, *June 6th*, 1871.

"I do not know how to thank you sufficiently for your admirable and memorable sermon, one I think of the most valuable gifts the Church has received in this generation."

[The two following letters refer to an incident in Convocation. On February 9th, 1872, the Bishop delivered an important speech on the Athanasian Creed, since republished in the "Remains," vol. iii. On May 3rd Bishop Wilberforce unexpectedly attacked it. On July 2nd the Bishop rejoined with a vindication of his former speech. See also "Bishop Thirlwall's Letters to a Friend," p. 279 :—]

To THE LORD ARCHBISHOP OF CANTERBURY.

ABERGWILI PALACE, *May 17th*, 1872.

"Will you have the goodness to inform me whether there is to be a meeting of Convocation in July, and if so, at what time, and for the transaction of what business. Is the question of the Athanasian Creed to come in any way under discussion? When I saw you for a moment at the Royal Academy, I knew nothing of what had passed the day before in Convocation, and afterwards read the Bishop of Winchester's speech with great surprise.   I had remained in the country, not being aware of anything that should take me to town sooner than I went up for the Royal Academy* dinner, and particularly not intending to say anything more on the Athanasian Creed.   But I found that the Bishop of Winchester had stated (on Friday) that he had given me notice of his intention to answer parts of my speech 'a week ago,' the fact being that I had only received a note from him to that effect on Wednesday, the 1st, and could not go up the next day.   I have had some correspondence with him on one portion of my speech, which he appeared to me to have quite misapprehended ; and I wished to have published my correspondence, but as he deprecates its appearance in the *Guardian,* I have not felt at liberty to do so, and must, for the present, remain silent, though feeling that I have been hardly treated.   I am not at all sure that the next meeting of Convocation will afford me such an opportunity as I should desire for defending myself.   But I have some other more special reasons for wishing to be informed when and for what purpose Convocation is to meet next."

To THE LORD ARCHBISHOP OF CANTERBURY.

ABERGWILI PALACE, *May 22nd,* 1872.

"My only object in going up for the meeting of Convocation, which on many accounts will be extremely inconvenient and disagreeable, would be to take advantage of the opportunity of replying to the Bishop of Winchester. I believe that I am able to vindicate all that I have said on every point on which I have been assailed, but have been

---

* Bishop Thirlwall was an Honorary Member of the Royal Academy as Professor of Ancient History. He was succeeded in this post by Mr. Gladstone.

in doubt whether it would be better to do so in a speech, or to reserve what I have to say for my visitation Charge. I am now inclined to take the earlier opportunity, though I suppose there will be but a very scanty attendance of Bishops. I wish, however, to be quite sure that, if I do go up, I shall have the opportunity, and shall be glad if you will kindly inform me whether on the ground of having to make a personal explanation I shall be entitled to precedence, so that—the Bishop of Winchester being present—I may speak as soon as the reporters are admitted."

To THE REV. CANON PEROWNE.

[On his vacating the Vice-Principalship of Lampeter.]

ABERGWILI PALACE, *February 28th,* 1872.

" It required no slight effort of abnegation for me to receive the intelligence brought by your letter in a proper spirit. Considering it only as concerns yourself, I should simply have congratulated you most heartily on the transfer from a field of work in which you have no doubt been most usefully employed, but have been exposed to most constant annoyance and obstruction, to one in which your merits and services will be duly appreciated.

" But as to the college and myself the loss caused by your departure is one which I can hardly hope ever to see supplied. Even if we should have the good fortune to find a worthy successor for your office, it would be too much to expect that he should be a person with whom I could stand on those terms of confidential intimacy, to which I have been indebted not only for so much pleasant intercourse, but such invaluable assistance as visitor of the college ; and I cannot help fearing that the difficulties of my position are likely to be greatly increased by the change.

"I must not, however, allow any selfish considerations to interfere with that which must be the feeling uppermost in the mind of all your friends, delight at the prospect of increased usefulness and comfort now opened to you. In that feeling I most fully share."

[On the same.]

To the Rev. Canon Perowne.

Abergwili Palace, *May* 10*th*, 1872.

"Will you be so good as to inform the Dean that I should be very glad to see the office of Vice-Principal filled as proposed, but that I am not prepared to take upon myself the responsibility of an innovation, by which the college for the first time in its history would be left without either Principal or Vice-Principal capable of teaching Hebrew, and might, as you have pointed out, find itself without a single professor who could do so. Still less should I be willing to expose myself to the charge of inconsistency by consenting in this case to that which I have resisted as a breach of faith in other cases. If any plan can be devised for avoiding the twofold inconvenience, it is for the Dean to suggest it, and the Board must be responsible for it—not I.

"I have been considering your suggestion about the puzzle in II Samuel v. 8.* I suppose there is no doubt it is unobjectionable in the grammatical point of view;

* [The suggestion was to render the last clause of the verse thus : " Wherefore they say (the proverb runs) 'The blind and the lame are there ; he (anyone) cannot come into the house (or fortress);' " the general sense being that the fortress is so strong that even the blind and lame can defend it.—J. J. S. P.]

but, on the other hand, I do not think it is required by the distinctive accent. If I am not mistaken, we have had many cases at the revision where that accent would be sufficiently represented by a comma, if, indeed, it requires so great a pause.

"If it is certain that the supposed prohibition never existed, the words cannot have the sense given them in the A. V., whether they belong to the original text, or, as Thenius believes, are interpolated. He produces no evidence of the prohibition, but the two cases, in Acts iii. 2 and John ix. 1 (compared with viii. 59), which strictly prove nothing but the custom of laying blind and lame beggars by the gate of the Temple, as might be done by the door of a cathedral where they were at full liberty to go in. If this be so I see nothing better than your interpretation, and only feel a little difficulty in the extreme conciseness of the allusion to the proverb, which, without the narrative, would be utterly unintelligible."

[On the difficulties of the Welsh Church.]

To ARCHDEACON CLARK.

ABERGWILI PALACE, *October* 28*th*, 1872.

"I had intended before now to return the papers you kindly sent me, but have been so much occupied with matters relating to my approaching visitation that I must beg you to allow me to keep them a little longer, perhaps until I see you at Haverfordwest. And I have now only time for a very few brief remarks. Mr. R.'s Paper is, I think, of all I have read on the subject the most unprofitable, and if any steps were to be taken for carrying his suggestions into effect, likely to be the most positively mischievous. . . . .

"You have certainly laid your finger on one chief cause of our low estate in that part of your most valuable summary in which you speak of our *poverty*.   I am, and have been, almost since I came into Wales, fully sensible of the supreme importance of the subject, but have never yet seen the way to a remedy. I should be glad to believe that I have overrated the difficulty, or underrated the ability and the willingness which would be forthcoming to supply the need. But I should like to know whether you have calculated the amount that would be required for an additional endowment, sufficient—I will not say to raise us to the average of an English diocese—but to tell upon the general condition of the clergy. My own belief is that the greater part of the landowners—who are with few exceptions our only rich men—live up to their incomes, and cannot be expected to make any sacrifice for other than local objects. As to the other hardly less important question—the habits and wants of Welsh congregations—I doubt whether you can safely draw an inference from your experience at Tenby and in the English-speaking parts of Pembrokeshire. It may be quite true that the Welsh everywhere would be grateful for kindness and pastoral care, and would feel respect and affection for a clergyman from whom they receive it. But it is not less true that they have a peculiarly strong craving for preaching, and greatly prefer that which is most exciting and sensational, while they have little relish for the services of the Church in themselves, and in the best worked parish, while they thankfully accepted the clergyman's good offices, would, if left to follow their own inclination, attend the meeting-house. . . . ."

[On the same.]

To Archdeacon Clark.

Abergwili Palace, *November 1st*, 1872.

" . . . . My own sense of the difficulty which will be found in providing for the physical wants of the Church in this diocese has been quickened by my own experience. My Augmentation Fund, with the grants it has elicited from the Ecclesiastical Commissioners, and Queen Anne's Bounty, has yielded between £30,000 and £40,000. Yet, compared with the need of further endowment, the effect is scarcely perceptible, and I am afraid it will be long before even this is doubled by any of the means you suggest. With regard to the Ecclesiastical Commissioners, I doubt whether you are fully aware how necessary it is for such a body to proceed by fixed rules, and how exceedingly difficult to exercise any discretion in relaxing those rules to meet the circumstances of each particular case, as for instance that of a mixed population, where the English-speaking congregation form a small minority. In all such cases a question arises as to how many of the Welsh understand English, and how many of the English understand Welsh. But these are points into which it is absolutely impossible for the Commissioners to inquire with any hope of ascertaining the truth. No doubt, where the English congregation consists of a few wealthy families, as is very frequently the case, they ought to provide the service they require for themselves. But I believe it is very rarely indeed that they do so. A few weeks back an Englishman, residing at St. Dogmael's, complained that he could not get the clergyman to perform a service for his benefit and that of a few coastguards and other English residents, the place being, as you probably know, within a short and pleasant walk of Cardigan, where there is an

English service. The effect of doing what he desired would have been to disperse the Welsh congregation; but about this the wealthy English seem never to feel the smallest scruple. I agree with you as to that which the Welsh under proper superintendence might become. But I am afraid the reformation of their spiritual tastes and habits is a work not less difficult than the provision of a sufficient endowment. You are no doubt aware that when the foundation of a Welsh college for the education of divinity students was first proposed, many thought that the funds collected for that purpose would have been far better employed in the founding of scholarships for Welsh students at Oxford or Cambridge. But no one could have foreseen the disastrous effect that would be produced on the character of the college by the government to which it has been ever since subject, an effect which its singular good fortune in the series of able and earnest men who have filled the office of Vice-Principal has been insufficient to counteract. During Canon Perowne's term of office, a party, which has often been a majority in the College Board, has been constantly bent on two objects : one the secularising of the instruction with a view to attract students who had no view to enter into holy orders ; the other, to fill every seat at the Board with a Welshman. I have been engaged in a continual struggle in opposition to these two movements ; and I inclose for your perusal a paper which I addressed a few years ago to the College Board with regard to the curriculum. It seems in general to coincide with your views. But I am not sure whether you are aware that the College has no power to transfer the emoluments of the profession of physical science to any other branch of learning. When you have done with it I shall be glad to have it again."

[On the Day of Intercession for Missions.]

To ARCHDEACON CLARK.

ABERGWILI PALACE, *November* 16*th*, 1872.

"The subject of the Intercession Day was brought before me two days ago by a letter from Mr. Bullock, Secretary of the S. P. G., inclosing the form of service authorised by the Archbishop for his diocese. I was obliged to tell Mr. Bullock that I felt a strong doubt as to the propriety of the measure. It seemed to me that there was something inconsistent in the clergy praying and exhorting their congregations to pray for a blessing which is already placed within their reach, but which they show no desire to obtain. Among those who will use the Intercession Service there are probably hundreds who might go out into the missionary field, with the certainty that there would be no difficulty in supplying their places at home. This is a thought which will probably occur to some in every congregation, and must, I think, tend very much to damp the fervour of prayer. But I do not wish on this account to place myself in opposition to the Archbishop. I only desire to leave the entire responsibility of the proceeding with him. I am ready, as I have informed Mr. Bullock, to authorise the form of service sanctioned by the Archbishop for his diocese, though there is hardly a sentence in it that appears to me really appropriate to the occasion, or that can be adapted to it without more or less of violence. (The command ' Pray ye the Lord of the harvest,' &c., was addressed to those who were themselves going forth.) But I do not believe that anything more to the purpose is to be found in the Prayer Book. My only wish is that the clergy should exercise their own discretion as to the use of the form, and I hope that they will abstain from making a collection on the occasion, as this would be likely to sug-

gest the suspicion that the whole was merely a new device
for raising money.   But if any think fit to do so, I cannot
prevent it, and should not like to seem indifferent to the
success of the missionary work."

[On the same.]

To ARCHDEACON CLARK.

ABERGWILI PALACE, *November 25th*, 1872.

"As your attention will for some time be a good deal
occupied with the subject of missions, I thought you might
like to see a pamphlet in the form of a letter to the Archbishop of Canterbury from the Bishop of Bombay, which I
received two or three days ago ; and I should like to
know your opinion of it.   To me it appears the most
disheartening view of the subject I have yet met with.
When translated out of what seems to me sadly misplaced
rhetoric, the upshot, as I understand it, is that the only
possibility of success for our Indian missions lies in the
adoption of the sacerdotal and sacramental system, in
which we take up the attitude of those which say to every
other Protestant missionary body, 'Stand by thyself, come
not near to me, for I am holier than thou,' while we make
ourselves pioneers of Romanism.   I shall be curious to see
whether the S. P. G. lends its sanction to this proposal,
and also how it is relished by the Church Missionary
Society.   I am in no hurry for the return of the pamphlet."

[On the same.]

To ARCHDEACON CLARK.

ABERGWILI PALACE, *December 26th*, 1872.

" I send you a copy of a sermon which I have printed,*

* On " Missionary Duties, Difficulties, and Prospects."

not for its literary merits, but because I wished to draw attention to a side of the subject which appeared to me to have been too much overlooked. I quite agree with you on your remarks on the Bishop of Bombay's letter. I feel very strongly with regard to it, and I think that the Committee of the S. P. G. ought to take some notice of it, at least to the extent of distinctly disclaiming any intention of acting upon its recommendation. If I believed that any part of their funds was to be so appropriated, I should feel myself bound to withdraw from the Society."

[On Adult Baptism.]

To ARCHDEACON CLARK.

ABERGWILI PALACE, *December 12th*, 1872.

" I receive a good many inquiries from time to time on the subject of adult baptism. It is unfortunate that the Rubric should be so obscurely worded—perhaps a consequence of its having been drawn up by a Welshman, Bishop Griffith, of St. Asaph—there being nothing to show what is the *purpose* to which it refers ; and it is the more to be regretted that it was left untouched by the Ritual Commission. The cause of the direction that notice should be given to the Bishop may perhaps be found in the fact— observed by Procter on Common Prayer—that it was originally designed for converts from heathenism or Judaism, and not contemplated as to be used in a Christian country, and therefore, as he says, whenever it is called for it is an occasion of peculiar solemnity. But I quite agree with you that this part of the Rubric has now become obsolete and useless. In the American Prayer Book it is altered to ' timely notice shall be given to the minister that so due care may be taken,' &c. This is all that can now be reasonably required. That the Bishop—an utter stranger to all the parties and circumstances of the case—should undertake to give directions as to the examination or instruction of the candidate appears to me one of the wildest of absurdities.   But though I *wish* that the Rubric was altered to suit the real state of the case, I am not at liberty to dispense with the observance of it so far as it is clearly intelligible.   The minister must be considered as a ' discreet person,' competent to give the required notice to the Bishop.   I am therefore obliged to submit to the annoyance, though I should be certainly disposed to deal very leniently with a clergyman who spared it me."

[The next four letters are part of a correspondence which arose out of an attack made upon the Bishop by the Rev. Malcolm MacColl.   In his "Damnatory Clauses" he expressed his regret "that the Bishop of St. David's should have been a party to the hounding of Dr. Newman out of the Church of England a quarter of a century ago." A correspondence ensued upon this in the *Guardian*, in which the Bishop showed in the clearest and most convincing manner how absolutely without foundation Mr. MacColl's charge was.   A letter also appeared in the same paper from Dr. Newman himself, procured through the intervention of Professor Plümptre, in which he exonerated the Bishop in a "perfectly satisfactory" manner from the accusation.   Dr. Newman had, indeed, in one of his works, referred to the "courtesy" of Bishop Thirlwall as a marked exception to his general treatment at the hands of the English Episcopate.   See also the "Remains," vol. ii. p. 353 :—]

To the Bishop of Argyle and the Isles.

Abergwili Palace, *January* 10*th*, 1873.

" I am thankful that I do not perceive any failure in my mental powers. In the last conversation I ever had with Grote, he observed that his most earnest hope was that he might not survive the decay of his intellectual faculties, and I most heartily sympathised with that feeling. But that has nothing to do with the abatement of physical strength which I experience in various ways, and which tells upon the amount though not on the quality of the intellectual work I am able to go through ; and I find increasing difficulty in meeting the demands upon my time. I am sorry that I have nothing in my portfolio which I could put into yours. But even in my best days I was never addicted to writing, and, in fact, never wrote anything without some special object, and without a view to immediate publication ; and that is now the case with me more than ever.

" I do not know whether it is an unavoidable incident of the time of life when the shadows are lengthening to take a gloomy view of things, but I must confess that I am very much disheartened by that which I see as to our prospects in Church and State. I think I perceive the approach of a tremendous struggle through which the next generation will have to pass, and to which I can foresee no limit or end. It is only the young who can look forward with pleasure to taking a part in it. Those who can be no more than passive spectators must wish to be spared the spectacle.

" I think you underrate Mr. MacColl's ability. That is not the side on which he appears to me most deficient. But whatever I might have thought of it, it was impossible to acquiesce in his assertion that I had been a party to hounding Newman out of the Church of England.

I have, however, taken my leave of him in the last *Guardian.*

"I hope you received a copy, which I directed to be sent to you, of my sermon on Missions."

To THE DEAN OF WESTMINSTER.

January 18th, 1873.

"I am extremely obliged to you for your kind suggestion ; but I do not intend to take any further direct notice of Mr. MacColl, and I meant to signify that intention at the end of my last letter to the *Guardian.* It is very difficult to say what suggested to him the idea that I had been a party to the 'hounding.' It may have been the passage of the 'Apologia' to which you refer, or that at p. 349, when he speaks of the 'unanimous expression of opinion from the bishops,' or it may have been the pamphlet from which he quotes. But it would be a mere conjecture, and would not much affect the state of the case. The material points which I should wish to be generally known are :—

"1. That all the 'hounding' must have been exclusively the work of my Charge of 1842. I find from records in my registry, that the Charge of 1845 was delivered for the last time in Cardigan, on the 25th of September. It could not have been published within a fortnight after that date, or before he had announced his intention of seceding in his letter of the 8th of October.

"2. The nature of the contents of the Charge of 1845 thus ceases to be of the slightest importance. But in it I said, 'I am not going to discuss the character of that movement afresh, but it is fit to state that I see no reason for recalling or changing any opinion I expressed with regard to it on the former occasion.'

"3. The context of the passages quoted by MacColl

clearly shows that they did not relate to Newman. If this was understood, it would be seen that there is absolutely nothing left for MacColl to stand on. But I do not believe that either facts or reason go for anything with him, or with those who are pledged to his party. I think, however, of sending the date of the Charge to the *Guardian*, for the benefit of those who are not willingly deceived but desire to know the truth. I have also to thank you for the sermon which I wanted very much to see."

To Rev. E. H. Plumptre.

Abergwili Palace, *January 18th*, 1873.

"Whatever may be the result of the step you have taken I shall be equally thankful for the kindness which prompted it. It certainly ought not to be doubtful what kind of answer you will receive, and I know one reason, unknown to any one else, for hoping that it may be a plain statement of the truth. And this is, that I am under a strong though vague impression that somewhere or other Newman referred to my Charge with some acknowledgment of obligation for the manner in which I spoke of his 'Lectures on Justification.' On the other hand it is, I am afraid, quite possible that he may decline saying anything to the purpose, partly through disinclination toward me, and partly through unwillingness to bear witness against MacColl, whom he may regard as a useful if not hopeful *protégé*. If he should write anything which you think proper to send to the *Guardian*, even if it should not be perfectly satisfactory in itself, it might afford me an opportunity of correcting some of MacColl's misstatements, which otherwise I should be forced to pass over in silence. . . . ."

"One fact, indeed, I mean to have placed on record, which will effectually dispose of three-fourths of MacColl's last letter, by showing that it was impossible for Newman to have seen my Charge of 1845 before he wrote that letter of the 8th of October ('Apologia,' p. 366) in which he announced his secession. My Charge was delivered for the last time on the 25th September at Cardigan, and could not have been published until about three weeks later; so that if I was a party to the 'hounding' it could have been only through the Charge of 1842, in which I took so much pains to defend his position in the Church of England against all assailants. Stanley informs me that he could not succeed in an attempt which he made to disabuse Newman of the illusion that 'he was driven from Oxford by the Liberals,' as he asserts ('Apologia,' p. 329). Stanley thinks that it was this passage which misled MacColl. I should rather suspect that it was another (p. 349), where he says, 'I could not stand against such an unanimous expression of opinion from the bishops.' That was in 1843."

To Rev. E. H. Plumptre.

ABERGWILI PALACE, *January* 21*st*, 1873.

"I am most deeply obliged to you for that which you have brought about. Newman's letter is perfectly satisfactory with regard to the Charge of 1842, and as much so as I could have expected under the circumstances in regard to that of 1845.

"I do not consider myself as placed in a position of antagonism to him, but I am thankful for the opportunity he has afforded me of showing—as I hope to do to the satisfaction of all impartial persons, himself included—that he is quite under a mistake as to that part of my second

Charge which he evidently understands as directed against himself. I could not have brought myself to do this by way of replying to MacColl's misrepresentations, but I may now write without taking any direct notice of his last letter, and mean to do so as soon as I see the correspondence in the *Guardian*.

"I return Newman's letter."

[On the Athanasian Creed.]

To THE REV. CANON PEROWNE.

ABERGWILI PALACE, *August* 22nd, 1872.

"I have read your sermon with great interest and satisfaction. It appears to me very seasonable and much wanted. I had observed with concern how greatly the occasional literature of the other side—all more or less tending to obscure and confuse the question—preponderated in bulk. I have never yet met with anything that appeared to me so well calculated to recall attention to the real issues, and to dispel the haze of sophistry and declamation in which they have been wrapped. It is quite lamentable to see a man of MacColl's abilities reasoning so wildly. I cannot still make out what it could have been that so affected the nerves of the young lady, or drove two of the congregation out of church. But the fact shows how much the sermon was needed, and I hope it will do much good."

[On the same.]

To ARCHDEACON CLARK.

ABERGWILI PALACE, *February* 4th, 1873.

"I am so completely in the dark as to the nature of the intended synodical declaration that I hardly venture to express any opinion upon it, as any remark I make may turn out to be inapplicable to it. I can only say that, subject to this proviso, I do not see how any declaration of the Convocation of Canterbury on the subject can be binding on any but those who choose to adopt it, and as little do I understand how it can meet the objections which have been made to the present use of the Creed. At all events, the two main points to be considered in the discussion would seem to be : 1. What is the warrant ? 2. Where will be the gain ? To the first question I should say *Nil ;* to the second, *Nusquam.* But there seems to be hardly any room left for reasoning when the strongest argument of the majority is the assumption that any change in the use of the Athanasian will involve a rejection of the Nicene."

[On Early Liturgies.]

To ARCHDEACON CLARK.

ABERGWILI PALACE, *March* 20*th*, 1873.

"No one who knows you will ever suppose that you make any statement without some good authority. My Buxtorf, with the sight of which I was once familiar, not having received a visit from me for a long time past, has now hid itself in some corner where I do not expect to find it until I have no further occasion to look at it. But a translation of the eighteen Prayers or Eulogies, with the addition of that which is said to have been added by Gamaliel as an imprecation against the Christians, is given, not only by Prideaux, but by a Mr. Bernard, in a work called 'The Synagogue and the Church,' which is condensed from Vitringa. Both are willing to believe that they are in the main the work of Ezra. But both observe that there are some which seem to have been composed after the destruction of Jerusalem, and Bernard-Vitringa refers the final arrangement to a Rabbi Simeon Gossypiarius. Considering the constant tendency of the Rabbis to carry the present as far back as possible into the past, and still more the character of the prayers themselves, I cannot believe that Ezra had anything to do with them, or that they became fixed before the fall of Jerusalem. At the same time I should think it highly probable that there was a nucleus, or nuclei, contained in the blessings of a much earlier date.

"'The writer of the article *Synagogue*, in 'Smith's Dictionary of the Bible,' thinks that 'the ritual of the Synagogue was to a large extent the reproduction of the statelier liturgy of the Temple.' But what was that liturgy? I cannot find a trace of any form of prayer prescribed to the officiating priest. There was a musical accompaniment conducted by the Levites, and the people prostrated themselves, either in mute adoration or secret prayer, as while Zacharias was burning incense in the Temple. But it is quite possible that the acts of the ritual were also accompanied by short traditional ejaculations, answering to the Eulogies—which are much more in the nature of Psalms, even to the Selah, than of prayers—and that, after the destruction of the Temple, these were retained, expanded, and at last fixed in the worship of the Synagogue.

" But I think our original question was, whether, assuming the fact of a fixed form of prayer in the Synagogue, we should be warranted in the inference that there was also one in the earliest assemblies of the Church. And as to this it appears to me clear that a Christian congregation could not have borrowed forms of prayer which either ignored, or, at least by implication, denied the coming of Christ as an event of the past. I cannot conceive that the Apostles ever entered a Synagogue simply to join in its devotions, or for any other purpose than to preach

Christ in their exposition of the portion of Scripture which happened to be read. The writer of the article in the 'Dictionary of the Bible' observes : 'From the Synagogue came the use of fixed forms of prayer.' But he admits (for his tendency is the other way) that 'the gifts of utterance which characterized the first period of the Apostolic Age led for a time to greater freedom, to unpremeditated prayer.' That the form was still in a state of flux, and the principal prayer unpremeditated, or not prescribed, seems to me incontrovertibly proved by Justin's ἐπι πολύ, and ὅση δύναμις αὐτῷ, though I could not agree with those who would draw the same conclusion from Tertullian's 'monitore quia de pectore oramus,' which would be quite consistent with the use of a Form of Intercession, though I do not believe that one was fixed in his time. And St. Paul's description of the state of things at Corinth (1 Cor. xiv. 26) seems to require the supposition of a long interval before it gave way to liturgical regularity."

[On the same.]

To Archdeacon Clark.

Abergwili Palace, *March 26th*, 1873.

" I do not think there can be the shadow of a doubt as to the general proposition that the earliest Christian worship was founded upon that of the Synagogue, adopting its order and framework. But when we come to examine its details, it is just in the matter of the prayers that a difficulty arises. Surely it was impossible that Christian worshippers should ever be satisfied with forms of prayer which at the best were non-Christian, and ignored the coming of Christ. In their own assemblies, however closely in every other respect they might have adhered to the order of the Synagogue, they could not have borrowed those forms, at least without supplements of Christian devotion which would entirely alter their character. And the question is whether it is credible that their Christian prayers were offered in prescribed forms. Before I could believe this, I should require the most precise and authentic evidence of the fact, which is entirely wanting, while such as we have points the opposite way. I am rather surprised at the way in which you speak of the passage of Justin to which I referred, and I think your memory must have misled you in your impression as to the nature of the services to which it refers. It is the most luminous description extant in Christian literature of the celebration of the Eucharist in the first half of the second century. The service it describes is the ordinary Sunday Service. (ἄρτος προσφέρεται καὶ οἶνος καὶ ὕδωρ, καὶ ὁ προεστὼς εὐχὰς ὁμοίως καὶ εὐχαριστίας, ὅση δύναμις αὐτῷ, ἀναπέμπει, καὶ ὁ λαὸς ἐπευφημεῖ λέγων τὸ ἀμήν.) A little before, speaking of the same thing, he uses the expression, εὐχαριστίαν ἐπὶ πολὺ ποιεῖται. Taken together the two expressions seem irreconcilable with the supposition of a fixed formulary of thanksgiving.

"But while I fully recognise the intimate connection between the Jewish and the Christian Synagogue in that part of the Service which answers to our Morning and Evening Prayer, when you speak of 'claiming the Synagogue worship as the original and pattern of Christian worship,' do you not overlook the fact that the Synagogue could offer no pattern whatever for the principal and most characteristic part of Christian worship, viz. the celebration of the Eucharist? And I need hardly say that the most difficult as well as the most interesting question connected with this subject is the development of the liturgy out of its original form. Bingham gives little help in this inquiry. Palmer shows that ours will bear comparison in point of antiquity with any other, but stops far short of the beginning.

"Nevertheless, that liturgical elements existed from the very first is manifest from Scripture. For what else were the words of Institution, the εὐχαριστία, offered by our Lord Himself, and the closing hymn in which He joined? But the process by which these elements were expanded, until they were crystallised in the extant liturgies, is probably beyond the reach of human research. That fragments are to be found in the Epistles and the Revelation I have no doubt, though it is incapable of strict demonstration. I am tormented by a vague recollection of having read somewhere a most ingenious and interesting Paper by Professor Plumptre, in which he made it highly probable that fragments of the most ancient Christian hymns are to be found embedded in the Epistles, but I do not know where to look for it.*

"Bunsen believed that he had collected everything relating to these questions in his 'Hippolytus and his Age.' Other Germans are still working at them.

"Pray do not trouble yourself about Buxtorf. I believe I have everything he gives in some form or other."

[On the Laying on of Hands.]

To ARCHDEACON CLARK.

ARERGWILI PALACE, *July 3rd*, 1873.

"Is it necessary to suppose that our Lord laid His hand on the children while He was embracing them? Is it not quite consistent with St. Mark's narrative as well as perfectly natural, that He should first have taken them into His arms, as a sign of affection (peculiarly

* See the close of Professor Plumptre's article on the "Lord's Supper," in "Smith's Bible Dictionary."

called forth by the conduct of the disciples), and then have set them down on the ground and blessed them with the imposition of His hands. They were παιδία, not βρέφη, and capable of *coming* to Him.

"In my own practice of confirmation I may have been unconsciously swayed by the preference which, by the common consent of mankind, is given to the right hand in all symbolical acts, so that I felt the laying on of that hand to be equally due to every candidate. But I quite admit that, for purposes as to which there is no difference in the physical power of the two hands, the one may serve as well as the other; and, in the absence of any express prescription, Bishop Hampden's practice is perfectly allowable, and has much to recommend it. Possibly I am quite singular in mine, having only been guided by the light of nature.

"With regard to ordination, I apprehend that it would be quite in accordance with liturgical principles that a distinction should be observed between the acts of the ordaining bishop and those of the assisting presbyters; so that, if it was necessary for the bishop to lay on both hands, it might well be sufficient for each of the assistants to lay on only one. The act appears to have been considered as the act of the bishop, while the assistants only testified their consent. Hence Jerome asked: 'Quid enim facit, excepta ordinatione, episcopus quod presbyter non faciat?' And there is a memorable illustration of the feeling which prevailed in early times on this subject, in the decision of a Spanish Council held in 618. A bishop had ordained a presbyter and two deacons with laying on of his hands; but a presbyter had given the blessing, the bishop being unable, through weakness of his eyes, to read the prayer. The Council ruled that the ordination was invalid, and those who had received it were deposed.

"Suicer observes that χειροθεσία is used in two senses:

1. εὐλογίας, benedictionis, non ordinationis, seu conservationis ; and, 2. χειροτονίας, seu, καθιερώσεως, conservationis. He gives a quotation from Chrysostom which favours the notion that one hand only was used by the ordaining bishop: ἡ χείρ επικειται του ανἐρός, τὸ δὲ πᾶν ὁ Θεὸς ἐργάζεται καὶ ἡ αὐτοῦ χείρ ἐστιν ἡ ἀπτομένη τῆς κεφαλῆς τοῦ χειροτονουμένου, ἐὰν ὡς ἐεῖ χειροτονῆται.

"On the other hand, he cites from Optatus the charge brought against Donatus in the words 'quod confessus sit se rebaptizasse et Episcopis lapsis manus imposuisse,' which looks the other way. But I should think it most likely that the early practice was not uniform in this particular.

"Suicer does not discuss the question as to the laying on of one or both hands."

[On the same.]

To Archdeacon Clark.

Abergwili Palace, *July 5th*, 1873.

"When we were talking about the 'laying on of hands,' I think we omitted to refer to the supreme authority, the example of our Lord Himself. Can τιθεὶς τὰς χεῖρας ἐπ' αὐτά (Mark x. 16) be understood in any other sense than that He laid both hands on each ? And even if He only laid one, could it have been any but the right ? And must not Acts viii. 17, ἐπετίθουν τας χεῖρας ἐπ' αὐτούς, be interpreted in the same way ? Whether the εὐλογία ought to be repeated at each imposition of hands may admit of a doubt. But if it is allowable to use the words less frequently, it seems merely arbitrary to limit the number of those over whom they may be pronounced during the imposition to two."

[On the same.]

To Archdeacon Clark.

Abergwili Palace, July 12th, 1873.

"Though the subject we have been discussing is certainly not of first-rate importance, it is interesting enough to make one wish to understand it as well as the state of the evidence permits, and I am glad to have my views modified and expanded by yours.

"I take the distinction between $\beta\rho\acute{\epsilon}\phi\sigma$ and $\pi\alpha\iota\delta\acute{\iota}\sigma\nu$ to be simply that every $\beta\rho\acute{\epsilon}\phi\sigma$ was a $\pi\alpha\iota\delta\acute{\iota}\sigma\nu$, but every $\pi\alpha\iota\delta\acute{\iota}\sigma\nu$ was not a $\beta\rho\acute{\epsilon}\phi\sigma$. I am not aware that there is any definition of the age at which the $\beta\rho\acute{\epsilon}\phi\sigma$ becomes a $\pi\alpha\iota\delta\acute{\iota}\sigma\nu$, and if there was, it would be quite arbitrary and conventional. We should say that a child ceases to be a baby when it no longer needs to be carried in the arms. But before that time it is able to run alone. I have an illustration of that fact constantly before my eyes in John's youngest child, who is the reigning baby of the house, and known only by that title, but runs up every morning to receive the caresses of the family. The children brought to Christ to be touched were no doubt not all of the same age; the taking them up in his arms implies that all were very young, but not that all were too young to stand and walk alone. It seems doubtful whether our Lord was expected to touch in any particular way, or intended to follow any traditional usage, or in fact treated all in exactly the same manner. In the case which you witnessed in the synagogue, the imposition of the right hand on each boy as he passed by would be the most natural form, whether prescribed or not. But in the case of a person kneeling before me, my natural impulse would be to use both hands. But this may be something peculiar to myself."

[The next six letters are part of a continuous correspondence arising out of mutual work in the Old
Testament Revision Company.]

[On Genesis i. 2.]

To THE REV. CANON PEROWNE.

BULKELEY ARMS HOTEL, BEAUMARIS, *July 6th*, 1870.

" I am much obliged to you for your report of the proceedings of our Company. . . . I should have liked to
know who were present. I approve of what was done as
to the italics and marginal notes. But I shall be grieved
to see ' hover ' even in the margin [of Gen. i. 2].
It seems to me a sad blunder. It can only suggest the
idea of a hawk ready to swoop upon his prey, instead of
one beautifully suggestive and more conformable to the
original text. It is no doubt good that we should proceed very deliberately, but if the first day's work was to
be a sample of our future rate of progress, I should hardly
expect to witness the completion of Genesis.

" We shall, probably, in time come to a tacit understanding as to the construction to be put on our instruc-
tions with regard to *faithfulness*. I once thought it might
be desirable to begin with some resolutions on the subject.
But I am not sure that any could be framed that would
not raise the same question, which will be better solved
ambulando."

[In reference to Exodus iii. 14.]

To THE REV. CANON PEROWNE.

ABEROWILI PALACE, *September 2nd*, 1871.

" . . . . I could not reconcile myself to the proposed
change even independently of the latter part of the verse,

where it would seem necessary to make 'because I am,' the answer to Moses' question. The rendering of the Vulgate is strangely marred by the variation, QUI EST, instead of QUI SUM. But that of the LXX. Ἐγώ εἰμὶ ὁ ὤν, and afterwards Ὁ ὤν, seems perfectly satisfactory. If the first four words stood alone, the best English for them would be, I think, I AM HE WHO AM (the French is, *Je suis celui qui suis*), but then the *Name* would be not, I AM (subject and copula), but the predicate HE WHO AM. It seems a confusion of the subject with the predicate to translate as the French, 'Celui qui s'appelle JE SUIS m'a envoyé vers vous.' What I proposed [I WHO AM] still appears to me the nearest approach to the right expression of the meaning. I was not able to follow the argument of Dr. Kay in favour of the future, in which the Dutch version follows Luther. It seems to me liable to the double objection of suggesting the same truism as I AM THAT I AM; and also the idea of a future, as distinguished from a present, being of God."

To THE REV. CANON PEROWNE.

ABERGWILI PALACE, *March 4th*, 1873.

"It is very unlucky that, not having heard of the Company's intention to take the Psalms immediately after the Pentateuch, I devoted the time which I should have given to them to Joshua and Judges. I expect, however, that they will prove a *pièce de resistance*.

"There is a little question which has often occurred to me, on which I should like to know your opinion. Our Version is often disfigured by the insertion of an *and* between two verbs in the same tense, where there is no conjunction in the Hebrew, *e.g.* Psalm v. 7. You, I think, generally avoid this by the repetition either of the

pronoun or of the auxiliary verb.   Compare Psalm lxii. 3.
It seems to me that in most of these cases the nearest
approach we can make to the force of the Hebrew, which
depends on the abruptness, and is quite ruined by the
interpolation of a conjunction, would be to turn the second
verb into a participle.   I only commend this to your consideration.

"I have not met with Conant, or ever heard of him
before.   Could you give me the title?"

To THE REV. CANON PEROWNE.

ABERGWILI PALACE, *March* 10*th*, 1873.

"I am very much obliged to you for your interesting
and luminous 'Dissertation on the Prophecy of Isaiah.'*
I was the more glad to possess it, because I have often
regretted that I did not keep the numbers of the *Guardian*
in which I think you discussed the same subject some time
ago.   I do not know whether your engagements at Cambridge will permit you to attend the meeting of our Company, which is to begin to-morrow.   But if you have means
of knowing what they are doing, I should be glad if you
would inform me whether they begin the revision of the
Psalms this session."

To THE REV. CANON PEROWNE.

ABERGWILI PALACE, *May* 31*st*, 1873.

" . . . . It is certainly to be lamented that the readings
of the Company should not represent the opinion of the
majority ; though it is a little consoling to think that when
they do not they are wrong.   In my future contributions
I shall confine myself to a few suggestions by which I fancy

---

* Chapters viii. and ix. ; printed first as a Prælection for the degree of
D.D., and afterwards in a volume of Sermons.

that the Version may be improved, and which I have not seen elsewhere. It is not to save myself trouble—for I shall continue as long as I am able to go carefully through the whole—but to save the time of the Company. In fact, there are very few passages indeed in which I should desire any change in the A. V. that I do not find in either your text or your notes, though there are several in which it might be made to run more smoothly. I should wish the Revised Psalter to combine the greater accuracy of the one version with the easier flow of the other. But such things can only be discussed orally.

"I found very little indeed of any use in Conant. You have probably observed that his 'Fair, Fair' was merely a translation of Ewald's 'Schön, Schön.' But he has not even judgment to pick and choose.

To THE REV. CANON PEROWNE.

ABERGWILI PALACE, July 22nd, 1873.

"I am much obliged to you for keeping me *au courant* of the Company's progress. I am the better satisfied with the decision on Dr. Schaff's question, as I do not expect a great deal from the American Company, and am afraid that Conant's 'Translation of the Psalms' may be considered as a fair specimen of their taste and judgment. I have never seen Leeser's work, but I have the Unitarian Translation, which I have often consulted with profit, and consider as a very creditable performance, though insufficient. Is Leeser readable? I find the style of all Jewish English books I possess extremely disagreeable.

"I was deeply grieved at the sad news of the Bishop of Winchester. To all appearance he had in him, and before him, at least ten years of unabated mental vigour, and perhaps increasing usefulness. Though for some time past his views on several important questions had been diverging from mine, I have no doubt that he was quite sincere in the memorable last words which he uttered in the House of Lords. But that which is now uppermost in my mind is the remembrance of his habitual kindness, and of the many instances in which it was shown to myself, and of the singular charm of his society."

To THE LORD ARCHBISHOP OF CANTERBURY.

ABERGWILI PALACE, *August 7th*, 1873.

"Thank you very much for your kind letter. I had some special reasons for lamenting the loss of the Bishop of Winchester, beside the closeness of our long intimacy and the remembrance of much kindness which I had received from him. I must always regret that the last occasion of our meeting was the only one in which we came into a disagreeable personal collision.* There is something, indeed, of comfort in the thought that it was the only one, but it is painful to me to reflect that I saw him under such circumstances for the last time, though I have the satisfaction of believing that he knew that what had passed had made no breach between us.

"I am very sorry for the change which has been made in the Final Court of Appeal by the Judicature Bill. I regard it as mischievous and ominous, and believe that the persons who introduced it were among those who least desired its inevitable consequences.

"With regard to your kind inquiry, I am much as I have been for the last year : pretty well equal to any work which I have to do here, not requiring a prolonged absence from home, but not fit for London life. I have not,

* See page 334.

however, made any resolutions as to my future proceedings, as they will depend on contingencies which I cannot foresee. Only in the ordinary course of things it seems too late for me to expect any considerable renewal of health and strength. What I most anxiously desire is, that I may not survive myself or live any longer than I am capable of some kind of work."

[The next three letters are on the subject of the Welsh name for the Feast of the Epiphany :—]

To THE REV. CANON PEROWNE.

ABERGWILI PALACE, *November 1st*, 1873.

" You pay me too high a compliment when you suppose that I can supply that which is not to be found in any of the Welsh lexicographers. Your friend's notion that *ystwyll* is simply *stella* in disguise is a very tempting solution of the difficulty, but I am afraid utterly irreconcilable with the laws under which Welsh words are formed from the Latin. There is no analogy to account for the *wy* as representing *e*. We are, therefore, apparently driven to suppose that the word is a compound, and that the second part is *gwyll, gloom or darkness*, the initial g being absorbed by the preceding *yst*. But the only way that I find hitherto proposed for bringing a star, or other light, to illuminate this darkness is Dr. Pughe's fancy, that *yst* means 'that which exists.' Join this on to *gwyll*, and you get 'that which exists in the darkness,' and then all that remains is to believe that this was 'an epithet of a star' (for which no example or authority is cited). But I must say that I had rather remain in the dark than follow such guidance."

Abergwili Palace, *November 14th*, 1873.

" I was quite aware that most, if not all, of the Welsh ecclesiastical terms are borrowed from the Latin, and also of the great number of words in which the prefix *y* was required by the Welsh organ for the pronunciation of words beginning with the sibilant, followed by a consonant.   It is hardly so great as that of the words which you find under *E* in a Spanish dictionary, in which *e* is prefixed for the same purpose : escribir, escuela, espacio, espuma, escuda, estupido, espera, &c., &c.   Among them, not in the least remarkable, is the Spanish representative of *stella*, which is not, as might have been expected, *estella*, but *estrella*.

" But as to the adoption of Latin ecclesiastical terms, if it is asked why they were adopted, I suppose the answer must be that there was no Welsh word exactly, if at all, corresponding to them.   This, however, was not the case with *stella*, which is not an ecclesiastical term at all, and is simply synonymous with *seren*.   There is no apparent reason why it should have been substituted for the word with which every one was familiar in his own tongue. The difficulty appears to me rather increased than lessened by the other description of the Feast to which you refer. I do not see how *seren-wyl* can be properly called ' another form ' of *seren*, or (if *ystwyll* = *seren*) of *ystwyll*.   Nor does *y seren-wyl* exactly express *gwyl ystwyll*.   The one I should render ' the Star Feast,' the other ' Feast of *a* Star.'   In other words, I should have thought that the article was required before *ystwyll*, as all the Sundays after Epiphany are described as *gwedir ystwyll*.

" The Breton form *steren* is merely a slight variation of the Welsh, and does not seem to have much bearing on our question.

"The geographical examples appear to me every way doubtful. What reason is there for supposing that in any one of them the Welsh was formed from the English ? The contrary would appear to result from the fact that they are all significant. Certainly *Tafwys* (Taf-water) could not have been derived from the Thames. The instance of *Eglwys* for *Ecclesia* seems more to the point. But a link is missing from the chain of the argument."

To THE REV. CANON PEROWNE.

ABERGWILI PALACE, *December 12th,* 1873.

"I return Mr. Sinker's letter, which I have not been able everywhere to read with certainty, and have thus, perhaps, lost a little of the force of his arguments. There is a proposition as to the labials being 'easily interchanged,' which seems to require some explanation or limitation, as it might be understood to mean that the use of them is not governed by any fixed law, which can hardly be Mr. Sinker's meaning, On the whole, I could not deny that his derivation is possible, and, as far as the letters go, I may say as much of the conjecture that the word is a corruption of Twelfth. The difficulty about this is, that it is not an ecclesiastical term. But certainly Twelfth Day is not a provincial description, nor was the Twelfth Cake a provincial institution. The name of Shakespere's play would, I suppose, be sufficient to prove the general use, and I have no doubt that the confectioners' shops in London continue to vie with one another, as they did when I was a boy, in the exhibition of Twelfth Cakes. It was then also usual to entertain the children with the 'drawing of King and Queen,' and other cards which were sold with the cakes.

"I am not surprised to hear what you have said about ——. The incumbent could not have been directly presented by Lord Bute, as he came to the living in 1866 before Lord B. was of age. But if he was appointed through Lord Bute's influence, one may easily understand his Romanising propensities. How far this was the case I do not know. I hope, however, that the fact does not indicate that this party is gaining ground in the diocese of Llandaff. I am not sorry to see that some of the most advanced are at loggerheads among themselves. My old friend MacColl has been battling with Orby Shipley in the *Church Review*. Orby Shipley cannot make up his mind whether he will accept the Decree of Infallibility or not. MacColl and the *Tablet* say that it is a question on which every clergyman ought by this time to have formed a decided opinion. There I think he is right. But that there should be any who are still hesitating is a curious sign of the times. Do I rightly gather from Mr. Sinker's letter that you have taken your D.D. degree?"

To THE REV. CANON PEROWNE.

ABERGWILI PALACE, *December*, 1873.

". . . . Passing to lighter and pleasanter topics, I believe there is a great mass of materials illustrating the spoken provincial dialects, though, no doubt, not exhausting the subject. I have several little books compiled for that purpose, in the form of dialogue; and I suppose the Philological or Early English Society has a complete collection. But after the article in the last *Quarterly*, one doubts whether any one now living will see the great Dictionary begun. I am afraid it will prove a Tower of Babel.

" You will find Dr. Vogan's letter to Denison very well worth reading. As he is evidently a candid as well as earnest man, I was surprised to find him reviving the outcry against my famous 'paradox' about Transubstantiation without noticing my own explanation of it.* At the same time he appeared to me to show that what I had said might be more properly described as a truism than as either a paradox or, as he prefers calling it, a 'contradiction.' However barren the tomes of Eucharistic controversy, which fill so many libraries, may be of any other result, I should have thought that they might have been allowed to prove the fact, that the same words (of the Institution) have been alleged with equal confidence of subjective 'certainty,' by conflicting parties in support of their opposite views.

" Are you trying to read the Archdeacon's 'Episcopatus Bilinguis?'   I find it hard work, and should prefer a page of Tertullian.   What can have possessed him to take to Latin—and Convocation Latin—in his old age?   Is it a sacramental mystery, or simply a development of the Romanising tendency?   The Pope would probably enjoy it, and possibly understand it."

To THE LORD ARCHBISHOP OF CANTERBURY.

ABERGWILI PALACE, *November 5th*, 1873.

" I think it not unlikely that I may have some occasion of stating my views on the subject of Confession, but I am less inclined than ever to bring out a pamphlet on any topic of the day, and have no reason to suppose that any opinion of mine would carry much weight with those who take a different view. It might be with a part of your Charge reproduced, as Mr. Baker suggests, by yourself.

* *See* the Charge of 1857 in the " Remains," vol. ii.

"I do not know whether you have seen Mr. Orby Shipley's article on the subject in the last number of the *Contemporary Review*. It seemed to me to invite a reply, which might be very useful, and which, after being inserted in the *Review*, might appear in the form of a pamphlet. I do not know whether to be glad or sorry to see that you are going to St. Petersburg in January. But the voyage or journey may prove bracing and invigorating, and I heartily hope that you may have reason to reflect with pleasure on having been there."

[In reference to a sermon on "Absolution."]

To REV. E. H. PLUMPTRE.

A. P., C., *November 20th*, 1873.

"I have read—I may say studied—your sermon with great interest. It is certainly a word in season, very much needed and likely to do much good. Indeed, I am not aware that anything has yet appeared in the way of mediation between the contending parties, or even aiming at the bringing of those who may be open to conviction to a better understanding with one another. Neither, I think, can find any pretence for complaining that you have not done justice either to itself or to the other. I do not know why the most strenuous opponent of Confession should feel himself concerned to deny that there may be cases in which it is practised with beneficial effects in the Church of England, as is undoubtedly the case in the Church of Rome, though he may believe that in both the evil preponderates immensely over the good. I could more easily conceive that advocates of Confession, like Mr. Orby Shipley, may be very loath to admit that it is ever opposed from right motives or on reasonable grounds. Your review of the history of the doctrine will, I am

persuaded, be very useful to all candid readers who are
not yet acquainted with it. A short summary of it is
given by Gieseler (Lehrbuch der Dogmen-Geschichte) in
which he notices two points of some interest : one, that
the new theory of the twelfth century derived its main
support from a forgery of a work ascribed to St. Augus-
tine, ' De Vera et Falsa Pœnitentia ; ' the other, that
Richard de S. Victor, while rejecting the doctrine of Lom-
bardus, still confined the absolving power of the priest to
the penalty of sin, and reserved the divine prerogative of
absolving its guilt, leaving it for Aquinas to get rid of this
last distinction between priestly and divine absolution.   I
am still more thankful for the frankness with which you
admit the deplorable blots in the Prayer Book, which you
notice in your notes.   It will be a great gain that
their origin should be understood and acknowledged,
even by those who regard them as a providential mercy,
precious relics of ' Catholic ' truth, and use them as a lever
for upturning the Church of England.

"There is only one point in which I cannot go along
with you, or at least adopt your language in what seems
its most obvious sense.   I have never been able to reconcile myself to the hypothesis—which I remember seeing
maintained by Archbishop Sumner—that the Apostles
received any ' special inspiration ' by which they
were enabled ' to read the hearts of men and thus
authorised to remit or retain sins.'   I understand you
to distinguish this gift of ' more than natural insight '
from the general operation of the Holy Spirit in its
enlightening and sanctifying influence.   And this is the
distinction for which I see no sufficient grounds.   In our
Lord Himself this insight must be presumed to have been
infallible (though this opens several difficult questions).
But in what sense did He Himself forgive sins ?   Not, I
apprehend, as by an act of power, but by a declaration

concerning the state of the sinner, that it was one of forgiveness. And nothing short of an infallible insight could warrant such a declaration. Even if it be supposed that this insight was communicated to the Apostles to its fullest extent, so that they were able to read the heart without any aid from the utterance of the lips, or other outward sign of that which was passing within, I do not understand how such insight could be properly described as a 'power to absolve.' And you yourself seem to represent it as admitting of gradations of 'strength and clearness,' therefore I should infer as not infallible. But then it does not seem to differ in kind from that which wise and holy men have possessed ever since without any special inspiration. On the other hand, the words [John xx. 23] do not appear to purport the conveyance of a *power* without any reference to a *gift* which was to qualify the Apostles for the exercise of the power. The hypothesis of the special supernatural gift may be convenient to guard against the idea that the Apostles were invested with an arbitrary power—which our Lord Himself never claimed— of forgiving sins. But it seems to me that the same purpose is better answered by the supposition that the commission, though in terms absolute, was meant to be conditional, and to be confined according to the general tenor of the Gospel. I am, however, not sure whether there is any material difference between us; and I am glad to think that there is none which affects any fundamental principles.

"My health for the last year has undergone no change but that which the lapse of time brings with it, and I have no prospect of any other."

[The next letter refers to a correspondence in the *Times* between Earl Russell and Sir G. Bowyer on the subject of the Falck laws and Bismarck's Church policy.]

To Rev. E. H. Plumptre.

A. P., C., *December 17th,* 1873.

" I was very glad to hear of the work you have undertaken, and accept with great pleasure the honour which you propose to confer upon me.*

I cannot help fearing that Lord Russell is going to lend himself to something very foolish and mischievous, which is likely to strengthen the Pope's cause among us. The ground which he takes against Bowyer is utterly untenable, as the 'ascendancy' claim by the Pope over every baptized person, whatever may be its meaning and extent, is at all events nothing new. But for any English statesman to commit himself to the approval of Bismarck's ecclesiastical legislation seems to me a portentous blunder. Lord Russell, with his usual *nonchalance,* allows Bowyer to have the last, and, as I think, decidedly the best of the argument, and while he makes a perfectly irrelevant reference to 'the part taken by the Whigs in remedying Roman Catholic grievances,' he does not even notice the slap on the face which Bowyer administers to the Pope when he boasts of principles of toleration and religious equality, which the Infallible has so condemned and denounced, in Syllabus and Encyclical, that they cannot now be maintained—unless by virtue of a dispensation *per economiam*—without heresy."

To William Thirlwall Bayne, Esq.

Abergwili Palace, *New Year s Day,* 1874.

". . . . When I stayed three weeks at Hastings, in the vain hope of recovering health and appetite, I visited most of the notable places in the neighbourhood. At Battle, as

---

* The dedication to him of a new edition of Hare's "Victory of Faith."

I had expected little or nothing, I was not disappointed. I know from experience that it is one of the most difficult things in the world to identify ancient battle-fields. I have been on many where, even with the aid of the most lucid description, I could not recognise a single point. I think you would be likely to find more to interest you in the remains of the Cinque Ports. . . . .

"I take an almost painful interest in the Tichborne trial, and long for the time when Kenealy will, if that be possible, have said his last. I have heard of the anagram, and it exactly expresses my sentiments toward the miscreant.

"I am glad to hear of your choice of books. Boswell's 'Johnson' is one of the most entertaining in the language. Our writers of the eighteenth century are too much neglected. I believe you would find Shaftesbury and Bolingbroke well worth reading; but I know of none so full of amusement and instruction, conveyed in the purest and raciest English, as Swift."

[The following letter, written in answer to an application for help, speaks for itself :—]

To THE REV. WILLIAM WILLIAMS.

ABERGWILI PALACE, *April 29th*, 1874.

"I believe that you are aware that I have already devoted between £20,000 and £30,000 to the purpose of the Incumbents' Sustentation Fund, and that you will not be surprised if I consider that as much as can reasonably be expected from me."

CHAPTER X.

BATH, 1874—75.

INTIMATIONS of the Bishop's approaching resignation
had been for some time apparent in his writings and utterances.   The Charge for 1872 had opened with valedictory
words of deep solemnity.   A combination of bodily
ailments, such as attend old age, had caused a " continual
contraction " of his physical powers, and this was " painfully sensible " to one who felt so deeply his episcopal
duties and responsibilities.   In May, 1874, he carried into
effect the gradually formed resolution, and resigned the
see over which he had presided so ably for thirty-four
years.   He retired to Bath, and there spent the short
remainder of his days, tended by the united care and
devotion of the family which was bound to him by such
strong ties of gratitude and affection.

Even now it was not the mind but the body only that
craved rest ; the intellect remained as keen and vigorous
as ever.   The remaining letters show " how he continued
with indomitable energy the task of acquiring new knowledge ;" how assiduously, till eyesight failed, he attended

to his work on the Revision Company; and how, to the very end, the old judicial powers of mind were brought to bear on every prominent question of Church and State.

To THE LORD ARCHBISHOP OF CANTERBURY.

ABERGWILI PALACE, *May* 11*th*, 1874.

"I enclose a formal application in accordance with the terms of the Bishops' Resignation Act, 1869. This is only the fulfilment of a purpose which I formed some two years ago, and which I intimated in my last Charge. I now feel that I must defer it no longer. The greatest kindness you can do me is to expedite the affair to the utmost of your power. There are circumstances which make it extremely important for the interest of the diocese that the vacancy should be declared and filled up as soon as possible, and on private and personal grounds I have the strongest reasons for wishing it."

To THE LORD ARCHBISHOP OF CANTERBURY.

ABERGWILI PALACE, *May* 13*th*, 1874.

"I am deeply obliged to you for your prompt compliance with my request, and for the kind terms in which it is conveyed, and I most heartily pray that you may be very long spared to watch over and defend the Church, in this critical period of her history, from her foes, and, when needed, from her friends."

To ARCHDEACON CLARK.

17, GREAT PULTENEY STREET, BATH, *May* 27*th*, 1874.

"It belongs to your character to depreciate your own merits and services; but I am too deeply conscious of the extent to which my own labours have been lightened by your co-operation not to set a very different estimate upon them. They have been to me quite invaluable, and far more than I had any right to expect.

"I feel sure that no act of my episcopate will have proved more useful to the diocese than my resignation. If ever there was a diocese which needed the full vigour of two active bishops it is St. David's. It has had of late only the half, if so much, of one, and he an invalid, verging upon eighty.

"But however it may be with others, the continual contraction of my power of work, of which I have been for some time past painfully sensible, arising not only from advancing age, but from various ailments which must be growing with lapse of years, made the burden too heavy for me to bear.

"I can most truly say that among all the good and pleasant things which I leave behind me, there is not one which I shall miss more keenly than the opportunity of intercourse with you and yours, which has been the source of an enjoyment I can never forget, or remember without the most earnest and affectionate wishes for the happiness of you all."

To THE REV. CANON PEROWNE.

59, PULTENEY STREET, BATH, *August 5th*, 1874.

"MY DEAR SIR,—As I receive the *Athenæum* only in monthly parcels, and do not always open it immediately, it has happened that I have only just read what you have written of me. I value it very highly as an expression of your judgment, but even more as a proof of your kindness, for which I am deeply grateful, and remain,

> "Yours ever faithfully,
>> "CONNOP THIRLWALL (Bishop.)"

[The next five letters refer to the passage of the Public Worship Regulation Bill through Parliament. The Bill was introduced by the Archbishop of Canterbury on April 20th, 1874, and passed with Lord Shaftesbury's modifications (Ecclesiastical Judge instead of Bishop and Assessors) in the House of Lords on June 25. Mr. Russell Gurney took charge of the Bill in the House of Commons. It was opposed by Mr. Gladstone with his famous 'Six Resolutions.' It was then taken up and supported by Mr. Disraeli. There was an unanimous vote on the second reading, showing, spite of Mr. Gladstone's eloquence and earnestness, how widespread was the repugnance to extremes of Ritualism. Mr. Gladstone surrendered on July 14th, and the Bill was finally passed on August 3rd. Lord Penzance was appointed the Ecclesiastical Judge.]

To THE LORD ARCHBISHOP OF CANTERBURY.

ABERGWILI PALACE, *May 7th*, 1874.

"I am sorry that I shall not be able to be with you on Monday. It is the great ecclesiastical event of the session. But I shall be surprised if the principle of your Bill does not obtain very general assent in the House of Lords. Its chief danger will, I think, be from a coalition of two opposite extremes, which may also obstruct its successful working."

To Rev. E. H. Plumptre.

59, Pulteney Street, Bath, *July 15th*, 1874.

"I was very glad to receive your kind letter. As to the Public Worship Bill, I am waiting to see in what form it will finally pass through the House of Commons before I form a judgment on its merits and value. I have always felt a doubt, which perhaps only experience can solve, as to its operation. I am afraid that, even as a check to farther innovations, its effect will be but partial and precarious, while, if applied to the past, it will provoke attempts at retaliation, which, whether successful or not, will disturb and weaken the Church. The best thing about it seems to me to be that it must sooner or later lead to a revision of the canons, and to some relaxation or enlargement of the terms of communion. I have unluckily missed your letters to the *Times* and *Guardian*, which I should very much wish to read, and I shall be very much obliged to you if you will let me know the date of each, as I have both by me.

"It may seem strange that a man who has retired from business should be in want of leisure, yet such is the case with me. The cause is not that I have so much to do, but that my working hours are so miserably shortened through weakness that I can sometimes do little more than my daily work of revision, and have only time for a cursory inspection of the newspapers. I shall also, I expect for some months to come, be occupied with putting my books and papers in order. At present they are partly in cases, partly in confusion on the floor, though I was obliged to dispose of a large portion of the books from want of room to stow them. To return to the Bill. I read Gladstone's speech with great pain and surprise. Nothing ever so shook my confidence in him. It is astonishing that he should bring down a set of resolutions cut and dried without having (as it would appear) asked himself what they mean or what they could effect. And what a bidding for the *popularis aura* from a certain point of the compass, in the statement that it was the duty of the House of Commons to pronounce a eulogy upon the clergy !

" *Hoc Ithacus velit,* and to-day will no doubt take advantage of the opportunity.

" *As to the treatise* (' Supernatural Religion ') *you speak of, I am so utterly a stranger to its contents that I never before heard of its existence.** I do not intend ever again to write to the *Guardian* (from whom I received the grossest insult the editor could offer), but I should be glad if there or elsewhere you would contradict the rumour in my name. Perhaps for all but the authors and propagators of the report, the words I have under-lined would be sufficient. . . . ."

To THE LORD ARCHBISHOP OF CANTERBURY.
59, PULTENEY STREET, BATH, *July* 18*th*, 1874.

" I thank you most heartily for the great kindness with which you spoke of me the other day in Convocation. I may now, perhaps, venture to congratulate you on the substantial success of your Bill. Beside the immediate good effect which may be expected from it in checking the license of innovation, it has brought to light something which, antecedently to experience, could hardly have been believed, and which I regard as in the highest degree cheerful and hopeful. I believe we should have to look back some centuries before we find so animated a debate in the House of Commons on an ecclesiastical

---

* In reference to a rumour which ascribed the authorship of " Super-natural Religion " to Bishop Thirlwall.

question. But that the Bill should have been read a second time without a division, and this notwithstanding Gladstone's opposition, which only served greatly to damage his reputation as a statesman, seems to me to have proved several things which could have been ascertained in no other way : 1st. The practically universal sense of the need of such a measure ; the unanimity of the country in its favour ; and, what is most important of all, the continued attachment of the great mass of the intelligent laity to the Church, as a Reformed Church, and the deep interest they feel in its welfare. So much, I think, may be fairly said whether the Bill be improved or not, as it passes through committee. More will depend on the way in which it is worked. I am afraid that it is almost hopeless that the bishops should come to a general understanding and agreement as to the exercise of their discretion. Of course it will not and cannot stand by itself, but I hope and trust will be so supplemented as to render your primacy an ever memorable and happy epoch in the history of the Church of England."

To Rev. E. H. Plumptre.

59, Pulteney Street, Bath, *July 20th*, 1874.

" I found that I had seen your letter to the *Guardian* though not that to the *Times*. I believe that I can enter into your views and substantially agree with them. But this does not prevent me from rejoicing at the passing of the Bill, after such a debate, without a division, and at the collapse of Gladstone's resolutions.

" Whatever may be the final issue, I consider this fact as a decisive and most valuable proof of the interest felt by the great majority of the House of Commons in the concerns of the Church, and of their attachment to it, on the condition of its remaining a Protestant Church. I cannot yet forgive Gladstone for overlooking or ignoring the radical and all important distinction between the High and Low party with regard to the observance of the Rubrics. It is I think notorious that the Low Church party drifted into a departure from the Rubrics from manifold causes, without the slightest consciousness of any doctrinal bearing in their practice. The Tractarian-Ritualistic party, on the other hand, have introduced innovations, avowedly for the sake of their doctrinal significance, and with a most distinct and deliberate design, which is no other than that of transforming the character of our Church until it becomes ripe for union with Rome. Those who do not at present contemplate this step would do something still worse. They would inflict on us all the evils of a thorough adhesion to 'all Roman doctrine'—except perhaps the Papal Infallibility, as to which Orby Shipley seems to be still hesitating— without any of the social advantages which might result from the union. The person who, next to Gladstone, has most lost ground in my esteem is the editor of the *Spectator*. It amuses me to observe that after all he would be reconciled to the Bill with Cowper-Temple's amendment, if he could only rely on the discretion of bishops— which of course he cannot. What a pity it is that he should never have explained his theory about bishops. Can it be that there is some mystical influence in the consecration of a bishop which impairs his mental faculties? or that, by a secret dispensation of Providence, bishops are invariably chosen from persons destitute of judgment?"

To THE LORD ARCHBISHOP OF CANTERBURY.

59, PULTENEY STREET, BATH, *August 20th*, 1874.

"Many thanks for your kind remembrance of me. I have no doubt that my successor will justify the Archbishop of York's favourable opinion of him. It gives me pleasure to reflect that some time ago I offered him a canonry of St. David's, which he was unable to accept, not having been the requisite time in holy orders.

"I believe, as I think I have already said, that the success of your Bill will be found to depend on the way in which it is worked, and therefore in a very great degree on the discretion of the bishops. I wish I could place unlimited reliance on the discretion of every one of them ; but recent occurrences have violently shaken my faith. The *Spectator* predicts that Parliament will repent of having preferred a system of restraint to one of comprehension, to which it seems a sufficient answer to say that not only the Church but the country has declared that it will not endure the system of comprehension or *laissez faire*, even when recommended by the authority and eloquence of Gladstone."

[In reference to Mr. Gladstone's article in the *Contemporary Review* on Ritualism and Ritual.]

To THE REV. E. H. PLUMPTRE.

59, PULTENEY STREET, BATH, *October 6th*, 1874.

"I am and have been for the last month confined to my couch, where I have some difficulty in writing ; and my nephew, who mostly does it for me, is laid up with a sharp touch of gout. I am extremely weak, but, though very slowly, regaining strength. I have not yet received your sermon, but want to say a word on Gladstone's article in the *Contemporary*.

"I read it with much surprise and concern. There is no doubt a great deal in it which, though not quite new, is very true and deserving of attention on the æsthetical aspect of Ritualism, much also that is highly edifying on its religious or spiritual aspect, but I think better suited to the pulpit than to the pages of the *Contemporary Review*. It strikes me that I have pretty often, though much less ably, preached it myself. But admitting all this to the fullest extent, I conceive that a statesman, who is also a political leader, is hardly at liberty to publish his thoughts on such a subject and at such a season, just as if they were simply those of a private person. If he handles it at all, it should be from the statesman's point of view. And from this the article appears to me utterly unsatisfactory and worthless. For it wholly overlooks and ignores the great, and in my view by far most important, practical question of the day, which is this : Shall any section of the Church, or any clergyman, be permitted to conduct the public services of the Church in such a way as to make it appear that the Church gives its sanction to a doctrine—I mean that of the sacrifice in the Romish and Tractarian sense—which the greater part of her members reject as false and mischievous ? So long as the Church is secured from this flagrant wrong, I (for one) am ready to allow the widest possible latitude that any heart can desire, both as to the quantity and the quality of ritual."

[The next letter refers to Professor Plumptre's edition of " The Victory of Faith," by Archdeacon Hare, with Introductions by Professor Maurice and Dean Stanley. It was dedicated to Bishop Thirlwall (see p. 372) as " one in whom the three writers here brought together recognised a friend and teacher whom they all alike honoured."]

To REV. E. H. PLUMPTRE.

59, PULTENEY STREET, BATH, October 17th, 1874.

" I have been forgetting myself very delightfully for the last hour or two, carried back into the past, in reading your Preface and the two Introductions to ' The Victory of Faith.'   I find the question to what school or party Hare belonged, and whether or not to the ' Broad Church,' brought so prominently forward, that I cannot forbear inclosing for your most private perusal a few pages which I wrote a few months ago in self-defence from the like imputation.   I wrote without any object beyond my own immediate satisfaction, nor do I now know what will become of the MS., but I thought you might like to see it.   I wish it, however, to be preserved, and will therefore beg you, when you have read it, to let me have it again.*

" I believe I may now consider myself as having entered on a period of convalescence, though I have a long way to make up before I am what I was before my illness."

[In reference to a sermon on the " Law of Progress in Theology."]

To REV. E. H. PLUMPTRE.

59, PULTENEY STREET, BATH, October 23rd, 1874.

" I received your sermon yesterday, and have read it both with the interest which the subject naturally inspires and with special attention to the point on which you desired to know my opinion.   I am afraid that many people would think that I am hardly a fit person to consult on such a question, as the whole tendency of my

---

* This paper is printed in the " Remains," vol. iii. p. 481.

theological opinions may well be supposed to have pre-possessed and pledged me in favour of the views opened in your sermon. I cannot but hail them with pleasure, for I never was less satisfied with the present condition of Anglican theology ; never, as it appeared to me, had our divines more need of a larger measure of modesty and reverence to prevent them from believing that they had mastered the whole counsel of God, or as much of it as is still accessible to human investigation, while they aimed at nothing more than vamping up an orthodox phraseology, so as to give it an air of novelty. But it also seems to me that the present state of parties among us is peculiarly unfavourable to any attempt in this direction, not only because public attention is absorbed by the ' infinitely little,' without even sufficiently studying that, but because all parties alike are afraid of incurring the reproach of doctrinal innovation, and, above all, of scepticism and rationalism, which they would gladly cast on one another. I am one of the last persons who could venture to guarantee the reception of your sermon among men of other minds and different habits of thought ; but I may say that I have found in it nothing at which any well-informed and intel-ligent reader could take just offence—nothing laid down for which the way had not been prepared by reference to authorities which none can dispute. I therefore think it is —however it may be received—a word in season, which can bear none but wholesome fruit."

To Rev. E. H. Plumptre.

59, Pulteney Street, Bath, *October 24th*, 1874.

"I am afraid that yours of the 19th has been in my possession two or three days unopened through some over-sight. I am quite willing that you should keep a copy of

c c

my Paper on 'Broad Church' as, for the present, a strictly private document. If it ever sees the light, I should wish it to be after my death, and with the consent of my representatives. I am the more willing, because it is more than a platitude to say that my continuance here is very uncertain. After I saw you I had a very severe attack of illness, which completely prostrated me, and confined me to my couch for a month. I am now slowly recovering strength, but do not expect to be ever again as well as I was at the end of my first five or six weeks at Bath. A very slight matter throws me back, and I have now the winter before me. I wanted to say a few more last words on an important practical subject, in which popular theology seems to me to have gone sadly astray, but I do not know whether I shall be able. The prospects of my eyesight are also uncertain, but certainly gloomy.

"You are quite at liberty to show the MS. to Mr. Maurice."

[The next eight letters are a continuation of the correspondence on the work of the Old Testament Revision Company.]

To THE REV. CANON PEROWNE.

17, GREAT PULTENEY STREET, BATH, *June 2nd*, 1874.

" I am very much obliged to you for your kind letter.

" I had indulged in a hope that I might be able to continue making some little contributions to the work of revision. But I find that it is very doubtful how long I may do so with safety. Some unpleasant symptoms induced me lately to consult an oculist, who holds out but a gloomy prospect, as the most cheerful part of it is

that the operation for cataract, which will sooner or later
—if I live—become necessary, is not painful. But I fear
that long before I come to this extremity I may be obliged
to give up reading Hebrew—which, from the contrast
between the thick and the fine strokes and the accents, is,
I think, more trying to the eyes than any other language—
and also such prints as Lange's 'Commentary.'

"Still I should be glad to know how the work of
revision is going on, and should be much obliged to you
if you would inform me from time to time what books are
to be taken in hand."

To THE REV. CANON PEROWNE.

59, PULTENEY STREET, BATH, *July 3rd*, 1874.

" Yesterday I dispatched a first instalment of my notes
on 1st Samuel to the end of chapter xiii., and intend to
send something more next week. You may easily conceive the interruptions arising out of a removal from
Abergwili to Bath. Not one-half of the books which I
kept have arrived, and I do not expect that they will be
in their places for months to come. But I hope that in
future I may be able to keep ahead of the Company's
work. I am thankful to say that I have experienced a
very great improvement in my general health and relief
from suffering since I came to Bath. But I find that my
right eye is worse than useless. With it alone I can distinguish nothing but the most hazy outlines, and see best
when it is shut. The chief inconvenience I suffer from it
is that I am forced to bring what I read immediately under
the good eye, and cannot read all parts of a folio page from
one position. It is a little ' thorn in the flesh ;' but I
should be only too happy if I was sure that nothing worse
is to come.

"I shall be glad to have from time to time *des nouvelles* of the Company's proceedings, and particularly to hear what progress they make this session."

To THE REV. CANON PEROWNE.

59, PULTENEY STREET, BATH, *October 7th*, 1874.

"I send my notes to the end of 2nd Samuel. I do not expect ever to send any more. I have been very ill, and am in a state of extreme debility and prostration, which looks very like the beginning of the end. God bless you."

To THE REV. CANON PEROWNE.

59, PULTENEY STREET, BATH, *September 9th*, 1874.

"I am still confined to my couch, and, though mending, am gaining strength very slowly indeed. Any work requiring continual reference will, I fear, for a very long time be wholly beyond my power. Many thanks for your account of the Company's proceedings . . . . I am glad that Isaiah is to be taken next, as I may hope, though unable to take part in the revision, to enjoy the pleasure of reading him again. I should be a little curious to know whether a like rigour prevails in the American Company."

To THE REV. CANON PEROWNE.

59, PULTENEY STREET, BATH, *November 27th*, 1874.

"I am very much obliged to you for your account of the Company's proceedings. I was rather puzzled by the notices I received. I am glad that the Company find they can utilise the Mondays, but do not know whether I am to gather that they mean to meet every fortnight or three weeks.

". . . . I consider myself now as convalescent, though I am not, and do not expect to become, what I was before my illness. My eyes give me a great deal of trouble, and very much retard the progress of my revision. I hope, however, to send you the first instalment of notes on Isaiah before the Company's next meeting, and having such a start, to keep ahead of them, unless they change their step for one of unexampled rapidity, which, in Isaiah at least, I do not expect or wish."

To THE REV. CANON PEROWNE.

59, PULTENEY STREET, BATH, *December* 11*th*, 1874.

"I send the promised instalment of my Notes on Isaiah to the end of chap. x. I could have sent as much more, but it seems very unlikely that the Company will go any farther in this Session, and I keep the rest by me for the chance of something better occurring to me here and there.

"I should rather like to know whether any of the Company—particularly yourself—approves of the change which I have proposed at x. 16.* I have not found it mentioned by any commentator. But for that, I should have thought it quite certain. But it may be open to some objection which I have overlooked."

To THE REV. CANON PEROWNE.

59, PULTENEY STREET, BATH, *January* 15*th*, 1875.

"I send a continuation of Isaiah to the end of chap. xxii., though not expecting that the Company will advance so

[* The substitution of " instead of his glory " for " under his glory."—
J. J. S. P.]

far this Session. I suppose the question as to the manner of printing the verses has been decided, though I do not know how, or whether it has been reserved."

To THE REV. CANON PEROWNE.

59, PULTENEY STREET, BATH, *February 7th*, 1875.

" The numbness which has for the present deprived me of the use of my right hand did not come on me quite suddenly, but began with a strike of the little finger, which refused to take its proper part in the work of the hand, and then gained the other fingers over to its side. It is no doubt a severe privation, but I have much more reason to be thankful for that which I am allowed to retain than to grumble about that which I have lost. I never before fully knew the value of the left hand ; and I think it is a capital defect of our physical education that children are not trained, as they might easily be, to use their left hands as fully as their right.

"But I want to say a single word about the question raised in your letter, which, though it relates immediately only to a matter of form, I consider as one of the very highest practical importance. It appears to me that the consideration which should govern the Company's decision is, which mode of printing will render the reading of the Bible most edifying and attractive, not to the learned and cultivated few, but to the great mass of readers. And from this point of view I should much deprecate the innovation in the mode of printing adopted by Bunsen and in the Unitarian translation, in which the prose form is a rare exception to the general rule. I think that the right course is the reverse of this, and that we can hardly be too chary of the poetical form. And this,

I collect from what you say, is your own view of the subject.”

[In reference to a Paper on “St. Paul as a Man of Business,” in the *Expositor* for April, 1875.]

To REV. E. H. PLUMPTRE.

59, PULTENEY STREET, BATH, February 16th, 1875.

“I am obliged to avail myself of an amanuensis, having for the last fortnight lost the use of my right hand. I am so completely disabled that I cannot even draw a rude cross without assistance to support and guide my hand. Happily I am still able to read, though the state of my eyes limits the use of them for this purpose also. I shall, however, be very glad to receive anything that you may have to send me. I have read your Paper with much interest. Your view of the relation between St. Paul and Philemon is not, as far as I can see, affected by the question whether St. Paul wrote from Rome or from Cæsarea ; otherwise Meyer’s argument in favour of Cæsarea seems to me very difficult to meet. It is also not quite clear to me what could have been the motive of Onesimus, when he had made his escape, in seeking a friend of his master’s. I must also own that I find some difficulty in reconciling St. Paul’s position as a capitalist with the straitened circumstances which compelled him to accept pecuniary assistance, as he says, from the Philippians (chap. iv. verse 16) at Thessalonica. I see from Meyer that several commentators have adopted the idea of a temporal partnership. Your view of the object of the last journey to Jerusalem appears to me free from objection, and to throw very valuable light on St. Paul’s character and conduct.

I believe that copies of my photograph may be had at
Elliot and Fry's, but of this you shall hear again as soon
as my nephew, who is at present laid up with a fit of gout,
shall be able to write."

[In reference to Mr. Gladstone's article in the *Contemporary Review*, entitled, " Is the Church of England worth
preserving ?"]

To REV. E. H. PLUMPTRE.

59, PULTENEY STREET, BATH, *July 15th*, 1875.

" I have been hearing Gladstone's article in the *Contemporary* more than once, together with a part, perhaps only
infinitesimal, of the literature which has already grown
out of it, and which is no doubt destined to assume much
larger proportions, none with greater interest than your
letter to the *Times;* but I find the ear so very imperfect
a substitute for the eye, especially in controversial writing,
that I am by no means sure I yet fully understand the
merits of the question.   You, I think, propose to let the
whole dispute turn on the answer which would be given
by Mr. Mackonochie and Canon Ryle to the question,
whether the Holy Communion administered in the way
they respectively dislike and disapprove of would not
nevertheless be a valid sacrament. You have not thought
it necessary to explain what you mean by a 'valid sacrament,' but I suppose it may be safely assumed that it is
nothing more than a real sacrament, a sacrament entitled
to that name; and in this sense I quite agree with you
that Mr. Mackonochie and Canon Ryle could only answer
your questions in the affirmative.   Canon Ryle could not
undertake to say how far an imitation of the Mass might
be carried without ' overthrowing the nature of the sacra-

ment;' nor, on the other hand, would Mr. Mackonochie deny that a real sacrament might be celebrated even in plain clothes, as Dr. Littledale in his last article in the *Contemporary* stated to have been repeatedly done by himself. But if I am not greatly mistaken, neither of these gentlemen would consent to let the question turn on this issue. Might they not say that though the reality of the sacrament was not affected by the mode of its celebration, its efficiency and value depended in a very great measure upon it, and might be greatly impaired, if not utterly lost, if it were made to convey inadequate and, above all, erroneous notions of its nature? They might, perhaps, observe that, after all, a sacrament is nothing more than means to an end, namely, the communication of grace, and that when this end is in any way defeated it can matter little that the rite is notwithstanding a real sacrament; it might be still neither acceptable to God nor edifying to man, as our Church does not admit the notion of an 'opus operatum,' but makes the efficiency of a sacrament, though not its reality, to depend on the inward condition of the communicant. Might not this opinion be illustrated and confirmed by the analogy of the Church? The Church, though not only disendowed and disestablished, but though split into numberless independent sections, and reduced to the lowest state of poverty and weakness, might still be a valid Church, *i.e.* a congregation of faithful men, in the which the pure Word of God is preached and the sacraments are ministered according to Church ordinance in all those things that are of necessity requisite to the same; but would any one consider that as a sufficient consolation under so great a calamity? I shall be thankful for any light that will satisfy my curiosity on this subject."

The last few letters are very touching in the indications they convey of the accession of bodily weakness and the tenaciousness of the mental powers. In April, 1875, the Bishop became almost totally blind, and lost the use of his right hand. His solitude was relieved as far as possible by those around him. He was kept acquainted with everything that happened, and his unabated interest in all religious and political matters was shown by the letters he dictated. His mind was kept in continual exercise; a letter from his nephew, written a short time before the Bishop's death, speaks of him as translating Sanscrit as it was read to him by one member of the family, Italian and Portuguese with another, and German and French with another. Even the little ones were employed in reading history and chemistry to him. His patience and gentleness touched the hearts of all about him. The loss of eyesight and the loss of the power of using his pen must have tried him severely, yet no complaint ever escaped him.

The end came suddenly and peacefully at last on the 27th of July, 1875. " With one call for him who had been as his own son on earth—with one cry to his Lord in Heaven, Who to his upward gaze seemed yet more visible and yet more near—he passed, as we humbly trust, from the death of sleep, and from the sleep of death, to the presence of that Light in which he shall see Light." *

His body found a fitting resting-place in Westminster Abbey, in the same grave with his old schoolfellow, friend,

---

* Dean Stanley's Introduction to Bishop Thirlwall's " Letters to a Friend."

and fellow-labourer in the fields of Grecian history The
stone which marks the spot is inscribed to—

CONNOP THIRLWALL

SCHOLAR, HISTORIAN, THEOLOGIAN,

FOR THIRTY-FOUR YEARS

BISHOP OF ST. DAVID'S.

BORN FEBRUARY 11, 1797.

DIED JULY 27, 1875.

COR SAPIENS ET INTELLIGENS

AD DISCERNENDUM JUDICIUM.

GWYN . EI . FYD.

INDEX.

A.

Abraham's Sacrifice, Dean Perowne's
    Sermon on, 326
        Thirlwall on, 326, 327
Addison, 11
Adult baptism, 344
Æneid, Dryden's translation of the, 5
    Pitt's translation of the, 5
Æschylus as a soldier, 26
    Professor Plumptre's translation
        of, 303
Æsthetics, 109
Airy, 113
Allen, Dr. Bishop of Ely, 159
American Prayer Book, Rubric on
    adult baptism in the, 344
American Revision Company, The, 362,
    388
"Ancæus," Thirlwall's Essay on, 100
Aquinas, 173, 370
Aristotle, The ethics and politics of,
    91
Arnold, Dr., 107, 151, 284
Arthur, Prince, visit to Wales, 243
Athanasian Creed, The, 171
    Speech by Thirlwall on, 334
    Bishop Wilberforce's attack on the
        speech, 334
    Sermon by Dean Perowne on, 350
Athenæum, The, 77, 376
Atonement, The, 310
Atrou, 231
"Auf der Höhe," 288
Austin, Charles, 53
Autobiography, J. S. Mill's, Extract
    from, 53

B.

Baker, Sir Samuel, 299
Bangor, 223
Basevi, Mr., 53
Battle, 372, 373
Baumgarten, 190
Bayard, 88

Beaconsfield, Lord, 53, 377
Bennett, Mr., of Frome, 306
Bertheau, 209
Bingham, on the "Common Prayer,'
    354
Biographies, 24
Bishops' Resignation Act, The, 375
Bismarck, 332, 371, 372
Blakesley, Dr., Dean of Lincoln, 103,
    284
Boethius, 203
Bolingbroke, 373
Bombay, Bishop of, "Letter on
    Missions" by, 343
Bonald, Fievée, 89
Bossuet, 89
Bourges, 238
    Archbishop of, 239
Bowyer, Sir G., 371, 372
Brantôme, 88
Bright, Mr. John, 228, 294
British Association, The, 149
"Broad Church," Thirlwall's Paper
    on, 384, 386
Brougham, Lord, 128, 129, 132
Browne, Bishop Harold, 192
Bulwer (Lord Lytton), 53
Bulwer (Lord Dalling), 53
Bunsen, 23, 49, 284, 355, 390
"Bunsen, Life of," 23, 284
"Bunsen, Baroness, Memoirs of," 23
Burdett, Sir Francis, 6, 10
Bute, Marquis of, 367
Buxtorf, 351, 355
Byron, Lord, 26

C.

Cæsar, Julius, 26
Cairns, Lord, 306
Cambridge, 3, 22, 113
Campbell, Dr. J. MacLeod, 272, 285,
    310
Candler, John, 3
Carlyle, 190